INSIGHT
GUIDES

Gran Canaria
Lanzarote
Fuerteventura
The Eastern Canaries

Edited by Andrew Eames
Editorial Director: Brian Bell

APA
PUBLICATIONS

GRan CanaRIa

First Edition (2nd Reprint)
© 1991 APA PUBLICATIONS (HK) LTD
All Rights Reserved
Printed in Singapore by Höfer Press Pte. Ltd

ABOUT THIS BOOK

Until the Spanish arrived in the 15th century, the Canary Islands were virtually unknown specks in the ocean somewhere out beyond Gibraltar, the stepping-off point of the known world. Their early history is still an unwritten book; the hieroglyphs of the Guanches, the original islanders, are still undeciphered. Later, the islands played key roles, particularly in the history of transport, serving as stepping stones for Columbus in his discovery of America, for coaling stops for the first steamships, and as refuelling points for early inter-continental airliners.

Such a legacy is not quickly overcome. Even today, few visitors are able to name all seven major islands in the group. Even more visitors would have trouble pinpointing them on a map. Yet each island has its own culture, preserved despite the waves of colonising or economic invaders.

The team behind this Insight Guide set out to pick their way through the rubble of the past, and paint a fair, entertaining and informative picture of the present. The task of assembling that team fell to project editor **Andrew Eames**, no stranger to Apa's philosophy, having edited its Cityguide to London and its Insight Guide to the Balearics. Eames is a freelance writer and editor now living in London. He is the author of *Crossing the Shadow Line*, his travel autobiography, as well as a novel and a cartoon book. In recent years he has worked for *The Times* and as a freelance magazine consultant.

The task of finding resident experts on the islands capable of writing with sufficient authority on a wide range of subjects was not an easy one to manage from London. Eames enlisted the support of **Mike Eddy**, a British archaeologist living and working on Gran Canaria. Eddy, the major single contributor to this book, is one of those expatriates who would rather not be recognised as such; his appearance (dark and bearded) and his rapidly-acquired Spanish make him look more Mediterranean than Anglo-Saxon. However, his wife **Moira**, a geologist and teacher who wrote the chapter on volcanoes, is unmistakeably Scottish. Special mention is also due to Hazel, their first child, who arrived during the incubation period of this book.

Ron Williams, the headmaster of the English school on Gran Canaria, has been on the Canaries for more than a decade and is therefore well positioned to write the chapter on Expatriates.

Sarah Simon, resident for eight years on the islands, has a multi-faceted past in journalism, starting on the smallest newspaper in the world, the *Que Que Midlands Observer*, in what was then Rhodesia. In her time she has worked in Africa, Cyprus, the Middle East and London, where she was the first woman sub-editor on the *Evening Standard*. She completed several chapters for this volume, including part of the extensive Travel Tips section.

A Flowering of Talent

David Bramwell (Flora and Fauna chapter) is universally acknowledged as the authority on the natural history of the Canary Islands, publishing his first volume on Canarian wildflowers in 1974. When he is on the islands, Bramwell oversees the Jardin Canario in the hills above Las Palmas, as well as several other island projects. Also locally based are **Austin Baillon** (Issues in the News)

Eames

Eddy

Fernandez-Armesto

and **Chris Goulding**, (Going to Africa), both on Tenerife. Special thanks is due to Austin and his wife **Julie** for a contribution that was not just limited to words and pictures.

The history chapters of this book were the province of **Felipe Fernandez-Armesto**, a fellow of St Antony's College, Oxford. His books include *Before Columbus*, *The Spanish Armada*, and *The Canary Islands after the Conquest*. He is now at work on a major history of Spain for Oxford University Press. Canarian history has been among his most persistent interests for nearly 20 years, and he has been elected to the Instituto de Estudios Canarios, a rare honour. "I detest travel," he writes. "The only journeys I like are made in the imagination, and my favourite means of transport are an armchair and a book."

Andy Gravette (sections on Fuerteventura and Las Palmas) first discovered the islands while working as a foreign correspondent in West Africa. He regularly took his leave on one or other of the seven islands. Gravette has completed several other guidebooks, particularly to the Caribbean, and he is currently writing a book on Christopher Columbus, including his connections with the Canary Islands.

Stuart Ridsdale is a name that will be familiar to regular Apa readers. Now based in London and working for a leading public relations company, Ridsdale spent two years working as editor in Apa's Singapore headquarters, and has contributed to many of the company's titles. He would like to thank **César Manrique** for his wit, eloquence and hospitality, and **Marymar Duarte**, for helping him to gain an insider's view of Lanzarote, about which he writes in this book. Duarte, a native Lanzaroteno, also contributed part of the Travel Tips section at the back of the book.

The photography in these pages draws heavily on the work of **Tulio Gatti**, an Italian in Gran Canaria, who has been there longer than he can remember and who has played a key role in presenting images of the islands to the outside world.

This book could not have been completed without the assistance of the Canarian tourist authorities, particularly **Señor Jose Torrellas**, and Air Europe.

Supervising the book's progress from conception into print was Apa's London-based editorial director **Brian Bell**. Vital cogs in the production machine were typists **Janet Langley** and **Valerie Holder**, proofreader and indexer **Rosemary Jackson Hunter** and computer tamers **Audrey Simon** and **Karen Goh**.

Simon   *Ridsdale*   *Gravette*   *Baillon*

CONTENTS

TRAVEL TIPS

DOES ANYONE
EAT LOCAL FOOD?

Television on the Canary Islands is a source of irritation to the Canarios. During the commercial breaks, while mainland Spain is watching advertising, the Canary Islands station relays a blank screen; advertisers on the mainland do not think it worthwhile targetting the Canarios.

The Canary islanders believe they have always existed at the whim of mainland Europe, taking what is handed out to them like a dog waiting by a table. Only once did the archipelago really come into its own: when it functioned as a staging post on the shipping routes between Europe and Central and Southern America during the boom of trade with the New World.

But the Canaries are no longer a bridge between the continents. Columbus used to call here on his voyages of discovery; more recently early steamers called in to refuel, and latterly airlines did the same. But modern shipping barely stops at all and modern aircraft have increased their range, transforming the Canaries from stepping-stones in the Atlantic to an island cul-de-sac, with all manner of people and customs accumulating on the shores.

Europe has long treated the islands as a seed-bed for various experimental industries; sugar, wine, tomatoes, cochineal, and bananas have all at one time or another completely dominated island trade. During their time these industries have made fortunes for their architects, but they have left little or nothing behind them for the islanders. Hundreds of thousands of Canarios have emigrated to Central or South America, where life is at least a little more predictable, if not actually easier.

The latest in the series of monocultures is tourism. Today seven million visitors travel to the Canaries every year, bringing new prosperity. But a questionnaire circulated among the sun-flattened tourists around a villa pool in harsh, barren Lanzarote, for example, would be poorly answered: does anyone know that Admiral Nelson lost his arm trying to grab a Spanish bullion ship in Tenerife? That the ancient, tertiary-era forests on the lesser-known islands are so damp that the trees are draped in a cloak of moss from top to toe? That Franco started the Spanish Civil War from here? Does anyone eat local food? Unlikely.

The new tourists don't come to the islands for the islands; they come because the islands play host to a predictable winter sun.

And yet there is an enormous corpus of knowledge about the Canaries, little of which ever gets presented to tourists. This volume is the first English-language guidebook to take these islands seriously; they are a continent in their own right, with capital cities, industrial and agricultural regions, local accents and customs, and inter-island jokes and rivalries, none of which most tourists will be aware of. This book lifts the lid off this mini-continent.

Preceding pages: straw-heads in Fuerteventura; the central mountains; sun-worshippers in Gran Canaria; Carnival ride in Las Palmas; Lanzaroteño with her bean harvest. Left, detail from a mini-continent.

Leonardo Torriani, the Italian engineer who chronicled the European colonisation of the Canaries, describes the conquest of the island of Hierro: "The Christians began to disembark, and they were received with great rejoicing and happiness. They seem'd to all the natives to be Gods and not mortal men like themselves; and with this illusion the heathens nearest to the shore began to board the lighters, as they wished to get out to the ships; and so many came on board that the ships were fully loaded. They were all taken to Lanzarote and afterwards they were dispatched from there to be sold in divers places."

Torriani, writing *circa* 1590, goes on to recount how the Europeans came back the following year in order to play the same trick on the naive islanders. Unfortunately on that occasion one of the shore party made too clear his intention to take one of the young women with him and her father struck him with his staff, drawing blood. Realising that gods shouldn't bleed, the girl's father rallied the islanders to prevent yet more Bimbaches (as the islanders called themselves) from being taken into slavery.

Whether Torriani got the story right is a moot point, but he certainly exposes one of the main interests of the European adventurers who visited the islands in the Middle Ages—slavery.

Human trade: Like all slave-raiders the medieval Europeans were mainly concerned with the natives' sales potential and what might be called product availability. "The country (the island of La Palma) is strong and well populated because it has not been so heavily raided as the other islands. They are people of comely proportions and live on naught but meat…"

Likewise on Tenerife, relates one trader, "there live many people, who are the most daring of all the other peoples that inhabit the islands, and they have never been attacked nor led into captivity like those of the other islands". Gomera, too, was first recorded as well-populated by powerful tribesmen, pro-

tected from raiders by "the marvellously great and deep ravines" of the island.

But Hierro, the smallest and the most westerly island, had suffered the effects of slave raids even before the con-trick that Torriani exposed. "It was once populated by many people, but several times they were made prisoners and led into captivity in foreign countries and today few people remain… The inhabitants are people of comely proportions, both the men and the women." So hurry now while stocks last.

The sales pitch of slavers, however, is not the only source of information about the original islanders. The first European conquistador—the Frenchman, Jean de Béthencourt—brought with him two priests (who wrote the descriptions quoted above) to save the souls of the heathen islanders and to protect his own. Like other evangelising priests they took a dim view of Canarian paganism and baptised in the wake of military conquest.

Whilst de Béthencourt raided and conquered throughout the islands, the two priests, de Bontier and Le Verrier, left thumb-nail sketches of each island and their

Left, Guanche figures in Santa Cruz. Right, slavers made off with many of the islanders.

and great hope of being a good Christian". And great hope of not being clapped in irons once again!

De Béthencourt's conquest was, according to his camp-following priests, "for the honour and exaltation of the Christian faith". Their contemporary report is, however, full of informative detail. "And as for the isle of Lanzarote, which is called in their tongue Tytheroygatra... it has a great number of villages and fair houses, and used to be well-populated, but... when M de Béthencourt arrived, there were only 300 inhabitants whom he conquered with much labour and great trials... There is a great number of springs and cisterns, pastures and good lands for tillage and great quantity of barley is grown."

The conquerors themselves wrote of their battle needs and the course of conquest, especially in the case of Gran Canaria, which was a royal enterprise rather than a private venture. The early colonial administration, too, records aspects of native life—a report to the Inquisition in 1502 of a burial by pre-conquest rite outside Telde, Gran Canaria, is a typical example.

Then there are the accounts of the travellers. The first Englishman to write about the islands, in the 16th century, Thomas Nichols, described the native islanders succinctly: "The people which first inhabited this land were called Canaries by the conquerors. They were clothed in goate skinnes made like unto a loose cassocke. They dwelt in caves in the rockes, in great amitie and brotherly love. They spake all one language. Their chief feeding was gelt dogs, goates and goates milke; their bread was made of barlie meale and goats milke, called *gofio*, which they use at this daie..." (and still use extensively at this day, too).

Early Canarios: Nichols' account touches on one of the main problems for archaeologists and prehistorians studying the native islanders—what should they be called? Each island had a different name and the people of each also had their own tribal names within their islands.

The easiest solution seems to be to mis-use the word "Guanche", which really refers to a native inhabitant of Tenerife, and apply it to all pre-conquest Canary Islanders in general. This practice has been widely adopted through the archipelago. Nevertheless each island had its own peculiarities within the over-all Guanche culture.

The Guanches of Gran Canaria—"Canarios" in all the chronicles of the conquest—probably take their name from a branch of the Canarii tribe, who lived around the area of Beni Abbas, on the Saharan side of the Atlas Mountains. Whether they earned their name from the habit of eating dogs, as Thomas Nichols and some classical authors say, is doubtful. No tell-tale bones have been found so far to suggest that dogs were eaten. Nevertheless, Nichols was right on most other counts. The prehistoric Canary Islanders did live in caves, though not necessarily in brotherly love. On Gran Canaria—which

was generally the most developed of the islands—some of the caves had painted walls. The Painted Cave at Gáldar is the best known; Cueva del Rey on Roque Bentaiga can also be visited, though there are no signs, no information and no protection for monument or visitor.

All the painted caves are artificial, excavated out of soft volcanic rocks, so the walls are fairly flat and lend themselves to the red, black and white geometric designs. What these caves were used for is unknown—popularly they are supposed to be royal dwellings (*Cueva del Rey* means King's Cave). However, they may be *harima-*

guadas—a sort of convent where young women were schooled in wifely tasks.

Several European chronicles mention the important role played by women in pottery-making, painting and storing the harvest. All these aspects of life on Gran Canaria were dominated by geometric art. The finest pottery vessels were decorated with red and black geometric designs, and the pottery was usually made almost exclusively by women working in their caves.

Interestingly most of these highly decorated pots are containers for liquids, and women played an important part in religious ceremonies by pouring libations of milk.

Painting, too, was a female preserve. A

chambers. These were placed in almost inaccessible cliffs, and housed the reserves of a particular tribe or perhaps headman.

Early housing: The Guanches on all the islands lived in caves, but in all three eastern islands (Gran Canaria, Fuerteventura and Lanzarote) they also built houses. On Gran Canaria these were "low and with very thick walls of large stones without mortar but set with puddled earth. They were covered with beams and boards of finest *tea* (pine wood) and other hard woods... On the beams and boards they put flag-stones, thin and flat... and on these flags they spread wet earth, and they trampled it so much that even if it rained for several days the water ran off the roof and

number of small clay stamps *(pintaderas)*, also decorated with geometric designs, were probably used to mark the security seals around grain stores.

In dwelling caves these grain stores are bell-shaped pits cut into the floor or wall. Sometimes a natural cave, separate from the dwelling cave, was used. But throughout Gran Canaria there are defended communal granaries of anything from a dozen (Cuevas Muchas in Guayadeque) to a hundred (Cenobio de Valerón, Gáldar) specially cut storage

Left, Jean de Béthencourt. Above, the Cenobio de Valeron, an ancient Guanche grain store.

did not penetrate inside." An excellent model of this type of house is on display in the Museo Canario in Las Palmas.

On Lanzarote and Fuerteventura the houses were grouped into hamlets around the edges of barren lava fields. They were "low, and the streets narrow so that two men could hardly pass". Temporary goat-herders' huts were made out of lumps of basalt slag among the lava fields.

What may be the "palace" of the king of Lanzarote has been excavated at Zonzomas, near Teguise, but, like so many Canarian sites, the excavations are neither published nor conserved, and certainly not open to the general public. The royal palace at Gáldar, Gran Canaria, was demolished over two centuries ago.

Guanche Kings: Lanzarote had only one king when de Béthencourt landed in 1402, but Fuerteventura and Gran Canaria were both divided into two kingdoms. De Béthencourt's clerics recorded a wall dividing Fuerteventura's two kingdoms—Jandía in the south, and Maxorata in the north. The remains of this wall, La Pared, still survive, cutting off the Jandía peninsula from the rest of the island.

La Pared is a low wall, in places barely a metre high, and elsewhere wrecked by holiday bungalows and the activities of the Spanish army. Built into the wall are a series of circular enclosures, probably livestock pens or meeting places. Behind it, on the Jandía side, two possible defensive works have recently been identified.

Gran Canaria's two kingdoms were centred on the towns of Telde and Gáldar. The boundary probably ran along the ridge separating Santa Brigida from Teror, and passing by the sacred mountain and former lake at Pino Santo towards that other sacred mountain, Bentaiga, in the centre of the island. From there southwards, marked by a low wall, it met the coast near Tauro, between Puerto Rico and Mogán.

The kings of Gran Canaria were called *guanartemes*, and beneath them were a number of nobles, *guayres*, presumably clan chiefs. Each *guanarteme* shared power with a *faycan*, "who was in the manner of a priest, a man of good example, who in time of want gathered the people together and led them as in a procession to the sea-shore, with boughs and branches in their hands, calling out loud, and they beat on the water with the boughs." This ceremony still persists in present-day, Christianised festivals.

Their principal deity, Alcorán, was a sky god and the Guanches worshipped him in small, circular rock-cut enclosures, known as *almogaréns* in Gran Canaria. There are examples at Bentaiga and Cuatro Puertas (Telde). Their religion, as far as the Catholic priests recorded it, was centred on rain-making and fertility. A recently discovered cave near Telde was decorated throughout with scores of unmistakable rock-carvings of the female reproductive organ! Other rock-carvings depict dancers, spi-

rals, networks of straight lines and even lettering akin to pre-Roman Libyan script.

The Guanche way of life was fairly well-described by the European chroniclers—the economic potential of the islands was an important consideration for the conquistadores. Their main agricultural products were, as Nichols recorded, goat meat and goat's milk together with *gofio*.

Economy and diet: *Gofio* is a finely ground, toasted flour, then made from barley but now from maize or wheat. Other crops were available—local fruits and berries, roots, and perhaps figs. Goats were the main food animals, though the Guanches also kept pigs and perhaps sheep. Fishing was an important

food source, and was also socially important as the *guanartemes* also took part in netting the fish. The king and his nobles hunted unknown quarry—perhaps wild pig, partridges and quails.

The peasantry, however, relied a lot on shell-fish, and shell-middens (refuse heaps) are known on all the eastern islands.

Agriculture was run on a communal basis. They aided one another in the sowing; the fields were held in common and remained theirs as long as the crop lasted. Each year the

Above, the Guanches mummified their dead.

fields were shared out. They had places where they locked up their barley and foodstuffs. In a separate storehouse they put aside a tithe of their crop as a reserve for the years of scarcity, when they divided it out as alms.

Their economy was based on a mixture of farming, herding, collecting and fishing. On the two easternmost islands goat-herding was much more important than farming because of the dry climate.

They had no knowledge of metal-working, and there are no ore deposits on the islands. Stone and bone were roughly fashioned into tools instead.

From bone they made needles, awls, punches and fish-hooks. Out of basalt they fashioned heavy knives, picks and chopping tools. Finer cutting tools were made from tiny pieces of obsidian, a black volcanic "glass" found on Gran Canaria, and from a poorer-quality brown obsidian found in Fuerteventura. Porous lava was shaped into circular mill-stones and into mortars, for grinding grain and mashing roots.

Containers were made from wood, leather, basketry and pottery. In Canary Island cave sites such materials are finely preserved in the dry, stable atmosphere. Small leather and basketry draw-string pouches are a relatively common find, and several are on display in the Museo Canario—even a leather glove and a leather trouser-leg have been unearthed during excavations.

Their main weapons were wooden spears and staves—the spears were not tipped with stone points but hardened with fire. This was, as the Spanish discovered to their cost, just as effective as a stone-tipped weapon. They also used sharp throwing-stones to great effect.

The Guanche way of death was remarkably complex, for they mummified their dead—not as well as the ancient Egyptians but quite adequately. The body was first washed in the sea by a caste of specialist undertakers/butchers, who lived a life apart from the rest of society—death and blood were taboo for the Guanche nobility. The body was then dried in the sun once the internal organs had been removed. Finally it was wrapped in leather or basketry shrouds for burial.

Some of these mummies were placed in caves on wooden litters or beds of stones, and others buried in stone-lined graves on top of which a low tower of stones was built. Further down the social scale the dead were covered with piles of lava blocks on the barren lava fields. Others were buried in simple graves around a more important personage's stone-lined grave.

Many of the burial caves and tower-like cairns were probably family tombs—the earliest burials in a cave were shoved to the back to make room for new arrivals in the other world.

Origins of the species: But where did the Guanches come from, and when did they reach the Canaries? The "where" question is easier to answer.

The Canarii were a tribe living in Morocco in Roman times; and Canarian place-names are shared with North Africa—the island of Gomera and the Berber village of Ghomara, for example. The few fragments of the Guanche language that can be reconstructed from place-names and a few recorded phrases show that they were Berber-speakers. The occasional letters carved on rocks and in caves throughout the islands are related to scripts used by the Berbers in antiquity and by the modern Tuaregs.

Fire-hardened spears, defended communal granaries, cave-dwelling and burying the dead under tower-shaped cairns are all Berber characteristics.

As for when the Guanches first arrived on the Canaries, that is more difficult. Much has been made of the racial types that made up the Guanche population before the conquest—the Cro-Magnon and the Mediterranean—and several waves of invaders have been suggested on this basis. However, since the introduction of scientific dating methods—especially radio-carbon dating—to Canarian archaeology, such racial distinctions are irrelevant.

All the radio-carbon dates so far point to the first or second century B.C. as the most likely time for the Guanches to have moved across into the islands. There are a couple of earlier dates, around 500 B.C., but these are not directly linked to human activity—just a few fragments of charcoal and lizard bones, both of which occur quite naturally on these volcanic islands.

But even at the earlier date the Cro-Magnon and the Mediterranean populations around the Mediterranean Sea had been long mixed into early Berber tribes.

THE CONQUEST

Like patches of twilight in the Sea of Darkness, the Canary Islands in the Middle Ages lay, never utterly unknown, but long unvisited, except in voyages of the imagination. Memories of the archipelago, transmitted from antiquity, became encrusted with legends of Merlin, St Brendan, St Ursula and the Earthly Paradise. The first genuine visit, at an unknown date probably prior to 1339, was attributed in most sources to the Genoese Lanzarotto Malocello who found the island which still bears a version of his name, Lanzarote.

The dating and authenticity of many of the earliest documents are so much debated that the circumstances and motives of his voyage—whether under Genoese or perhaps Portuguese auspices, whether of reconnaissance, conquest or trade—are matters for speculation. But his chivalric name, vagabond career and attainment of fame are features of the tradition of explorers and conquistadores who visited the Canaries over the next century or so.

The excitement of discovery was rapidly spread by merchants, like the Florentine of Seville, who reported on their voyages when they got home; or by map-makers like Angelino Dulcert who recorded the findings of Lanzarote in Genoa or Mallorca or by humanists like Boccaccio, who transcribed a detailed account of a voyage dated 1341.

Gold-hunters, slaves and would-be conquerors followed. Four sailing licences for voyages from Mallorca to the islands (including one project of conquest) have survived from the month of April 1342 alone. For most of the third quarter of the 14th century, after the Black Death, the effort seems to have slackened, except for spiritual conquerors. Mallorcan missionaries concentrated their campaign on Gran Canaria, where they founded the diocese of Fortuna at Telde. The mission lasted precariously from 1351 to 1393.

French adventurers: Traders and slavers in Castile, especially in Seville, became in-

creasingly active towards the end of the century, but the first enduring attempt to establish a European presence in the islands was launched from France. For among the men who contracted to serve on the Duke of Bourbon's crusade to Barbary in 1390 were two who were to play a crucial role in the history of the Atlantic world: Jean de Béthencourt, lord of Granville in Normandy, and Gadifer de la Salle, of the cadet line of a noble Poiteven house.

De Béthencourt had cousins by marriage in Seville, among families which had already professed an interest in the Canaries. Gadifer had no known Castilian connexions nor any allegiance outside France. It may have been the attraction said to exist between opposites that drew them together.

Gadifer, with no patrimony of his own, was an inveterate adventurer. Reckless and improvident, he was steeped in conventional piety and the chivalric romance that resounds in his very name—a preincarnation of Don Quixote, with the insular ambitions of Sancho Panza.

De Béthencourt was the more practical partner. For him the conquest was as much a

Left, the conquering Spaniards put the islands on the map. Right, Lanzarotto Malocello, who gave his name to Lanzarote.

financial gamble as a chivalric escapade. He manoeuvred his comrade-in-arms out of any share in the spoil, protected his inheritance at Granville from all-comers—Englishmen, creditors, cousins—and pursued the entire adventure in the Canaries as if more for gain than glory.

Recruiting manpower locally and raising loans widely, the conquerors sailed from La Rochelle on 1 May 1402. Undermanned and inadequately equipped, the expedition needed a base closer at hand. By November, 1403, de Béthencourt—to his partner's apparent chagrin—had transferred allegiance to the king of Castile. The change was pregnant with consequences. Henceforth, Castile after dissensions en route, only 63 arrived.

De Béthencourt did make subsequent recruitment efforts in Normandy. He also had agents around the western Mediterranean hawking indulgences procured from the anti-pope, Benedict XIII, in order to recruit more manpower. But Castile and especially Seville, were the most productive sources of conscripts. Such was the strength of the Sevillian complement that when, in 1418, de Béthencourt's nephew contracted to sell rights in the islands to the Sevillian cousins, the only vestige of the original "Norman" conquest remained in Castilianised versions of a few French personal names.

Going native: Colonisation was not the

was to occupy a privileged position in Atlantic colonial expansion.

In the long run, the Canaries proved to be the most significant of the Atlantic archipelagos, in strategic terms, because the wind system linked them to the New World.

Thus it was that a Frenchman, de Béthencourt, founded a distinctly Spanish colony. The complement of the original expedition was mainly Norman and Gascon. We know that women were included because of a chronicler's claim that Spaniards tried to rape them. But those who originally embarked contributed little to the colonisation: of the original complement of 280 souls, conquerors' main objective. Their avowed motives were "to convert the natives" and to establish a base from which to find "the River of Gold"—the fabled source of the Saharan gold traffic, which was erroneously thought to lie on the latitude of the Canaries. Only in 1405, when hopes of an easy conquest or a quick killing on the gold-run had faded, did colonisation begin in earnest.

Even then, de Béthencourt touted mainly for carpenters and masons—potential creators of a fortified base. In the expedition's chronicle Gadifer de la Salle is said to have exhorted his companions to "kill all the native men, take their womenfolk...and live like them". This "going native" remained an option throughout European colonisation of areas inhabited by primitives.

The colony which emerged was not, however, the result of sad desperate acts. In the three conquered islands—Lanzarote, Fuerteventura and Hierro—the natives do all seem to have died off or disappeared into slavery abroad, the women along with the men. In their place, the labour needs of the new society were met by a settler-peasantry, and women were brought in from outside.

There were no large proprietors. De Béthencourt distributed the lands among peasants and artisans "to each as seemed good and as suited his rank". The settlers over-reliance on goat husbandry.

When they wanted to bring an action at law against their lords (de Béthencourt's successors), they begged the king of Castile to give them the services of a notary because they could not muster enough literacy between them to understand the documents in their case. The reality of life in the "Fortunate Isles", beneath the civilised airs and chivalric graces affected by early colonisers, was nasty, brutish and short.

Balance of trade: The economy was geared to slaving and raiding the African coast and victualling ships. The products de Béthencourt brought in with his settlers were pigs, cattle and wheat. The goods they yielded

brought with them the crops, livestock and ways of life of home: far from going native, they sustained a feeble imitation of metropolitan society.

Despite the romantic illusions with which they were associated in chivalric literature, islands in the late middle ages normally supported only poor and precarious lives. In their earliest surviving self-characterisation, the colonists of Lanzarote called themselves "poor, miserable and needy folk", victims of scant harvests, rare rainfall and economic

Left, Gadifer de la Salle, a brutal coloniser. Above, harsh and unhelpful landscape.

were durable provender—lard, bacon, ship's biscuit, hard cheese.

But de Béthencourt's sketchy new agronomy did not entirely succeed in domesticating the new animals. Potential exports listed in the earliest chronicle show the balance between new and traditional products: "Several sorts of merchandise, like leather, fats, orchil, which is worth much money and serves as a dye, dates, dragon's blood and several other things".

Orchil and dragon's blood were naturally occurring commodities, the first a moss-like dye gathered from rocks, the latter a resin from the *el drago* tree, also used in dyeing but equally exploited medicinally: "it is good for medecines", said a 16th-century source, "and for putting flesh on one's gums". Pastoralism and gathering were features of the traditional economy of the islands which survived long into the colonial era, even when there were few natives left to pursue such economies.

De Béthencourt's conquest was only a partial success. His declared objectives had been the large, fertile and populous islands of Gran Canaria and Tenerife; even the three conquests he completed were achieved against native populations enfeebled and depleted by years of slavers' depredations.

On Lanzarote, de Béthencourt and de la zarote and launch assaults on other islands. The example of a castle erected by Lanzarotto Malocello was before their eyes; but the classic pattern of Norman conquest was being followed in this last Norman conquest of all. The castle was the first in a series they erected in Lanzarote and Fuerteventura, thus extending by intimidation a conquest which was begun by guile.

Portuguese threat: The fortifications were needed, not, as it turned out, against the natives, but against the Portuguese. The islands' usefulness as a potential staging-post, and their appeal in their own right to the ambitions of Prince Henry the Navigator, ensured that they would be a battleground of

Salle established themselves by subterfuge: they posed as defenders of the natives, whom they promised to take "as friends rather than subjects", guarding them "from all who would want to do them harm"; this could only been understood as a reference to the same Sevillian slavers who were increasingly to become de Béthencourt's suppliers and close associates. The goodwill thus procured from the natives gave the conquerors a chance to erect a fort, at Rubicón in the south-east of the island—the present ruins of Guanapay probably belong to later fortifications on the site.

From there they could dominate Lan-Iberian rivalry for most of the 15th century, during Portugal's long quest for access to the sources of African gold.

However, every Portuguese effort was thwarted. Lanzarote and Fuerteventura remained in Castilian hands; but conditions for a further extension of the conquest were unfavourable and de Béthencourt's dream of conquering Gran Canaria remained unfulfilled by his successors. Not until the 1470s was there any decisive new departure in the history of the eastern islands.

Castilian interlopers in the African trade had attracted Portuguese complaints in the previous three decades, but the war of 1474-

79, in which Alfonso V of Portugal challenged Ferdinand and Isabella for the crown of Castile, acted as a catalyst for Castilian activity. The monarchs were open-handed with licences for voyages of piracy or carriage of contraband; the Genoese of Seville and Cadiz were keen to invest in these enterprises, and Andalusian mariners, including many who were to ship with Columbus or who made transatlantic journeys after him, were schooled in Atlantic navigation. Portuguese ships battered the defences of the settlers of Lanzarote.

The islands' importance increased. When Ferdinand and Isabella sent a force to resume the conquest of Gran Canaria in 1478, a

Portuguese expedition in seven caravels was already on its way. The intervention of the Catholic monarchs thus has the character of a pre-emptive strike against the Portuguese.

Other, longer-maturing reasons also influenced the royal decision. First, the monarchs had other rivals than the Portuguese. The lordship established by de Béthencourt had eventually descended by marriage to Diego de Herrera, a minor nobleman of Seville. His claim to have made vassals of nine "kings"

Left, the colonisers had to be permanently on their guard against pirates. Above, Guanapay castle on Lanzarote.

or native chiefs of Tenerife and two of Gran Canaria was, to say the least, exaggerated. He had merely raided those islands, erecting intimidating stone turrets in the manner of earlier conquistadores.

But such large and indomitable islands could not be conquered by the private enterprise of a provincial hidalgo. Even had Herrera been capable of completing the conquest, it would have been unwise to permit him to do so. He was not above intrigue with the Portuguese; he might have become a turncoat, like many peripheral lords; and he was the sort of truculent paladin whose power was an affront to the crown.

Profiting from a local rebellion against Herrera's rule on Lanzarote in 1475-76, the monarchs seized the chance to enforce their suzerainty. In November of that year, they initiated an enquiry into the juridicial basis of the lordships of the Canaries. Its findings were embodied in an agreement between seigneur and suzerain in October 1477: Herrera's rights were unimpeachable, but "for certain just and reasonable causes", which were never specified, the right of further conquest should revert to the crown.

As often in the history of Latin involvement in the African Atlantic, gold was the spur. According to a privileged observer, the king's interest in the Canaries was aroused by a desire to open communications with "the mines of AEthopia"—that is, Africa.

Royal struggle: It proved almost as hard to advance the conquest under royal auspices as under those of Herrera. It took six years of hard-fought campaigns to reduce Gran Canaria to submission. The ferocity of native resistance was responsible in part; but finance and manpower proved equally hard to command.

At the nerve centre of the monarchs' war effort, scraping contingents together, assembling groups of financial backers, was Alonso de Quintanilla, a treasury official who was one of the most influential architects of policy in the reign of Ferdinand and Isabella. He seems to have been given responsibility for organising the conquest from 1480, when dwindling returns from the sale of indulgences caused a crisis of finance. He devised a wide range of expedients, including the mortgaging of royal booty and recourse to Italian, chiefly Genoese, capitalists. In doing so he foreshadowed the circle that would later contribute to the financing of Columbus.

Two observations made by contemporary chroniclers are helpful for an understanding of the conquest of Gran Canaria. Although the natives were neolithic "savages", their strategems and the defensible terrain brought them frequent victories over technically superior adversaries. And the conquest made continuous demands on the scant resources which the Castilian monarchy could spare for the task. The chronicler Hernán de Pulgar, remarked of Gran Canaria that it would have been an insuperable task of conquest, but for the internal rivalries which the conquistadores exploited. As in Naples,

plains where the natives grew their cereals and other crops, the gentler hill-sides up and down which they shunted their goats.

It was a strategy of mere survival, not of victory. Between raids, the invaders remained in their stockade at Las Palmas, where inactivity bred insurrection.

The arrival of Pedro de Vera as military governor in 1480 inaugurated more purposeful strategies: he planned amphibious operation to the otherwise barely accessible West coast and the erection of another stockade— a second front—at Gaete. But his first major victory was the result of a miscalculation by the defenders, who descended to the plain of Tamaraseite near Las Palmas, to offer con-

Granada, Mexico and Peru, Castilian conquerors were the beneficiaries of indigenous civil wars.

Undermanned and irregularly provisioned, for the first three years of the conquest of Gran Canaria the Castilians contented themselves with making *entradas* or raids by land on native villages. Working for wages, and therefore with little incentive to acquire territory, the recruits from urban militia forces did not touch the mountain fastnesses on which the Canarios used to fall back for defence. Rather, they concentrated on places in the low plains and hills, where food, not fighting, could be found—the

ventional battle with disastrous results. If the partisan chronicler can be believed, de Vera slew the most formidable native chief with his own hand.

Befriending the locals: Towards the end of 1480 or early in 1481 the natives' sowing brought a lull in hostilities, probably formalised by a mass baptism, to which the natives would have submitted cheerfully enough, without understanding much of its religious significance. Certainly a group of chiefs or notables whom the Spaniards had captured and in some sense converted, arrived at the court of Ferdinand and Isabella in, 1481.

The Catholic monarchs wished to impress

these new subjects with their clemency as well as their power and, urged by ecclesiastical advisers, desired to speed the conversion of other Canarios by a display of charity.

They bestowed a letter of privilege, declaring that they had taken the people of Gran Canaria "beneath our protection and royal defence, like the Christians they are" and guaranteeing their right to move and trade among Castilian dominions on an equal footing with Castilian-born subjects, as well as promising freedom from enslavement. For the time being these stipulations held good and the recipients of this charter must have been satisfied.

From that time on, the movement of

around his power base in the north of the island, to submit to Spanish rule.

Yet victory still proved elusive and, frustrated by the inaccessibility of the insurgents of the south who held out in the central mountains, beyond perilous goat walks and precipitous defiles, Pedro de Vera turned to a policy of terror and of scorched earth.

Innocent natives were burnt to death in reprisal for the loss of Spanish soldiers. Supplies and livestock were seized to deny them to the enemy. Gradually, coerced by these tactics, or persuaded by the eloquence of Don Fernando, the natives surrendered. Some abandoned hope and ended their struggle by ritual self-immolation, flinging

"loyalism" among the natives grew, so that in coming campaigns, Pedro de Vera was able to play off rival factions as a means to final victory. In particular, the capture and conversion of one of the most important chiefs, known to tradition as Tenesor Semidan but better identified by his baptismal name of Don Fernando Guanarteme, in February 1482, immeasurably strengthened de Vera's hand, as Don Fernando was able to induce many of his compatriots, especially

Left, the Spanish defend their acquisitions. Above, Los Letreros, undeciphered Guanche writings on the island of Hierro.

themselves from terrible heights, scenes that were described by Spanish chroniclers.

A small band continued resistance with justified confidence, for even in the winter of 1483, they were able to win a remarkable victory by their usual practice of precipitating an avalanche against the enemy column.

De Vera, implicitly acknowledging that force could not prevail against them on their chosen terrain, withdrew to Las Palmas and invited his adversaries to make honourable terms. Apart from rebels who roamed the mountain-tops for a few more years, without inflicting any serious damage, the entire island was held to have submitted by 1483.

Compared with the older colonies of Lanzarote and Fuerteventura, early colonial Gran Canaria was a land of opportunity. The easternmost islands were short of natural advantages, with their scant rainfall, low reliefs and sandy, stony soil. They were, moreover, lands of intermediate lordship and difficult landlords, where the hold of the local seigneurs interposed between subjects and the crown.

In the Spanish monarchy of the 16th century, it was proverbially more desirable for subjects to be ruled directly by the sovereigns and, though there was no reoccurrence on either Lanzarote or Fuerteventura of the rebellions against intermediate lordship which characterised the 15th century, the inhabitants smarted under a fiscal regime that was generally less favourable than that of their neighbours. It became necessary to restrict migration from the seigneurial to the royal islands by law.

Gran Canaria, by contrast, had exploitable soil, an enviable geographical position and a favourable form of government which, for a while, was unique not only in the archipelago but also in the entire Spanish monarchy.

Early government: The most conspicuous of the institutions by which the island was ruled was the governorship. The very name betrays the transitional nature of this phase of the islands' history. When Pedro de Vera was first appointed to the office, the name had inescapable military connotations: it suggested the commander of a fortress or garrison town. For the first time in Castilian history, in the Canaries the title came to have the modern sense of the word "governor"— the administrator of an outlying province or dependency, representing the monarchs with sovereign powers.

De Vera lasted for ten years in the job. As the military side of the governor's functions diminished in importance and civil preoccupations came to the fore, the nature of the dignity changed and a new type of man, a civil servant rather than a soldier, was needed. The image of Sancho Panza's island, in which "letters and arms are equally

Left, Pedro de Vera, first governor of the islands.

needful" was realised in successive stages of the history of Gran Canaria.

A succession of governor-bureaucrats unfolded rapidly. Short tenure was a device by which the monarchs controlled the abuse of power in so remote a province. Each new governor conducted a judicial investigation of his predecessor's conduct on arrival, and as a result, there were occasional level stretches of even-handed government.

Under the governor, there were two representative institutions: the assembly of citizens, which continued to meet in Gran Canaria well into the 16th century, at a time when communal and popular institutions had elsewhere fallen into disuse; and the *cabildo* or island council, where real local power resided.

The *cabildo* was a self-perpetuating oligarchy, chosen by lot from among the nominees of six electors, who were themselves appointed by members of the outgoing council. Only the monarchs could tamper with this cosy process by decreeing nominations and expulsions. The *cabildo* was both the main administrative organ of the island and the court of first instance. Because Gran Canaria had no resident aristocracy, it was a genuinely bourgeois institution, almost exclusively dominated by merchants and the agents or kin of big sugar-producers, who were engaged in a thoroughly capitalist industrial enterprise.

It was in the nature of the government of Gran Canaria that the excesses of gubernatorial power, which otherwise might have accrued from the island's remoteness from the throng, were thus checked by popular and oligarchic institutions and frequent interventions by the crown. This system was an outcome of the peculiar circumstances of the conquest. Unlike the seigneurial islands, it had been conquered by royal initiative, and the crown could therefore impose the institutions—quaintly called *fueros* or liberties— which it wanted; unlike the islands to the west, Tenerife and La Palma, the finance had been raised in the royal circle, and it was therefore not necessary to pledge profits of justice or administration to a "private sector" in advance.

In 1526 the royal share of power was extended when a permanent royal court of appeal, of which the judges were royal nominees and normally outsiders in island society, was established in Las Palmas. The expense in time and money involved in supervising the administration of justice and hearing appeals was cut at a stroke "in order", as the royal writ explained, "that the residents should encounter no vexation nor fatigue in coming to prosecute their suits". It was the kind of expedient that was being tried in all the distant fringes of what was by now a world-wide monarchy.

The court's jurisdiction extended throughout the Canaries and, as time went on

ish capitalists created a society which was all the more diverse for being small.

In June 1502 the governor in Las Palmas reported that "great thanks to God, this island grows every day, especially this town". In the second decade of the century, baptisms showed an average 50 percent annual increase over the previous ten-year period and settled down only in the 1530s.

Even at its peak, however, the entire population of the island—to judge from the estimates of cereal requirements, which are the only surviving evidence—is unlikely to have surpassed 20,000 in the 16th century. The total was only 20,458 in 1678, according to an episcopal census.

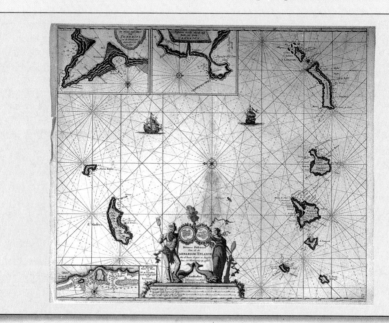

and the tribunal gradually swallowed up many of the administrative functions of rival institutions into its judicial role, it tended to unify the archipelago and to make Las Palmas the capital of the "Kingdom of the Canary Islands".

For a while at least, Gran Canaria's peculiar and conspicuous status made it attractive to settlers. For a brief spell, intensive settlement from far and wide made it the most cosmopolitan colony in the monarchy. Between the mid-1480s and the mid-1520s, Castilian planters and artisans, Portuguese share-croppers and technicians, Jewish and Morisco refugees, Catalan, Italian and Flem-

The most elusive element, in every sense, was the indigenous population of the Guanches and their descendants. Pedro de Vera's security policy involved mass deportations and illegal enslavement for export. Conquest and colonisation, moreover, took a heavy toll in deaths and inflicted unfamiliar killer-diseases and lethal culture-shocks.

Plagues in 1514 and 1522-3 reduced the numbers of surviving natives to insignificant levels. They were not merely displaced by the colonists, but engulfed. In contrast, for

Above, the Canaries and Madeira, an early navigational map.

example, to Tenerife, no native names figure among the lists of land-grants.

Comfortable prosperity: The period of successful settlement of the island came to an end by the middle of the 16th century, when an anonymous chronicler of Gran Canaria complained, "If the Indies had not been discovered, where all go who determine to migrate in search of fame and out of greed for gold and silver, then would Gran Canaria become a second Cyprus, and if it were fully cultivated and settled, truly it would become a major kingdom in its own right."

Yet even when the boom years were over, a comfortable level of prosperity remained, and the colonisation of the New World, if it deflected settlers, increased economic opportunities. The basis of the economy for most of the 16th century was the sugar trade. With her sister-isles to the west, Gran Canaria became a rival spicery, supplying Europe with the only Atlantic product that could compete as a high-value condiment with the spices of the east.

As with tea and coffee in the 18th century or chocolate in the 19th, popular taste quickly responded to a supply-led cycle and sugar became fashionable. The first mill was erected at Agaete in the year after the completion of the conquest. A rich Genoese of Seville advanced the capital for it and quickly bought in the mortgage; the large scale of investment required to set the industry up—planting the canes, irrigating the fields, building the mills, organising the labour for the refineries and providing water, or horsedriven power meant that the island suddenly acquired a rich foreign élite.

The Rivarolo family, for instance, based, like most of the island's prolific Genoese capitalists, in Seville, threatened to gain a stranglehold on the export of sugar and dyes, surviving Castilian settlers' attempts to expel or dispossess them.

With the Genoese planters came Portuguese technical advisers and share-croppers from the already established sugar industry of Madeira and black slaves, not for plantation work, which was all done by more cost-effective European labour, but for the more demanding heavy work in the refineries: boiling and carrying the liquid.

In 1535, the biggest mill on Gran Canaria had 23 slaves, 20 of them black. The small and specialised nature of the black labour force helped to ensure that the Canaries would be protected from racial problems that have bedevilled the history of so many other erstwhile plantation-lands of the Colonial Atlantic world.

Lucrative as the sugar-trade was, it could not last. The New World gradually established a sugar industry of its own which could undercut that of the Canaries; meanwhile, transatlantic colonies were growing, offering a tempting market for Canarian wines, which could also be exported to the northern European outlets, especially in England and the Low Countries, which had bought in large quantities of Canarian sugar.

Gran Canaria, however, could not benefit from the wine boom as she had from that of sugar. Tenerife had better soil for viticulture and, at Santa Cruz, an ideal port for the transatlantic trade. Sugar production had probably peaked by the mid-16th century, and the rapid growth of Tenerife's wines from then onwards marked the beginning of Gran Canaria's long relative decline, during which the islands of the eastern archipelago became a rather depressed "colony" of the comparatively rich and successful Tenerife. Gran Canaria's agriculture industry came to serve chiefly to supplement the other islands' food supply.

Forgotten islands: If Gran Canaria was relegated to second rank in the first great era of the islands' long-range trade, the seigneurial islands of the eastern archipelago, Lanzarote and Fuerteventura, were almost by-passed.

They went unmentioned in the instructions for navigators to the Indies printed by the protectors and promoters of Atlantic traffic in Seville. Their lack of sugar and little exportable wine made them of little interest to the international mercantile community. They lived by a cruder form of exchange than commerce—by piracy on the seas and raids on the coasts of Africa.

The words of the seigneurs in a late 16th-century petition to the crown may be exaggerated but are surely suggestive: "Since these islands were conquered, they have lived by war both in the conquest of the other islands and thereafter in attacking and making war on the Moors". By that period, captives from Barbary constituted the biggest element in the population of Lanzarote.

Piracy made for a precarious way of life, as did the other marginal activities of early-modern Lanzaroteños who made a living from the pickings of long-range trade through smuggling, interloping and fraud.

In the Lanzarote valley of Miraflores, south of Teguise, the Franciscan church is all that remains of the richest monument of the seigneurial era—the Herrera family pantheon, burned by pirates in 1618 and poorly restored with inadequate alms. The image of the Virgin of Guadelupe in Teguise still bears a corsair's sabre-cut in her cheek.

Yet the pirate war was gradually won and, over the 17th century as a whole, security fitfully improved. The port of Arrecife replaced Teguise as the main centre of population: instead of cowering in the hinterland,

the inhabitants could seek to prosper from passing maritime traffic from behind the relative safety of the Castle of San Gabriel.

In 1610, the New World trade was officially opened to residents of the Canary Islands trading from their home ports. This remained a peculiar privilege of the Canaries for 150 years. Lines of business once clandestinely drawn up could now be legitimately exploited, and the transformation wrought in the economic prospects of the seigneurial islands prompted a century of fierce lawsuits among rival claimants to the inheritance of the Herreras.

Mariana Enríquez Manrique de la Vega,

widow of the first Marquess of Lanzarote, married four more times after her husband's death in an effort to secure the island for her heirs. Now that it was linked to the New World even Fuerteventura was desirable enough to draw the gaze of the most cupidinous pair of eyes in Spain: those of the corrupt Duke of Lerma, Philip III's favourite, whose attempt to appropriate the island was only just beaten off.

Rivalry with Tenerife: Gran Canaria's loss of supremacy within the archipelago, to Tenerife, resulted in the 17th century in the displacement westwards of the centre of gravity of island government. La Laguna on Tenerife became the normal residence of a supreme official, called the Captain-General, with authority superior to that of the Audiencia, which remained in Las Palmas, its administrative competence increasingly limited to local affairs.

The modest charm of the Vegueta, or old town, of Las Palmas, contrasts with the Baroque grandeur of the capital which succeeded it in Tenerife. For the best part of three centuries, political life on Gran Canaria was dominated by the need to preserve the relics of bygone pre-eminence— the Audiencia, the episcopal see, and the tribunal of the Inquisition—in Las Palmas.

Rivalry with Tenerife dominated issues of national and international significance. In 1776 Bishop Severa founded at Las Palmas the first Economic Society of the islands— an "improving " body dedicated to devising practical application of the idea of progress; in 1781 the island council provided the funds to build a new cathedral in Las Palmas to forestall La Laguna's plans.

Even the most bitterly parochial controversy of all—over whether the image of the Virgin of the Pine-tree at Teror, Gran Canaria, should be censed more often than a similar statue of the Virgin with a different following in Las Palmas—was related to the inter-island rivalry; the Virgin of Teror was the patroness of Gran Canaria, whose élite were anxious to enhance her statue to compete with the cult of the Virgin of Candelaria. The latter claimed the allegiance and devotion of the entire archipelago from her shrine in Tenerife.

Rival virgins...(left) of Candelaria in Tenerife, and (right) of the Pines in Gran Canaria.

THE STRUGGLE FOR IDENTITY

Gran Canaria's opportunity for self-assertion came with the Napoleonic invasion of mainland Spain. Within a fortnight of the popular uprising in the peninsula on 2 May 1808, the news of the invasion had reached the islands by brigantine.

Following the model of the provisional government in Seville, notables in La Laguna on Tenerife gathered to form a Junta of Defence to continue the functions of government on behalf of the Spanish state for the duration of the emergency. All the other islands subscribed except Gran Canaria, which proclaimed a Junta of its own.

The reaction of the central provisional government was stern: island institutions were suppressed and direct rule from the peninsula became more comprehensive than under the Habsburg and Bourbon "absolutisms" of the previous two centuries. Gran Canaria's position looked inauspicious. Tenerife had a virtual monopoly of the archipelago's long-range trade and her agricultural production figures towered over her rivals: she produced six times as much wine as Gran Canaria, two-thirds as much again of wheat, more than three times as many potatoes. Only in low-value animal fodders was Gran Canaria the islands' main producer.

Intellectual life was centred in Tenerife, in the salons of the aristocrats of La Laguna and the proto-university of San Fernando. Gran Canaria failed to obtain concessions from the national convention which met in Cadiz in 1812: the suppression of island councils and the creation of numerous small municipalities tended to strengthen, by comparison, the institutions located in Tenerife. Gran Canaria remained obsessed with its relationship with the other Canary Islands.

Ripples from the mainland: New opportunities arose with the period of constitutional instability that began in the mid-1830s, new challenges with the era of 1808 were echoed in a new crisis in 1840. A coup in Madrid provided a pretext for the proclamation of rival Juntas in Tenerife and Las Palmas; the

latter demonstrated its progressive credentials by ordering the demolition of a dissolved Convent of St Clare to build a secular theatre, before submitting to the government's order to disband. It had been an inglorious adventure, but it did help to make the voice of Gran Canaria heard in Madrid.

Experiments with the status of Tenerife's subject-islands—a failed legislative measure to divide the archipelago into two provinces, a short-lived attempt to create vice-governorships in important islands—were

tried in the 1840s. In the next decade, the confidence of Gran Canaria increased and on two occasions—briefly, in 1852 and 1860— her deputies secured laws in favour of a division of the archipelago into two provinces of equivalent power.

In the 1860s the unfairness of Tenerife's dominance seemed apparent: she virtually monopolised road-building funds; her ports served almost half the archipelago's total traffic; Gran Canaria was denied resources to adapt her harbours to long-range steamship trade; and the minor islands still had no steamship services at all.

Spokesmanship for the islands' cause in

Government from Madrid meant the imposition of unfair practices, closed doors (left) for Gran Canaria, and military presence (right).

Madrid was shifting to Las Palmas, where Agustín Millares Torres created an intellectual and antiquarian circle, whose work on Canarian history was inspired by a strong sense of identity and a feeling that the Spanish state had neglected this remote province.

On the economic front, the introduction of cochineal—a real "river of gold" according to Millares Torres—and the growth of an important tobacco industry equipped Gran Canaria to compete more effectively in the second half of the century.

It is by no means apparent that Fuerteventura and Lanzarote wished to follow Gran Canaria into a future free of the tutelage of Tenerife. In most of the constitutional crises

which erupted near Yaiza and burned for seven years, enriched the soil with a layer of volcanic ash and facilitated a new form of irrigation because of the way dew collects in depressions. Though the island, with Fuerteventura, could still be wracked by famine at the end of the 1760s, diversification and production made steady progress.

While Fuerteventura remained limited to dry farming for low yields of wheat and fodder, Lanzarote in the 19th century could export wine, linen and silk and produce good crops of green and root vegetables. On the other hand Fuerteventura remained the "thirsting rock" brilliantly evoked in a sonnet by Unamuno; she was in no condition to

of the 19th century, the authorities of the easternmost islands continued to acknowledge the supremacy of the acknowledged capital of the archipelago, though Fuerteventura's attitude was sometimes equivocal. The parliamentary deputies tended to favour local autonomy, but not necessarily splitting the Canaries into two provinces or creating a regional capital at Las Palmas.

Changed fortunes: Lanzarote, in particular, did well out of the economic changes of the 18th and 19th centuries and had no particular interest in a political movement inspired by economic and cultural jealousies. Lanzarote's extraordinary seismic blast of 1730,

influence the political destiny of the archipelago. Lanzarote settled down to enjoy unaccustomed comforts and was therefore in no mood to get involved in politics.

Changes in land ownership were anyway tending gradually to forge an alliance between the élites of all three eastern islands. The Vega Grande and Manrique de Lara families, for instance, had built up huge properties. The islands were under the local political control of quasi-feudal bosses whose relations with their tenants and labourers were good—there were no agitations by peasant-anarchists in the large estates of the Canaries to match those of Andalusia—but these bosses stirred up common antipathy towards the bourgeois politicians who ran the western islands.

Key figure: Late in the third quarter of the 19th century, Gran Canaria found a political "man of destiny" whose influence was to have a genuinely transforming effect.

The background to the rise of Fernando León y Castillo is formed by the "democratic" revolution of 1868 in Spain, which expelled the Bourbons and plunged the constitution into the crucible. For all the historic communities of Spain, devolved, autonomous, federal or separatist status were all up for grabs.

News of the revolution had the customary

immediate effect in the islands. Self-proclaimed Juntas took over in Tenerife and Las Palmas, the latter asserting its direct responsibility to Madrid, and instantly effecting measures of old-fashioned anti-clerical liberalism—turning, for instance, the site of the main Roman Catholic convent into an intended botanical garden.

Perhaps the most extraordinary proclamation was that which suspended celebrations of the anniversary of the completion of the

Left, cochineal beetles carved out a brief prosperity for Lanzarote. Right, Leon y Castillo transferred the seat of power.

15th-century conquest on the grounds that the conquest was an "anti-humanitarian manifestation...against a valiant and greathearted people who sought only to defend their independence." The Junta's real enemy, however, was in Tenerife.

The Las Palmas Junta's revolutionary rhetoric was ignored by the people, who voted with their bosses, and it reluctantly yielded power, along with other local Juntas, in December 1868.

The broad-suffrage elections of the following year revealed a decisive anti-democratic and anti-republican majority. Among the successful candidates, León y Castillo stood out as peculiarly qualified by wealth, competence, eloquence and metropolitan connexions to play a leading role.

He made his mark by opposing the federalist republican constitution of 1873. His professed reasons were all generalised and sophisticated: federalism was inconsistent with the national character of Spain; it was an anachronism in the age of the nation-state; it tended to foster the inefficiencies of subdivisions into cantons.

But León y Castillo's real motive was left temporarily unvoiced: he conceived federalism as unfavourable to Gran Canaria, which would, he feared, be permanently consigned to a subordinate place in the archipelago if the proposed constitution prevailed.

On 11 June 1873, the deputies for the Canary Islands were summoned by Nicholás Estévanez, a cabinet minister who happened also to be a deputy for Tenerife, and made to sign a "compromise" imposing single federal status on the archipelago. León y Castillo signed, but devoted himself to making the new status unworkable and to advancing the cause of Gran Canaria.

His methods were twofold: within the islands, he built up an electoral machine and network of alliances with members of the élites of other islands; the aim was to create an anti-Tenerife block of votes. In Madrid, meanwhile, he cultivated liberal politicians.

Castillo's opportunity: The packet boat which brought the news of the restoration of the monarchy in January 1875 was received with general approval in the islands but with mixed feelings by León y Castillo. The federal constitution was now dead, but a conservative reaction was inevitable, which would keep his own alliance out of power.

Indeed the new governor, Vicente Clavijo, was a tough old lawyer who took dictatorial powers, ruled uncompromisingly and closed down such institutions of popular education as the Gabinete Instructive, which León y Castillo had been using to promote his own programme.

Luckily for the cause of Gran Canaria, the new regime's blatant bias towards Tenerife helped León y Castillo to win friends in every other island: particularly resented were Clavijo's orders restricting migrant-carrying traffic to the ports of Tenerife and his selective channelling of funds. In 1878 the Captain-general—that is, commander of the armed forces' garrisons throughout the

The liberal government fell in 1884, to great rejoicing in Tenerife, but by then it was already too late. Work in Las Palmas had been urged on at an astonishing rate. From 1887, Gran Canaria had the best part of the steamship trade passing through the islands.

Within the archipelago, León y Castillo's efforts to promote Gran Canaria's interests through a multi-island alliance were crowned with success in 1893, when the islands' electoral college gathered to make its elections to the national Senate.

The meeting took place in the port which was Las Palmas' biggest rival, Santa Cruz de Tenerife, and the results provoked a riot.

The deputies from two of the minor is-

islands—showed his disapproval of the conduct of the civilian governor by building headquarters in Las Palmas and Tenerife.

A change of government in 1881 gave León y Castillo his great chance. As Foreign Minister under the new liberal premier he was in an ideal position to secure for his home island what he saw as a potentially decisive economic advantage. He rushed through a programme of improvements to the port of Las Palmas which were designed to make it the archipelago's major port by the end of the century. At about the same time, Las Palmas was adopted as a stop on the new steamboat schedule to the West Indies.

lands of the west had voted with those from Gran Canaria, Lanzarote and Fuerteventura to overturn the usual Tenerife majority. León y Castillo himself and his ally Weyler headed the poll. Hotheads at home wanted León y Castillo to follow up his triumph by hurrying through a measure to divide the islands into two provinces or at least to divide the status of capital so that Las Palmas enjoyed equality. A group even revived the Conservative Party of Gran Canaria—defunct since 1881—to demonstrate disapproval of the boss's apparent tepidity.

Perhaps because he preferred to proceed with moderation, León y Castillo refused to be rushed. It is at least possible that he was intending no longer merely to obtain equality for Las Palmas, but supremacy: he may have been aiming at the transfer of all the islands' chief institutions to his home ground. Gran Canaria, certainly, continued to grow in wealth and importance, but not, for the time being—though in 1903 a bill to divide the archipelago only just failed—in political status.

Foreign influence: León y Castillo was the political architect of Gran Canaria's revival, but his work was consolidated in the economic sphere by the efforts of a British businessman, Sir Alfred Lewis Jones, who moved the vast coaling station of the British

and African Steamship Company from Sierra Leone to Las Palmas.

Steam navigation and seaborne refrigeration were transforming the importance of the Canary Islands generally; and thanks to León y Castillo's sagacity, Gran Canaria was the main beneficiary. Britain and Germany vied to secure a base in an area that promised to be of key strategic significance for the control of access to Africa and for mastery of Atlantic sea-lanes generally.

The coming of steamships and refrigeration boosted trade. Above, Alfred Jones, pioneer of the coaling industry.

More than any other individual, Jones turned Gran Canaria into a sort of informal colony of the British Empire. He founded the Grand Canary Coaling Company; helped to get Elder Dempster to open up their fruit business in the island; encouraged the Bank of British West Africa to do the same; built the first ice factory; opened the luxurious Santa Catalina and other hotels; laid out the charming Barrio de Ciudad Jardín (Garden City) in Las Palmas; helped set up the Exposición Provincial in 1892, which proved to be a major stimulus to the encouragement of foreign investment; and, by the way, helped decisively to promote two of the islands' most important 20th-century industries: banana-production and tourism.

A happy result of the sudden economic miracle of the last two decades of the 19th century was the limited political impact of the Cuban War of 1898. The cochineal trade, on which the economy of the archipelago had come to rely in the mid-century, had been hit by the development of artificial dyes, and had peaked in about 1870. If a way had not been found out of the ensuing depression, economic discontent might have generated political violence.

Though the Canaries were formally a part of metropolitan Spain, and though the island élite had never had a "creole" mentality, the islands, especially the self-consciously backward and exploited eastern group, had an unmistakeable colonial air. Successive monocultures—sugar, wine, soda, cochineal—had boomed and collapsed in turn, condemning the economy to vulnerability and dependence. The Cuban and Filipino independence movements, which culminated in the war of 1898 and defeat for Spain, might have come to the Canaries, too.

Clinging to the mainland: In fact, the reverse happened. Canarios' sense of their Spanish identity was intensified by the loss of the last oceanic colonies. The novelist, Benito Pérez Galdós, who happened to have been born in Gran Canaria, spoke for most of his fellow-countrymen when he proclaimed the islands "Spain's advanced guard in the midst of the Atlantic". An independence party, inspired by the Cuban example, achieved a certain intellectual éclat, but little real support.

By the early years of the 20th century, Gran Canaria, and Las Palmas in particular, had recovered and exceeded economic par-

FRANCO GOES TO WAR

The summer of 1936 was hot and sticky in the Canaries. Winds from the Sahara brought a constant succession of scorching winds and choking dust. A paunchy little man called Franco, once Commander-in-Chief of the Spanish Army, must have found his Canarian posting gruelling.

In March of that year Franco had been removed to Tenerife by the Republican government, fearful of his reputation as a soldier and of his right-wing sentiments—he was suspected of being involved in a series of plots aimed at setting up a dictatorship under a fellow officer, General Sanjurjo. While Sanjurjo was exiled to Portugal, Franco managed to wriggle out of charges of complicity.

In Sanjurjo's absence the military plotters were headed by General Mola. Just before he left for the Canaries, Franco, Mola, and another principal leader of the "Glorious Revolution" of 1936, General Goded, agreed at a secret meeting to back Sanjurjo, who was then in Germany seeking arms and ammunition.

In spite of this promise of support Franco refused to commit himself to any firm plan of action until barely a week before the rising. Nevertheless he joined the other discontented officers at their meetings in the woods of La Esperanza in Tenerife or in the English-owned hotel of Los Frailes on Gran Canaria.

Only the promise of command of Spain's best troops—her tough Moroccan mercenaries and her ruthless Foreign Legion—succeeded in bringing Franco into the plot. Within 48 hours a Dragon Rapide bi-plane had been chartered from the old Croydon aerodrome near London.

On 14 July 1936 the Rapide touched down at Gando, now Las Palmas airport and then the only one in the islands. On board was a select party of English tourists—a retired army major, Hugh Pollard, his daughter Diana, and her friend Dorothy Watson. The family went sightseeing. In Tenerife Pollard contacted one of Franco's officers and delivered his message—*"Galicia saluda a Francia"* (Galicia greets France).

On 16 July the ex-RAF pilot of the Dragon Rapide was warned to have his plane ready. On the same day, the commanding officer of the Las Palmas garrison, General Amadeo Balmes, died conveniently as he cleaned his pistol. By nightfall Franco had obtained the War Office's permission to travel over to his fellow-officer's funeral.

At midnight Franco, his wife and daughter boarded the little Clyde-built steamer, the *Viera y Clavijo*. Shortly after docking in Las Palmas, Franco found the North African garrisons had started the uprising prematurely. An arms search of the rebel HQ in Melilla on the Moroccan coastline had forced the plotters to strike early.

During that hot and hectic afternoon Franco left Las Palmas for the airport. Perhaps fearing an assassination attempt—he had survived three during his short spell on Tenerife—he commandeered "a scruffy tug-boat" to get him there.

By the early hours of 18 July, Franco was in North Africa to broadcast his manifesto, promising "to make real in our homeland, for the first time and in this order, that trinity, Fraternity, Liberty and Equality."

The Canary Islands were in Franco's hands by 20 July. On the island of La Palma a false normality was maintained for a further eight sweltering days until the capital, Santa Cruz, was finally bombarded by a pro-Franco cruiser, and surrendered.

Within hours the repression began. Trade Unionists, teachers, left-wing or democratic politicians, and writers and artists were imprisoned or murdered.

Lieutenant Gonzalez Campos, the only officer in Tenerife to oppose the rising with arms, was given a summary court-martial, along with the civil governor and his staff, and shot. The governor's "crime" had been to shout, "Long live libertarian communism", though he was neither a libertine nor a communist, and independent witnesses had heard only the words "Long live the Republic".

Republican prisoners in Tenerife were herded into Fyffes' warehouse, near the present football ground in Santa Cruz. There they sweated it out, waiting to be shot in batches in the appropriately named Barranco del Infierno (Hell's Ravine) until the sport got tedious. The oil refinery now marks the spot.

ity with Tenerife and the rival port of Santa Cruz. León y Castillo was now an elder statesman, dignified with the apt title of Marqués del Muni, which reflected the role which the African steamship traffic had played in his island's *Wirtschaftswunder*, or miraculous economic recovery.

Yet no political realignment with the archipelago had taken place and economic success only nurtured Gran Canaria's political ambitions. In 1903, the Partido Local Canario was formed, with a programme advocating division of the archipelago into two provinces.

The effect was twofold: demands for autonomy were stimulated among opponents

countered with a "Canarian Assembly", meeting under a seven-starred flag; representatives of La Palma suggested that the rivalry of the big islands should be resolved by moving the capital to La Palma; the government's suggestion—alternating capital status for both Las Palmas and Santa Cruz—pleased no one; but a strong consensus did emerge in favour of restored *cabildos*.

In 1911 Gran Canaria hosted an assembly of its own, attended by representatives of Lanzarote and Fuerteventura, where, however, opinion was still divided. The national legislature held one public inquiry, which declared for provincial unity; the government held another, which favoured division.

of division as a means of diverting popular sentiment from the Partido Local, and all political interests advocated a return to *cabildos*—the island-wide councils founded at the time of the conquest—to sustain the interests of single islands, whether that be in an autonomous archipelago or in a pair of provinces.

In 1908 a new local government law created an opportunity for deputies of the Partido Local to table amendments calling for a division of the islands; the autonomists

Above, Las Palmas as it was at the turn of the century.

A return to *cabildos* was effected in default of any alternative consensus. Almost at once, it was realised that Gran Canaria had triumphed "by the back door": the *cabildos* could associate freely, effectively splitting the province. Provincial unity was reduced as the prime minister observed, to "wreckage on the beach".

The First World War threatened the newest of the Canaries' monocultures—the banana—with collapse. British control, of seaways and the internal economy alike, made Canarian involvement in the war more intense, and its effects more severe, than that of any other part of Spain. Between 1913 and

1917, banana exports fell by over 80 percent and the unit value by nearly as much.

Emigration, especially to the New World, became a flood. The recovery of trade after the war was slow, periodically rent by global depression or recession. Formalisation of the division of the archipelago in 1927 brought no new economic solutions, but it did, perhaps give the eastern islands new hope and self-confidence.

The proclamation of the Spanish Republic in 1931, and the expectations it excited of a new quasi-federal constitution were perceived in Gran Canaria as a threat. The autonomist leader was Gil Roldán, a romantic dandy with green bow tie and flowing

pocket-handkerchief. Gran Canaria held aloof from the assembly he convoked in May to call for devolved government in the archipelago; a deputy from Tenerife, Andrés de Orozco, foreshadowed the present Spanish constitution by calling for the entire country to be split into 14 more or less equally powerful regional committees, of which the Canaries would be one.

Franco: It looked as if Gil Roldán's case might win government backing, when, in July 1936, General Franco flew from his command in Tenerife to launch the Civil War. Under Francoism, the islands remained divided and Las Palmas preserved its status—for what it was worth under an authoritarian and centralist regime—as a provincial capital. The islands were rewarded for their loyalty to Franco by the combination of a favourable fiscal regime and government investment policy.

As with the rest of Spain, for the eastern Canaries prosperity under Francoism was long deferred, but spectacular when it arrived. Lanzarote and Gran Canaria, in particular, were able to exploit the tourist boom, begun in the sixties, that increased the average number of annual visitors from 40,000 to four million.

Tourism became the last of the islands' monocultures—but within a more diversified economy than ever before, with a strong agrarian sector, based on tomatoes and bananas, complemented by a fishing industry which has continued to grow despite disputes over zones and quotas, and the enormous benefits to the infrastructure that tourism has brought.

Fortunately the consequent over-exploitation and over-population of tourism has—no thanks to the planners—been steered by topography and climate away from the areas of traditional settlement, particularly in Gran Canaria, so that traditional life has not been utterly smothered by the industry's overpowering embrace.

Since the new constitution of 1978, regional autonomy has at last arrived—uncontroversially, unbedevilled by the bitter interisland rivalries of the past. It took the Franco regime's blend of political inertia and economic vitality to enable the islands to outgrow their internecine squabbles.

Talk of separatism, past and present, is a joke, diverted from Mickey-mouse terrorism into the invention of a "native" language. The sublime irony is that after centuries of the supremacy of an endogamous and introspective culture, characterised by net emigration for most of the time, the present generation, which has witnessed so massive an influx of Germans, Scandinavians and Britons, has renewed the diverse character of settlement in the islands, as was established after the conquest, theoretically by the French, 650 years ago.

Left, the Canary banana, once a symbol of prosperity. Right, surfers offshore from Playa Canteras, Las Palmas.

Quite who Canarios were and how they lived before the arrival of conquering mainland Europeans is still more a matter for supposition than of fact. But it seems appropriate that the islanders should have an insubstantiality about them; the islands themselves have a shadowy form, figuring in various mythologies, some more modern than others, but none with any real founding in fact. Beyond the sphere of man's knowledge of the world until as recently as the 13th century, the Canaries feature in legend over and over again.

Atlantis: If you want to write a convincing history of a place that never existed, be sure to give it a good long, dry bibliography. J. L. Borges did this for his invented land of Uqbar, and Atlantis, an invention many centuries older than Uqbar, has its long, dry bibliography, too. "We can make the acquaintance of one 'eminent Atlantologist' after another in bulky works," as the Swedish archaeologist Carl Nylander put it. In other words, if a thing is written three times it becomes history.

But there are different kinds of bulky works. In the case of Atlantis, they are bulky works "of somewhat unnecessary learning, where references and footnote systems seem to have a decorative rather than clarifying effect." Like the literature of Uqbar, that of Atlantis is fundamentally fantasy and never really refers to reality in any of its varied and verbose passages.

Borges invented Uqbar, as Thomas Moore invented Utopia and Plato invented Atlantis—to make a point. All three existed only as metaphors for society, real or imagined, repressive or ideal.

The "historical" evidence for Atlantis is to be found in two of Plato's dialogues, *Timaeus* and *Critias*, which describe the visit of Solon, an Athenian scholar, to Egypt, which for contemporary Greeks was *the* cultural mecca. Solon made his trip around the beginning of the sixth century B.C. but, from an aged holy man in Sais, a city in the

Nile Delta, he heard what was supposed to be the true history of the Greeks.

Beyond the Pillars of Hercules, in the western ocean, had once lain Atlantis. Nine thousand years before Solon's time it had been the superpower of its day—wealthy, strong and ruled by the wisest of men. The capital of Atlantis was circular in plan, the centre being a huge pillar of gleaming bronze on which were inscribed the laws of Atlantis. Here, too, was the temple to Poseidon, God of the Ocean, and the palace. On one side was

the ocean and on the other the vast, well-ordered irrigated plain.

But power corrupts, and the rulers of Atlantis set out on a path of world domination. Only heroic little Athens stood up to Atlantis. And Athens won.

The victory though was pyrrhic. A series of dreadful natural calamities destroyed Athens in 24 hours. Out in the west, Atlantis sank without trace to the bottom of Poseidon's ocean. Only Egypt came through the world-wide catastrophe, guardian of this ancient lore.

The Atlantis myth, if it reflects reality at all, is probably a dim memory of the destruc-

Left, myth and artistic licence unite in an intriguing playground figure. Right, chieftain statue on Tenerife, perpetuating the Canary mythology.

tion of the Minoan civilisation based in Crete. The location given by Plato—beyond the Pillars of Hercules, the Straits of Gibraltar—is little more than a literary convention; just as today we would place our imaginary societies in outer space. The Atlantis tale was the Star Trek of its day.

And the fall of Minoan Crete was in all probability as cataclysmic as the submersion of Atlantis. Nine centuries before Solon's trip to Egypt the volcanic island Thera, 70 miles (112 km) from Crete's northern coast, blew up. The Cretan civilisation ended with a horrendous bang.

Nevertheless, innumerable scholars have sought to locate Plato's Atlantis. Often the the Azores, Madeira, the Canaries and the Cape Verde islands.

Of course, such suggestions take little notice of minor inconveniences like geography and geology. The Azores lie on the mid-Atlantic ridge, over 600 miles (1,000 km) from the Canaries, which are themselves loosely attached to Africa. The Cape Verdes are located approximately 1,300 miles (2,000 km) south of the Canaries.

And between the Azores and the Canaries are trenches reaching depths of four miles (seven km). Mount Teide on Tenerife would have been, by this reckoning, higher than Everest is today. Moreover, the forces involved in the feat of removing a block of land

location of Atlantis coincides with the author's own country of origin—the Swede Olof Rudbeck placed its heartland in the Uppsala region, and there is a German work entitled *Atlantis, The Home of the Aryans*. The interests of more recent German anthropologists have focused more on the Guanches themselves.

The less patriotic, and the less xenophobic, have looked to the Atlantic Ocean, beyond the Straits of Gibraltar, and have lighted on the Canaries as the surviving mountain peaks of Atlantis. One Frenchman in the last century managed a marvellous reconstruction of the lost continent's outline—it took in the size of the present European Community would have destroyed the rest of the world as well.

The Guanches: The "increasing flow of misguided learning, lack of critical discernment, or simply downright lunacy" that surrounds Atlantis has been transferred to Canarian prehistory at various times, creating the "mystery of the Guanches". Tall, blonde lost Vikings; primitive, club-swinging throwbacks; or last survivors of an Atlantean master-race—you pay your money and you take your pick, according to your particular prejudices. A lot of theories have popped out of the woodwork.

Almost as soon as Blumenback started his innocent collection of human skulls at Göttingen University in West Germany, the Canary Islands were seized on as a laboratory for the "proving" of racial theory. Towards the end of the last century, physical anthropologists, like the Frenchman René Verneau, began working on the islands, measuring and sizing up the skulls of the living and the dead.

According to theory, developed in the wake of Darwin's theory of evolution and the system used by Danish antiquarians to classify ancient finds, mankind passed through a series of developmental stages equated with present-day races. The differ-

ences between present-day human groups are more or less easy to define—though they depend more on dress, foods and social customs than on more fundamental distinctions. But bones are bones.

In those days, a system of classifying human skulls was worked out on the basis of the breadth and length of the skull. Verneau and the Harvard scholar, Hooton, were using the most sophisticated research technique they had. Later investigators were not.

Left, the Guanches—lost Vikings or survivors of an Atlantean master-race? Above, Guanche monument in Las Palmas.

Indeed, in 1941 Himmler asked the SS's *Ahnenerbe* (Cultural Division) to look for evidence to connect the Stone Age inhabitants of central Europe—the makers of the big-bottomed "Venus" figurines—with the Hottentots and Bushmen, whose womenfolk also have well-padded posteriors. Some of Himmler's ethnographers looked towards North Africa for the link.

A Franco regime in the Canaries, with its own obsessions with "purity of the blood", and the isolation of the islands in prehistory made the archipelago a favourite haunt of racial theorists.

On the basis of skull shape alone, a complex series of invasions was suggested; the more "primitive" inhabitants being driven further inland until they finally died out—the islands have very little inland areas to be driven into!

This was misguided learning—the same "frightening and pathetic muddle of ravished science" that produced the literature of Atlantisology.

However, even if the Guanches are not the lost tribe of Israel or shipwrecked Vikings, there are interesting questions to be asked about them.

Apparently the Guanches had no boats when the Europeans arrived. So were they either brought to the islands as prisoners by the Romans or the Carthaginians, or had they simply "forgotten" how to build boats? Only one European chronicler mentions a boat—a dug-out dragon-wood canoe with a matting sail—but he was writing his account a century after the conquest.

The earliest European chronicles describe the native islanders as "swimming" out to the ships, but off the coast of Morocco one-man reed-bundles served until very recently as inshore boats. They are used pretty much as a buoyancy aid. Much bigger craft are still used on Lake Chad, and Thor Heyerdahl has sailed one across the Atlantic, passing by the Canaries.

And in 1404 the French adventurer Jean de Béthencourt brought a slave from Gomera to act as an intermediary with the slave's "brother", the chief of Hierro. If there were no boats in pre-conquest times, how could the two men be related? From Hiero to Gomera is a very long swim.

San Borondón: Still, strange things do happen at sea. Islands come and go and even

COLUMBUS ON THE CANARIES

In 1415 man knew of the existence of Europe, North Africa, and the Near East; by 1550 world maps had been enlarged to incorporate North, Central and South America and the rest of Africa. The Canaries played a key strategic role in those discoveries, spearheaded by one man, Christopher Columbus.

Columbus is one of those almost mythical celebrities who almost every country claims a connection with, and the man himself was sufficiently stateless to be suitable material for a tug-of-war between nations. Honest readers may admit to having believed during early school days that Columbus was of their nationality, but if the Canary islands and mainland Spain had their way you'd soon be brainwashed into believing that Cristobal Colón was a born-and-bred Spaniard, so heavily is supposed Colombiana spread over places Spanish, not least the Canaries.

Mallorca claims to be the birthplace of the great man, and there are two supposed burial places on mainland Spain, one at Santo Domingo and one in Seville. In the Canaries there is hardly a town without a Calle Colón and the island of La Palma boasts a massive cement model of one of his ships, even though La Palma is about the only island that does not claim a direct connection with the navigator.

In fact Columbus was the son of an Italian cloth-weaver in the city of Genoa, then one of the world's greatest maritime cities. However it was the Spanish court, not the Italian, who eventually sponsored his expeditions. The extent of his brief flirtation with the Canaries has for a long time been the subject of much local discussion, fuelled by inter-island rivalry.

It was on his second voyage of 1492, a crucial journey that ended with the discovery of Cuba, that Columbus definitely stopped at the Canaries, putting in at Gomera. Quite why he chose the smallest island is a point of discussion: some suggest it was because he already knew and had been attracted to Beatriz de Bobadilla, the Countess of the island, and others say it was because

Gomera, being the westernmost island, was the last stepping off point of the known world.

Gomera was by no means the best port in the islands, and Columbus evidently knew that, because when one of his fleet of three ships, the *Pinta*, broke a rudder in heavy weather, he left it to divert for repairs in Las Palmas on Gran Canaria while he hastened on to Gomera with the *Santa Maria* (his flagship) and the *Nina*.

Columbus himself described passing Tenerife (the last of the islands to be conquered, Tenerife was then still in Guanche hands, and staunchly resisting Spanish attacks) at an opportune moment, as he noted in his logbook: "As we were passing...we observed an eruption of the volcano. The smoke and flames, the glowing masses of lava, the muffled roaring from the earth's interior caused panic among the crew. They believed that the volcano had erupted because we had undertaken this voyage." Unfortunately Columbus's logbook does not go on to detail his movements through the islands on this and further journeys. Certainly the *Pinta* remained in Las Palmas for some time, and it is thought that Columbus went in search of it, although some local historians are adamant that he did not touch ground on Gran Canaria. Nevertheless Las Palmas leads the way in Colombiana, with a museum, a Casa Colón, a statue, and a church where he supposedly prayed before setting out for the New World, a claim also made of the church in San Sebastian de la Gomera.

The Las Palmas museum itself, although stimulating and atmospheric, has a collection of maps and objects relevant to Columbus's time, and includes an exhibition of South American objects of a similar period, but has none of Columbus's personal possessions.

Publications about the Canaries are divided about the course of the navigator. Some maintain that the only time Columbus did not make landfall in Las Palmas was during the second journey, when they acknowledge that he was clearly in Gomera. For the first, third and fourth journeys they say his resting place was Las Palmas. Others say that Columbus also stopped in Maspalomas on Gran Canaria and on the island of Hierro, and others still do not commit themselves at all.

move around. Beyond La Palma lies the island of San Borondón, though how far beyond is an open question. According to some Portuguese sailors who passed it in 1525, San Borondón is 220 sea miles nor'-nor'-west of La Palma; other 16th-century seamen put it another score of miles further off. One Renaissance geographer shifted it almost to the American coast.

No wonder, then, that two La Palma sea-captains, Hernando Troya and Hernando Alvares, could not find it in 1525, nor could their fellow-islander, de Villalobos, who set out in search of it 45 years later.

Others had more luck, they say—the Carthaginians and Caesar first, then Span-

iards fleeing the Moorish invaders. By the 16th century the island was well-known to Portuguese, English and French pirates, who hid there safe in the knowledge that the strong currents around the island would keep pursuers at bay. How they got on with the archbishop, his six bishops and the inhabitants of San Borondón's seven cities has never been revealed.

The Italian military engineer Giovanni Torriani even went so far as to draw a map of the island, 264 miles (422 km) from north to

Above, the current around San Borondón supposedly prevented most ships from landing.

south and 93 miles (148 km) from east to west, San Borondón is almost cut in two by major rivers. Torriani shows all seven cities on his map.

The Portuguese who landed in 1525 said it was full of tall trees. A Spanish nobleman turned pirate, Ceballos, confirmed that the forest came right down to the shore, and added that the woods were full of birds "so simple that they could be caught in the hand". There was a beautiful long sandy beach, but in the sand Ceballos had seen the footprints of a giant.

A French crew putting into La Palma after a storm, said they had left a wooden cross, a letter and some silver coins at the spot where they landed. Another ship-load of Portuguese saw oxen, goats, sheep and more giants' footprints in the sand. They had ended up leaving three of their crew there because of the strong current.

The power of that current was clearly shown in 1566 when Roque Nuñez, a Portuguese sea-dog, and Martín de Araña, a La Palma priest, set out for San Borondón. After only a day and a night at sea they saw land, but as they argued over which of them should land first the ferocious current drove them off the shore again.

The elusive San Borondón has not been picked up on any Satellite photo yet, but nevertheless some say you can see it, sometimes, from Tenerife and La Palma. The direction is right—nor'-nor'-west of La Palma—and about a couple of hundred sea-miles off. You can see its high peaks poking through the clouds; an optical illusion with its own mythical history, perhaps linked with the lost world of Atlantis.

Atlantis, the mystery of the Guanches, San Borondón—all are products of the Canaries' own history. Semi-mythical islands in the west, settled during the Renaissance when fantastic New and Old Worlds were being explored, the Canaries attracted their own mysteries.

Even in provable history, the history written down by the first European visitors, Stone Age tribesmen (the Guanches) kept the Spanish invaders at bay for nearly a century. The islanders had to be a little bit super-human to do that, and once you've begun to endow them with the strange origins of ancient mythology, then almost anything goes.

IN SEARCH OF THE TRUE CANARIO

Canarian tourism was never planned, as such planning anyway is neither a Canarian nor a Spanish characteristic—and you may never meet a Canario during a two-week sun-and-fun package holiday. Certainly not if you never venture out of the purpose-built (but not purpose-designed) resort centres.

On Lanzarote these days many waiters are beginning to forget what the words *café con leche* mean, and those foreigners familiar with the phrase learnt it during their first trip to Benidorm 20 years ago. Elsewhere, as most Canarios will tell you, the multi-lingual hotel receptionist is more likely to be a *godo*—a Goth, or peninsular Spaniard—than a Canario. Even many of the chambermaids, waiters and gardeners in the aptly-named tourist *apart-hotels* are probably Andalusians and Galicians attracted by comparitively high wages.

So how do you find a Canary Islander? And how do you know you have found the real thing?

On the larger islands it is easier. Hire a car and head inland, or take a service bus to Las Palmas, Santa Cruz or Puerto Rosario. Or head west from Tenerife to one of the other islands—the German hippies on Gomera and the British and Swedish astronomers on La Palma are easily identified birds of passage. But if you are on Lanzarote the only way to find a Canario is to take the ferry from Playa Blanca to Fuerteventura.

Cartoon Canario: The caricature countryman is Cho' Juáa, who made his first appearance in 1944 in the *Diario de Las Palmas*. His expansive belly rests on the waistband of his sagging trousers. Somewhere around what would once have been waist level is a broad cloth belt out of which pokes the handle of his *naife* or Canarian knife. On his feet a pair of *closas*, over-sized down-at-heel boots, and on his head the ubiquitous black felt homburg that has seen better days—though when those days were is anybody's guess.

Over his well-filled shirt he wears a waist-

Preceding pages: welcoming suburbs. Left, Alfred Diston's 1839 illustration of men from Gran Canaria (left), Fuerteventura, and Lanzarote (right). Right, a Lanzaroteño.

coat, unfastened and unfastenable. And below his *bandido* moustache, a cigarette stub adheres to his lower lip—except on high days and holidays, when it is occasionally replaced by a cigar stub.

Cho' Juáa is no fool though. Like his more literary counterpart, Pepe Monagas who appears in several Canarian short stories by Pancho Guerra, he has an eye for a bargain—and for a mug. In his business dealings he is aided and abetted by Camildita, his shrewd and shrewish wife.

Not that Cho' Juáa is really mean, he is just canny. And there is nothing he loves more than an opportunity to show off his largesse. What appear to be the verbal preliminaries to physical violence break out when two Canarios attempt to pay the same bill.

The Cho' Juáas and Camilditas of these islands are a dying breed. They can still be found on the smaller islands, or in villages like Teno Alto or Chinobre, on Tenerife, or Artenara and Tejeda in Gran Canaria. Occasionally they are to be seen in Las Palmas or Santa Cruz, but there is no place for their sharp negotiating skills—the market for three-legged goats was never large but in the cities it does not exist any longer.

A new breed: Cho' Juáa is now increasingly dependent on his city street-wise successors. Better-educated, taller and less corpulent, the new Canarios grew up with the tourist boom. They have all picked up a smattering of "Beach English" (often rude), and maybe a bit of Beach German, Beach Swedish and even Beach Finnish.

From Cho' Juáa they have inherited the ability to sell the same piece of useless *barranco* (ravine) slope twice over, and at varying market rates according to the buyer—double for Germans, a fifty percent mark-up for the Brits, the going rate to another Canario, and anything they can get away

table, and each table competes for the attention of the others. The waiters do deafening one-man shows in the midst of it all—the Canarian waiter is capable of bellowing an order across a rowdy restaurant like a parade-ground sergeant, but he keeps your attention at table by rattling off the menu in a low, almost inaudible, whisper. You must concentrate on him and him alone to find out what is on today—and, of course, *caballero*, he would never insult you by referring to the price of an individual item.

Like other Spaniards Canarios love a *fiesta*—anything from an *asadero* (a country barbecue) to a *verbena* (loosely translated as an all-night street party), or from a *trínqui*

with if the sale is to a *godo*. Nevertheless they will insist on taking you out to a slap-up dinner to seal the bargain.

In this respect Canarios are really no different from other Spaniards. They love the chance to take the leading role—no matter how insignificant the play, nor how small the audience. But five acts and a full house are preferred. Lines are never mumbled but projected across a crowded bar or bus, competing with all the other dramas being performed in the same small space.

Canarian restaurants at Sunday lunchtime are bedlam as three, or even four, generations compete for attention at the same

(drinks) to a *mogollón* (a much-longer-than-all-night street-party that grows out of *Carnaval*). An invitation to *tomar una copa* (to take a glass) really means to have several—so that tongues are loosened and stage-fright well and truly drowned. Should conversation flag then *arranques* (ones for the road) are ordered.

To keep in top conversational form a Canario, in the best Cho' Juáa or Pepe Monagas tradition, will pop into a bar for a rum at nine in the morning; for a *gin tónica* at eleven; and a bottle, or two, of *vino tinto* for lunch. But to stave off the tongue-tying effects of too much alcohol, it is taken with *tapas* or just a *bocata*—a *bocata* is literally a mouthful of food, a *tapa* slightly more.

Coffee, too, is an essential—small, strong and black (*café solo*); small and strong with a thick sludge of sickly condensed milk (*café cortado*); or a cup or glass of white coffee (*café con leche*). Coffee is invariably stiffened with liberal quantities of sugar. Even fresh orange juice, pressed out of little, sweet oranges, is heavily sugared by Canarios—a tradition derived from the Canaries' first export industry, sugar-cane growing.

Bad habits: If the sugar-industry, rum and *tapas* gave Cho' Juáa his sagging belly, it was one of the Canary Islands' other former staples—tobacco—that completed the cari-

this is called *individualismo* (individuality) when applied to yourself; *insolidaridad* (lack of social responsibility) when referring to others in general; and *barbaridad* (barbarism) when addressing the man who has just flicked his still-burning cigarette stub out of the bar door onto your brand new Lacoste sports shirt.

The Canario also shares mainland Spanish attitudes to women, children and the Church. He likes his women "*morena, bajita, gordita y con tetas grandes*" (dark, short, plump and well-endowed)—not that his preferences would check his interest in any other female shape, size or colouring. He has his *machismo* to maintain. Even Cho' Juáa is a Don

cature. Wherever Canarios congregate there is a fug of cigarette smoke—and the new anti-smoking legislation passed in the Madrid parliament is treated with the usual disdain reserved for any Madrid initiative.

This disregard for minor inconveniences—like "No Smoking" signs, parking restrictions, traffic lights, road signs and rubbish bins—is something else Canarios have in common with other Spaniards, though particularly in Las Palmas this has been developed into an art form. In Spanish

Left and above, attitudes are changing with the generations.

Juan, and every woman is *guapa* (gorgeous).

In Franco's time Canarian women could be divided into five types most of whom were dressed in black: children, expectant mothers, nursing mothers, nuns, or overmade-up characters from the last chapter of Orwell's *Animal Farm*. Since the demise of Franco there is, happily, a sixth type—curvaceous, vivacious, brightly and smartly dressed.

Whilst the average Canarian male is still ambivalent about the woman in his life—is she a whore or a Madonna?—both sexes absolutely adore children. As one Canarian teacher put it to me contentedly, pointing out a group of boisterous gum-chewing youths with attached ghetto-blasters: "these people, they are the future".

And nothing is too much for the future—private education for the uninterested, extra classes for the dull-witted, and presents for every child's birthday, saint's day, Christmas, Epiphany, first communion or just for the sake of giving. In the Canaries there is no segregation of the generations—even the smallest of children accompany their parents to *fiestas*, *verbenas*, political demonstrations, classical concerts, the cinema, and that other social attraction, church.

Even the most irreligious Canario goes to church several times a year—for baptisms,

taste for bull-fighting, *godos*, and Canarios from any island except your own; it is a secret affection for cock-fights and dog-fighting, a love of Canarian wrestling, of Canarian music no matter how grating and of Canarian rum no matter how rasping; but above all it is distance and accent.

The Canary Islands are further from Madrid than they are from Dakar. From Fuerteventura you can see the coast of Morocco—and there is virtually no difference between Jandía (southern Fuerteventura) and the Sahara.

For Canarios geography outweighs all else. Even Canary Islanders with classic Latin features and Spanish surnames as far

first communions, weddings and funerals of the various members of their extensive families. But services are not so much an act of worship as an act in the on-going drama. The priest plays to a full house, but the congregation is as uninterested in his performance as the audience in a northern Working Men's Club would be in Gregorian chant.

Lo nuestro: So what is it that makes Cho' Juáa and his heirs different—or, at least, to see themselves as different—from other Spaniards?

Perhaps it is best summed up by the words *lo nuestro*—"our own". *Lo nuestro* is *gofio* and milk for breakfast; *Lo nuestro* is a dis-

back as anyone can trace them will swear blind that they are the direct descendants of pure-bred Guanches. Most have a deep-rooted distrust of *godos*, and some an even deeper loathing of the *metrópoli*—Madrid.

The *metrópoli*, especially during the various agricultural recessions of the last century and in the Franco years, was seen as stifling Canarian enterprise and imposing unwanted officials on the islanders. Sending Franco to the Canaries as military governor in 1936 was one such metropolitan infliction. Today, even with autonomous government taking over some aspects of regional administration, there is still considerable disgruntlement about the number of *godos* in high places and the need to seek the permission of central government for often minor changes. And bureaucrats in Madrid are renowned for their relaxed approach, treating the Canaries as a colony, in the opinion of some.

Alienation from the mainland is most obvious in the language. Canarians do not pronounce the letter "z" as a lisped "th", like the peninsulares, but as an "s", like the people of south and central America.

Islanders will refer to "Lah Palmah" or "Ma'palomah" or "Santa Cru'" rather than Las Palmas, Maspalomas or Santa Cruz. Particularly on Gran Canaria consonants are clipped so sharply they cease to exist—so,

with a campaign of re-education. Such lessons do not just concentrate on accent, they include vocabulary.

Words like *baifo*, a goat kid, is a Canarian peculiarity and comes from the native pre-Spanish language. Others like *naife*, *chóni* and *canbullonero* derive from the British commercial connection—*naife*, a Canarian knife; *chóni*, a foreigner, from the English Johnny; and a *canbullonero*, from the expression "can buy on", is a dock-side "fence" who buys stolen items of cargo from sailors in the port. Locally a cake is known as a *queque*, and a *yora* is a passenger from a Yeoward Line Ship.

But perhaps the most Canarian idiom of all

for example, the name Juan becomes Juáa. Words are slurred together into a torrent which makes comprehension impossible on occasions—even among Canarios!

On some of the islands the local patois is less demanding, and on La Palma (beware the confusion with "Lah Palmah") the accent is particularly soft and clear, though still a South American Spanish. If you have already picked up some Spanish on the peninsula, Canarios will either react blankly or

Left, traditional costume, worn regularly in a feast of fiestas. Above, pronounciation and accents differ from island to island.

is *Ustedes* as a plural form of "you" instead of the peninsular *vosotros*. On the mainland *Ustedes* is reserved for two or more people you have never met before or whose status is considerable—in the Canaries it is used amongst the closest of friends and family. *Vosotros* is thought of as almost an insult.

It is difficult to define *lo nuestro*. It is a weird mix of the Spanish *picaresco*, or roguishness; South American "magic realism"—Canarios are always a little larger than life; and that distinctively Canarian sentiment that *Canarias no es Europa, somos Africanos* (the Canaries aren't Europe, we are African).

MANRIQUE: USING NATURE AS BRICKS

"The pleasure I derive from my way of life and work has its origins in the great wisdom of nature itself, something I have always loved and studied." Thus speaks the man who is credited with preserving Lanzarote's distinctive aesthetic appeal, according to his own code.

"It is my belief that mankind alone amongst living creatures is able to inflict such atrocities upon itself and that only mankind is incapable of adjusting naturally to our earth. Proof can be seen everywhere. If man would not be so far removed from nature as he is today and still possess the natural instinct for true life, then he would still be building his villages and towns as he did 80 years ago—with an eye for the free space and pleasurable aspects of life."

For a radical insight into Lanzarote you can do no better than to turn to César Manrique, the island's oft-quoted celebrated artist and exemplary supporter of good native architecture.

You don't have to look at his paintings to be able to understand his work. And you don't have to be an intellectual. His inspiration is always near at hand—in the Monumento Campesino, Mirador del Rio, Jameos del Agua, and the El Diablo restaurant in Timanfaya National Park.

In each case, the most visible evidence of this artist's work is actually built into Lanzarote's stark landscape. That's no accident: César Manrique is more than an artist, he is an architect and a designer. Above all, he is an environmentalist—not of the "save-the-whale" school of thought but in the sense of being a guardian of good sense and good taste. For more than two decades he has set an inspired example amid the gathering momentum of the island's construction boom.

Born on 24 April 1920, in Lanzarote, the young Manrique achieved important early successes. He held his first exhibition in Arrecife in 1942, another a year later in Las Palmas and by 1944 had notched up an exhibition in the Museum of Modern Art in Madrid. In 1945, he won a scholarship and moved to Madrid to study at the San Fernando College of Fine Art.

When he began his career in the early 1950s, Manrique was a traditional painter who specialised in subjects related to the sea, agriculture and vineyards. He soon moved towards abstract art and became one of the founders of that movement in Spain. His first exhibition of abstract art was held in Madrid in 1954—a turning point in his career. From then onwards his *curriculum vitae* is a long series of prestigious exhibitions and growing international recognition.

During the past 30 years, his work has been shown in Spain, Europe, the United States, South America and Japan. As early as 1955 he took part in the prestigious biennial exhibition in Vienna and had his first major exhibition in New York City in 1966 at the Catherine Viviane gallery, one of America's most influential showcases.

For most of his early life, César Manrique was an expatriate artist. He spent 20 years in Madrid and four years in New York City. In 1968 he returned to Lanzarote to paint. Today he lives and works in Taro de Tahiche, a spacious and innovative house just a few minutes drive northeast of Arrecife.

In 1986 Manrique made a speech to the International Press Institute, held in Vienna, saying: "I believe that the artist should be an integral part of the environment...that he should develop within the environment..." It was a statement which summed up much of what he had been working towards in the 18 years since he had returned to his native home. Not only has Manrique made a name as a painter of international renown; he has also set himself the role of being an artist whose chief aim is to conserve the environment.

While his many paintings show clearly the influence of the volcanic scenery of Lanzarote, Manrique's biggest achievements lie elsewhere in the island. In 1968, the year his "environmental period" is said to have started, he built the striking Monumento Campesino, dedicated to the agricultural labour of Lanzarote's peasants. He also built his own home, Taro de Tahiche, on the island, a model scheme for what could have been done at many other locations on Lanzarote.

Sited on top of five hollow spherical spaces in a lava field, Taro de Tahiche incorporates these natural "volcanic bubbles" into the way his house is designed. The result is a home that is more a sculpture than a construction, living proof that there can be a symbiosis between art and nature.

Manrique has since carried this idea of building with nature as the bricklayer through to his many creations around the island, all of which exist in sympathy with the land on which they are built and the landscape of which they are part.

Phrases such as "exist in sympathy" sound as if they have been lifted straight out of a high-minded treatise on the theory of art. Yet the beauty of what Manrique has done is that you don't have to be a highbrow to enjoy the results. Try writing down the five most memorable places in Lanzarote and the odds are that César Manrique's influence is involved in some, if not all.

The environmental connection in Manrique's works around Lanzarote, and elsewhere in the Canary Islands, is obvious. In 1970 he created a mural out of lava rock in the Gran Hotel Arrecife, following this with one at the Cristina Hotel in Las Palmas. He tried his theory further afield, two years later, when he created another large composition using rocks from Salamanca for the Post Office Savings Bank in Madrid. In 1973, he inaugurated the Mirador del Rio at one of the highest viewpoints on Lanzarote, built from the rock of a basalt precipice of the Famara Massif.

Jameos del Agua, which dates from 1968, and the auditorium,

added in 1976, repeat this theme of an artistic creation growing out of nature. In 1977 Manrique designed the gardens and swimming pool of Las Salinas Hotel on the Costa Teguise. His efforts were awarded the Ecological Prize of Berlin.

César Manrique didn't set out simply to build a collection of inspired tourist sites. His wider aim was that his work should inspire everybody on the island to strive for a clear and aesthetic style through which Lanzarote could grow. In the face of the profits that developers could achieve and the rush to acquire land, his aims may have seemed to be just wishful thinking.

He expressed many of his ideas in a book called *Lanzarote Immortal Architectura*, published in 1975. In his eyes, Lanzarote had developed a simple and rudimentary building style that had

achieved great beauty. His aim was to preserve that style and to unify it with the building boom that he and many others saw coming.

In 1980 he said: "Lanzarote was born some 15 years ago when it stepped out of its previous anonymity. Following the great reconstruction efforts during this relatively short period and the search for an individual style for this burned-out island with its more than 300 volcanoes, we began to give back the island its own original, volcanic character, to emphasise its unique landscape and to impose a clear, sober, elegant and popular style of architecture."

Manrique describes his work as "dreams that capture the sublime natural beauty of Lanzarote". It is his duty as an artist, he says, to protect the natural environment against the worst excesses of modern technology. Only in this way can nature, the source of art, be saved, he thinks.

Wherever he was involved in creating a style, Manrique's personal vision became reality. Elsewhere on the island, in Arrecife especially, critics say that his architectural utopia is an impossible dream that has failed to influence construction projects. Some would say that he has achieved little more than to encourage the distinctive use of green paint on white buildings right across the island.

The pressures of profit have often pushed Manrique's ideals aside. The lure of speculation has frequently outweighed his recommended good taste. And while agricultural landowners sold their holdings and achieved overnight wealth, Manrique's "clear, sober, elegant and popular style of architecture" inevitably took a back seat—he doesn't deny it.

"My battle to save the environment and the originality of the island has been violent," he says, "and has often enough failed to make headway against authority and the power of the state, which could hamper our work by its inability to appreciate aesthetic criteria."

He reserves his biggest criticisms for Arrecife. "The capital of our island is a prime example of this. It is crushed by cruel concrete blocks and buried under asphalt and traffic. Will this devastating development only be stopped when the inhabitants can breathe and live there no longer?"

The Canary Islands had to be discovered three times before they were truly on the world map.

Lost in antiquity and re-discovered in the middle ages, they descended into renewed obscurity in the early 19th century, when shrinking wine markets and revolts among Spain's American colonies seemed to make the archipelago economically redundant.

But it was the gloomiest era in the islands' economic history—the mid-19th century, when the wine trade had collapsed and only the short-lived cochineal industry offered any hope for the future—which saw the beginnings of what, in the long term, was to prove to be the Canaries' most exploitable industry: the interest of foreign visitors.

Scholastic attraction: The first re-discoverers of this period were scholars attracted by the islands' peculiar geology, climatology, botany and ethnography. They included Leopold von Buch, who made the first attempt to compile a systematic natural history of the island from observations made in person, and the German scientist Alexander von Humbolt. The most influential of these early observers, however, was Sabin Berthelot, a Frenchman and a diplomat who arrived from Paris in 1820, at the age of 26. His main interest was in the acclimatisation of tropical plants and fauna.

The Canaries had been selected as a place of experiment in this field in the reign of Charles III and, though the results had been disappointing, the Botanical Gardens of Orotova remained a magnet for an enterprising student of the subject. During a first stay of ten years, Berthelot became Director of the Botanical Gardens, played a major role in the acclimatisation of cochineal and developed a passionate interest in every aspect of Canariana, especially the archaeology and anthropology of the pre-Hispanic era.

In 1839 he published a miscellany of Canarian life and landscape, enlivened by engravings which introduced the Parisian

public to the romantic scenery and dress of the archipelago. In 1842 *L'Ethnographie et les Annales de la conquête* followed. Eight further volumes, written with the collaboration of the English botanist, F. B. Webb, gradually completed his *Histoire naturelle des Iles Canaries*.

After an absence of some years, Berthelot returned to the islands as French Consul in Santa Cruz de Tenerife. "My friends," he declared on disembarking, "I have come to die among you". The prophecy was true, if

long delayed. He died on Tenerife in November, 1880, "an islander at heart", as he himself said. With his compelling enthusiasm he proved the most tireless and effective propagandist for the islands abroad.

In the 1850s the islands became newly accessible because of steamship navigation from Cadiz to Las Palmas and Santa Cruz de Tenerife. A public whose interest Berthelot had excited could now come to see the islands for themselves, and the Frenchman's friendships and collaboration with English scientists and artists helped to ensure the extension of the islands' appeal abroad.

In the previous 300 years English resi-

Preceding pages: Tenerife, painted in 1817 by James Bulwer, while on a naval spying mission. Left, the locals were considered romantic and stylish. Right, Alexander Von Humboldt.

dents had been well established in the Canaries, always as merchants or prisoners of the Inquisition: indeed, 80 percent of the penitents who passed before the tribunal of Las Palmas in the 18th century were English subjects. Few, however, had felt much love of or attraction to the islands.

Notable exceptions were Thomas Nichols, a 16th-century sugar merchant, who published *A Pleasant Description of the Fortunate Islands*—a work notable for containing the first description in English of the sensation of eating a banana—and George Glas, who in 1764 produced a somewhat capricious translation of a history of the islands originally written by a late 16th-

E. BERTHELOT.

century Franciscan. From the mid-19th century, however, a continuous tradition of English interest began.

Elizabeth Murray: The initiator of new English interest was a remarkable woman who arrived as the wife of a newly appointed British consul in 1850. Elizabeth Murray was the daughter of a reputable portraitist who had been in Spain in 1812 to paint Wellington and his staff.

Born in 1815, Elizabeth was exhibiting at the Royal Academy from 1834. She had already visited Italy with her father, and had classes from Horace Vernet. When her father died in 1835 she was able to exploit the

connections he had built up to pursue a surprisingly independent way of life. Having, as she said, "neither master nor money", she travelled in the Mediterranean and finished her artistic preparation in the most fashionable manner.

In 1835 she was commissioned to paint views of Malta for Queen Adelaide; from there she went to Constantinople at Sir Stratford Canning's invitation, and developed a talent for street-scenes with a romantic and exotic flavour. In Athens, she painted King Otto and his family. She found her ideal milieu in Morocco, where she spent nearly eight years from 1842, in observation, sketching and dalliance; in 1846 she married the British Consul, and it was his posting to Santa Cruz that removed her to the islands via Seville and Cadiz. She was received with enthusiasm by the intellectuals, led by Berthelot, and the artists, who had recently organised themselves as a Provincial Academy.

At first, Murray contributed mainly Greek and Moroccan views to their exhibitions, but the scenery of the islands had captured her from afar; from the ship that brought her to the Canaries, she declared the view of the islands, "a spectacle which has nothing to match it in any other part of the world". She was indefatigable in seeking out subjects in the hinterland of Tenerife, accompanied only by a couple of servants, or staying with friends in the major settlements.

The fruit of her sketches and observations was the greater part (16 chapters out of 27) of *Sixteen Years of an Artist's Life in Morocco, Spain and the Canary Islands*, which appeared in 1859. The result in the islands was a sensation of a most unfortunate kind, for the Canarian intelligentsia, who had welcomed her so heartily, now felt betrayed. In the book, Mrs Murray declared Las Palmas "rather gloomy and uninteresting"; moreover Santa Cruz, she said, "does not contain anything which is of remarkable interest to the visitor".

She found Canarian religion distasteful, dress risible, architecture modest and mendicancy offensive. However lavish her praise for the islands' topographical beauty, Canarios found their own image was unflatteringly presented. They seemed to see themselves depicted as they feared they really were: coarse, brutish, backward, isolated and culturally impoverished—"like Blacks", a Las Palmas newspaper complained, "speaking in dialect and living in caves". The press, which had begun by publishing extracts from her work, soon suppressed it and began printing shocked denunciations of the authoress. It was fortunate that her husband was recalled in 1860.

Outside the Canaries, however, Mrs Murray's book was a positive influence, which helped to divulge an agreeable, and marketable, perception of the islands. What mattered were Mrs Murray's charming pictures, not her rather affected prose. The view of Orotova which forms the frontispiece of her second volume is typically enchanting. The steeply sloping city in the middle ground, with its Baroque towers and cloisters, and the gleaming pyramid of the Teide beyond, can still be appreciated as an almost unspoilt view by today's visitor.

Mrs Murray had a representative Victorian eye. She selected the romantic, the sentimental, the lavish, the exotic and the picturesque in her Canarian genre scenes and landscapes. Nor was she above heavy-handed social comment in her portraits of urchins, beggars and priests. Images which outraged the islanders were calculated to appeal to audiences abroad.

Paradise in paint: Elizabeth Murray never returned to the islands, but she influenced other image-makers of the Canaries, including Marianne North, the well-connected daughter of an MP. On a visit to Tenerife in 1875 to escape the English winter, she painted a large collection of oils of exotic plants, many sketched in the Botanical Gardens of Orotova, together with views showing the environment of the Canaries' unique native flora. She bequeathed her entire *oeuvre*, which included paintings made in the course of travel in six continents, to Kew Gardens, in London.

Her written recollections of Tenerife, though not published until 1892, reached a wide readership. The Canaries were depicted as a sort of paradise, where climate and views were perfect, where roses never smelled so sweet and where, "I scarcely ever went out without finding some new wonder to paint, lived a life of the most perfect peace

and happiness, and got strength every day with my kind friends."

Last, most influential and perhaps most formidable of the British Victorian viragos who travelled to the Canaries was Mrs Olivia Stone, who toured the islands in the winter and early spring of 1884. Mrs Stone was self-consciously a professional travel writer whose aim was to equip the tourist with a practical guide and to facilitate travel. Her aim was to establish "the best way of going round the islands in order to see the scenery". In a letter to *The Times*, her husband declared her findings, that the Canaries "require only to be known, to be much resorted to by the English." A prediction that has most cer-

tainly been proved correct.

Her husband, as her assistant, was able to make the first extensive photographic record of the islands on the course of the tour: on the basis of his work, her book appeared with lavish illustrations. Her inspection of the archipelago was exceptionally thorough. She was the first English writer to visit every island and claimed to be the first Englishwoman ever to have set foot in Hierro.

In some ways, Mrs Stone was an unlikely propagandist for the islands. She was a Protestant bigot who derided many Canarian customs. She flew the Union Jack from her tent, taught Canarian hoteliers to make plum

Left, Sabine Berthelot. Right, islanders at the turn of the century.

pudding and argued that the islands would be better off under the British Empire than as part of Spain.

Paradise in print: The notes Olivia Stone wrote up daily on donkey-back yielded another Arcadian image for the readers of her book. The archipelago, she concluded, was "the nearest approach to an Earthly Paradise of which a Morris could sing or a Tadema paint". It was a land where rainy mornings were so rare that people rose to look at them and where poor health could be transformed by exposure to a uniquely salubrious climate. The first edition of her *Tenerife and its Six Satellites* appeared in 1887. Mrs Stone could be pardoned for congratu-

lating herself, by the time of the appearance of the 1889 edition, on the fact that "visitors have poured into the islands" as a result.

The most illustrious of these visitors was the Marquess of Bute, the most distinguished Scottish Catholic convert of the 19th century. He enjoyed wealth, leisure, a scholarly disposition and dazzling linguistic skill. In the 1870s he had devoted these gifts partly to civic and philanthropic works but particularly to travels in Italy and the Near East which produced an important series of academic and devotional translations, mainly from Latin, Hebrew, Arabic and Coptic. On Mrs Stone's advice he went to Tenerife to improve his health, with—temporarily, at least—satisfactory results.

Guanche scholars: Bute became passionately interested in the archaeological and ethnographic remains of the Guanches. Since Berthelot's work on the subject, the field had largely been abandoned to local scholars, except for the efforts of René Verneau, who studied the physical anthropology of the Guanches in the 1870s and whose *Cinq années de séjour aux Iles Canaries* was an intriguing and popular record of his stay on the islands.

Bute's attempts to augment the literature on the islands were modest: he concentrated on the philological problems which lay in his own particular field, but his dissertation *On the Ancient Language of the Inhabitants of Tenerife* was an unprofitable work, devoted to demonstrating a fantastic connection between pre-conquest Canarian languages and those of some American Indians. Nevertheless, in his effort to compile materials he bought up almost the entire records of the early Canarian Inquisition, erroneously believing that they might contain some transcribed fragments of native speech.

He had these materials translated and then presented the originals to the Museo Canario of Las Palmas. As a result, the Canaries are the only province of Spain still to have their early Inquisition archives *in situ*. All others have been removed to Madrid.

The last figure in the great tradition of scientific curiosity among foreign visitors was Dominik Josef Wölfel, a Viennese anthropologist, who was fired with wonder about the pre-conquest islanders at a seminar in 1926, when he heard Eugen Fischer read a paper on the Guanches' fate.

Wölfel's many publications had slight influence on the image of the islands in the wider world because he almost always wrote in Spanish, but he founded an Institute in Vienna for the study of the subject. His transcriptions have now been superseded, and the ferocity of his partisanship on the Guanches' behalf is thought by many scholars to have distorted his judgement, but he remains a major influence in Canarian studies and a striking example of how the islands have captivated their discoverers.

Left, the Marquess of Bute in fancy dress. Right, Marianne North, recording nature on canvas.

The lady had just finished a game of tennis; mixed doubles. She was small, chic and very French. She stopped in front of us, squared her shoulders, and declared, with obvious pride, "I serve two clean arses!"

The resident expatriate population of Gran Canaria, and to a lesser extent Lanzarote, is cosmopolitan in the extreme. Danes, Dutch, Germans, Indians, Japanese, Koreans, Norwegians and the British are all well represented. The *lingua franca* between them is not Spanish but English, with a range of national variation in pronunciation, like the French lady and her clean aces. Criminals and colonials, busy businessmen and idle rich, young refugees and elderly retired, all create their own communities and sub-communities on the islands.

Asians: Not everyone is here for reasons of recreation: the Koreans and Japanese are on the islands for the business of fishing (major fleets from both countries are based in Las Palmas) and in most cases stay for only a few years before returning to their home country. Nevertheless both groups have had an impact on the local and expatriate communities.

The Japanese have established their own small school, packed with Sony and Toshiba audio and visual teaching aids. The students display the traditional politeness of their race and are popular and successful competitors in cultural activities. The small Japanese Club boasts a tennis court and is set in the quiet of Tafira Alta.

Japanese cuisine, in the form of several restaurants, is as popular with the Europeans as with the Japanese and the ritual of saki and raw fish is one of the minor culinary delights of Las Palmas.

Korean cooking has become so popular that there is a small supermarket for the more exotic ingredients. The Koreans have several small but thriving churches, many Koreans being Christians, but send their children to British or American schools. The children tend to complete their education in the United States, probably a reflection of the close ties between the two countries in recent years. Both Korean and Japanese celebrate their own festivals, particularly at New Year.

Rather surprisingly, by far the largest expatriate group on Gran Canaria is the Indian community. Indians are known the world over for their ability as traders and entrepreneurs and for their willingness to work long hard hours to build up their business and the Las Palmas Indian

businessman is no exception; he will sell you anything from a Design Centre award-wining one-sided wine rack to a bulldozer with a four-in-one bucket, from a "genuine" Korean made, self-winding, Cartier watch to a plastic eggtimer.

Many Indians are engaged in the import-export business and thus live near the port. However the Indian shopkeepers are tending to move to the south of Gran Canaria to cater for the ever-increasing tourist trade. Strangely there is no real Indian restaurant in Las Palmas, but delicious tandoori chicken is served at cricket "Test" matches arranged with visiting Indians from Tenerife.

Preceding pages: British residents at home on Gran Canaria. Left, croquet on the lawn. Right, a German photographer, resident on Lanzarote.

Europeans: The British were the first Caucasian settlers. Originally their interest was the wine trade and Shakespeare mentions Canary wine in a couple of his plays, but over the years bananas, potatoes, tomatoes, piracy and bunkering ships en route to South and West Africa have all proved profitable ventures. Most of these activities continue. The modern equivalent of the pirate is the resident of dubious background who came out to live—in some style—in rather a hurry, identifiable by the fact that he never returns to his homeland for Christmas or family occasions.

The resident Germans and Scandinavians are in the most part on Gran Canaria to

Dornier flying-boat named *Do X* and it was damaged while trying to take off in heavy weather. After an enforced stay of three months on the island the passengers eventually completed their rather nerve-wracking journey at an altitude of barely 100 feet (30 metres) most of the way to Rio de Janeiro via the Cape Verde Islands.

During World War Two the German Navy established a secret U-boat base on the southern tip of Fuerteventura which at that time lacked any sort of modern amenities or comforts, and German sailors regularly came to Triana, then the main street of Las Palmas, in search of what is euphemistically called R and R, Rest and Recuperation.

provide facilities for tourists from their home countries. They have established churches, schools and clubs. In and around Las Palmas there are German, Swedish, French, American and British schools whilst in the south there is a small but quite beautiful Norwegian school. Swedish-German and British churches in Las Palmas and the south share a general ecumenical attitude of mutual help.

The Germans were among the first tourists. In the early Thirties a group travelling by what was the world's largest aeroplane stopped here en route to Brazil. The aeroplane was a twelve-engined

There are German sailors buried in the British cemetery.

However it was the Scandinavians who came here first for the sun, the sand and the swimming, not to mention the bars, the beaches and the baring of breasts.

I first became aware of this while living in Helsinki some years ago, when the cashier in my local bank suddenly had a mahogany tan in mid-winter; two weeks earlier he had been like me, a wan, white, pasty-faced, sun-deprived, winter-wrapped resident of Northern Europe, but he had been to the Canaries for his winter holiday.

By the early Sixties the tourists began to

leave the dark winters of Sweden and Finland for the Canaries. Preceded by a deserved reputation for their ability to consume huge quantities of alcohol, it was not unusual for casualties to occur. One such was the man who was delivered unconscious to one of the excellent international clinics. Reeking of drink, blood oozing from a scalp wound, he was received with scant sympathy, treated and admitted. Only when he regained consciousness was he able to explain that he had reached for a bottle of his favourite vodka high on a supermarket shelf when the shelving had fallen towards him and brought hundreds of bottles cascading and exploding around his ears.

notario (a commissioner for oaths), who witnesses the signatures to the transaction to everyone's satisfaction.

The process is straightforward but the pitfalls are many, as indeed they are anywhere in the world. Do check that the property is registered with the land office, that there are no outstanding taxes and if there are who is going to pay them, and most important that the *escritura* (the deeds) show that the seller does indeed own the property and has not sold it to anyone else already. Many a house has been sold to two clients at the same time.

The days of buying a cheap, rustic old camel stable and converting it to a minor

Settling: Renting property on a long-term basis is difficult and expensive. If you wish to buy, the first decision is where to live, on the coast or in the hills, near Las Palmas or in the south. The process begins with an *imobillaria* (estate agent) of whom there are many and who advertise in the local press and sometimes in overseas media. Having chosen your property you progress to an *abogado* (a solicitor), who handles the legal side of the purchase and draws up the necessary documents. The final call is to a

Left, Swedish mother and twins on Lanzarote. Above, catering for British tastes.

baronial mansion have long gone, but despite the complexities it is still possible to buy a property which will be easy to live in and a pleasure to own.

Spanish taxation is as complex as anywhere else but taxes in the Canaries are lower than most places. The maze of regulations is the business of *gestoria*, best described as an expert in bureaucracy and queuing. For quite a small sum your personal tax return, due at the end of June, can be completed and sent to the Ministerio de Hacienda. The various *Gestorias* specialise, and it is as well to find one whose forte is taxation.

Expatriate residents are certainly united on one subject: the pleasure of the climate. They say that the world's best climate is found 300 ft (91 metres) above sea level in the south of Gran Canaria. Lanzarote and Fuerteventura enjoy similar conditions, but there can be tremendous variation even on a single island like Gran Canaria. Las Palmas and the coast are never cold but can be windy; the south enjoys almost endless fine and sunny days while the mountains inland have greater extremes of very hot days and quite cool, even chilly, nights.

Rain is looked on as something of a luxury to ease the island's water shortage and in some years the small town of Tejeda, the

island's highest, has snow. The snow never lasts very long; on these occasions Las Palmas city dwellers drive the winding road to Los Pechos, the highest point, build a conical snowman on the roofs of their cars and return rally-style back down to town to show their friends real snow before it melts.

Despite official statistics September and October seem to be the hottest months, because this is the time when the humidity increases, though rarely to an uncomfortable level. The only real discomfort occurs when the *levanta* blows. This wind from the Sahara brings *calima* (fine sand dust) to the Canaries, and has even been known to carry

this as far north as Southern England.

However the atmosphere in the islands is usually the clearest in the Northern Hemisphere, the main factor in the relocation of the Issac Newton and William Herschel optical telescopes from the Royal Greenwich Observatory to the new Los Muchachos site on the island of La Palma. The same clarity makes sunbathing something to be done with care and brings nights of unparalleled stillness and beauty, with millions of stars glittering in a dark, silent, velvet canopy of sky.

Recreation: The city of Las Palmas is a traffic nightmare with prohibitions, impossible parking and horrific traffic jams, most of which are like a red rag to a bull to Canarian drivers. Outside the city driving is still something to be enjoyed—once you have become used to the narrow twisting roads which are quite hair-raising in the way they cling to perpendicular cliffs. Away from the tourist beaches, the sheer beauty of the island, stark, dramatic and fascinating in its variety is unending. In Spring, provided that there has been some rain, the mountains are covered in flowers in a kaleidoscopic carpet of colour.

For the active resident or visitor there are plenty of potential hobbies to participate in. Riding schools offer pony-trekking into the mountains, which also offer a variety of walks. From the beaches board-sailing, scuba-diving and big game fishing are all excellent. There are some 20 world records held for tuna, bonito, barracuda and other game fish in Canary waters.

Jeep safaris rock and roll their way along the rougher off-road tracks. There are many tennis and squash courts and two excellent golf courses, that at Bandama being the oldest in Spain and having the biggest 19th hole in the world—a volcanic crater some 650 ft (200 metres) deep. In the garden you can grow virtually anything if you have water; without it you face heartbreak.

All in all it is an island like that in Shakespeare's *Tempest*, "full of noises, sounds and sweet airs, which bring delight and hurt not," increasingly popular with foreign residents.

Left, Mike Eddy, a British archaeologist in Las Palmas. Right, year-round sun and sailing, ideal for some.

INFLUENCES AND INDEPENDENCE

When the first autonomous government came to power, some bright spark came up with the slogan "A Bridge between three Continents" as part of a campaign to widen the islands' economic base. As a piece of advertising hype it was convincing: geographically, the islands are stepping-stones between Europe, Africa and the Americas, and they have been so ever since Columbus sailed across the pond.

But the slogan ignored the stranglehold monopoly that Iberia and Trasmediterranea—the Spanish national air and sea carriers—have on communications to and from the islands, and even between them. As a result the Canaries are more of a cul-de-sac than a bridge.

The attempts made by the Canary Islands' autonomous government to foster South-South trade between Africa and South America have foundered on the rocks of these monopolies. Instead of being a three-way bridge the islands are the end of the line for charter flights or just refuelling stops. And yet the Canaries do still maintain links—often long-lasting—with all three continents.

The European connection: This is the most obvious of the continental bridges. The islands form two provinces and one autonomous region of modern Spain, and are part of the European Economic Community, though they enjoy a specially negotiated position within the Community which guarantees cheap booze and no VAT on goods on the islands. It also guarantees excessively high prices for Canarian farm produce compared with countries like Morocco and Israel. Belatedly the island government is trying to renegotiate before Canarian agriculture finally disappears under a thick layer of rotting tomatoes and bananas.

The European connection existed even before the conquest in the 15th century, but at the time it was limited to slaving and trading. Nevertheless some Europeans had mixed with the native population before and

during the conquest; Mallorcan sailors may have introduced figs and architectural improvements and the Portuguese were once allied with the islanders against the Spanish.

The majority of the first European colonists were Spaniards from the frontier regions of Extremadura and Andalucia. Portuguese, Italian and even English merchants soon followed as the islands' first industry—sugar—began to develop.

Thomas Nichols, who wrote the first book in English on the Islands, came to the Canaries to trade cloth for sugar and wine. Others, like John Hill of Taunton, settled in the Canary Islands to farm land that "bringeth foorth all sortes of fruites"—Hill had the only vineyard on El Hierro in Nichols' time.

But even before Tenerife and La Palma had been reduced by Spanish arms, the Spanish maritime empire had been born. Columbus and those that followed him used the Canary current to coast past the North African shore, through the islands and on westward to the Americas.

As ships began to move freely and confidently more Spaniards settled in the islands, whilst some of the descendants of the origi-

Preceding pages: country madonna. Left, African dancers perform to tourists. Right, the street stalls reflect African influence.

nal islanders and the first European settlers moved on to the Americas. During the 16th and 17th centuries the Canary Islands were busy commercial centres through which passed much of Spain's American sea traffic. The ports of Las Palmas (Gran Canaria), Garachico (Tenerife) and Santa Cruz de La Palma (La Palma) flourished, until Garachico's harbour was destroyed overnight by a volcanic eruption in 1706.

However, the fortunes of the ports were so tied to the Spanish mainland that Las Palmas and the other ports stagnated, along with the Spanish empire and economy, during the 18th and early 19th centuries.

The essential elements of Canarian soci-

into various manifestations of the Virgin Mary. Over the course of the 18th century the "folk" costume of the Canary Islands took on its present form as the process of "civilising" the islanders went on.

Yet the North African roots of the islands' population never really died. They either went deeper underground—like the native martial arts, *juego del palo* and *lucha canaria*—or adapted to changed circumstances, as in the festival of the Rama in Agaete or Guía (Gran Canaria). Spanish became the accepted means of communication but it still contained a lot of Berberisms.

Almost from the earliest days of conquest native islanders joined their new masters

ety had been welded together by the time Garachico was buried by boiling lava, and European and native were inextricably mixed.

African roots: On the lesser islands and in the mountainous interiors of the larger ones the native islanders survived in enclaves and lived almost as their Berber-speaking ancestors had done. But the power of the Inquisition—especially as the empire turned inwards during the 18th century—gradually imposed the trappings of Christianity on these African communities.

By 1800 the principal native pagan festivals had been taken over by the Catholic Church, and the heathen deities converted

first in attacks on the other islands and later in the destruction of the Aztec and Inca empires. Gran Canarians and Gomerans found themselves in the front line during the conquest of Tenerife. And before the 16th century was out Canarian wrestlers were putting on demonstrations of their prowess for the Spanish viceroy of Peru.

South American exodus: But it was the agricultural recessions of the last century that drove many islanders west to Argentina, Colombia, Venezuela and Cuba. And, like the Irish who emigrated to the States, these Canarian migrants took with them their ill-defined ideas of liberty from foreign oppression and welded them into a coherent form in the Americas.

In 1810 Canarios had called for "a patriotic government, independent of that of the peninsula, to watch over all the Tribunals set up in the Province". In that same declaration, made as British and French forces slogged out the future of Europe on the Iberian peninsula, the Canarian Junta raised for the first time the Canarios' desire "to get rid of all the Spaniards now here and to put the people of this land in their place".

The same view was echoed in Spain's American colonies. Simón Bolívar, the liberator of most of Spanish America, referred to "Spaniards and Canarios" as quite differ-

ent peoples. In some of Bolívar's decrees he even included the Canaries in his list of Spanish colonies to be freed.

In time the Spanish empire in America was whittled down to just Cuba and Puerto Rico, which many Canarian emigrants continued to use as stepping-stones to the newly independent nations of continental America.

One of the most influential Canarian emigrants of the late 19th century, at least for Canarian politics, was Secindino Delgado,

Left, a quayside demonstration shows solidarity with Africa. Above, Castro lookalike in a carnival procession.

who at the age of 14 took advantage of a Spanish government offer of a free passage to the island of Cuba for anyone prepared to work for a year there. This offer was introduced in the same year that slavery was abolished by Spain in 1886 (over 80 years after it was abolished in Great Britain), and was designed to replace the lost cheap labour on the plantations.

Intimations of independence: In Havana Delgado lived "in the greatest harmony" with the Cubans, whose character contrasted with the pretentiousness of the *peninsulares*. There he met left-wing emigrés from the Canaries and mainland Spain and got to know members of the Cuban independence movement. During a trip to the United States he met the father of Cuban independence, José Martí (whose mother was a Canario); shortly afterwards he began to work for the Cuban freedom movement, writing for an anarchist paper *El Esclavo*.

Forced to flee Cuba in 1896 he returned for a short time to the Canaries where he developed his ideas about the future independence of the islands. The following year, in Venezuela, Delgado founded *El Guanche*, a newspaper devoted to promoting the cause of Canarian independence.

El Guanche seems to have been a short-lived venture, though it was re-established in 1924. Since then the title has been used for publications of the Canarian Nationalist Party, the Free Canary Islands Movement, the Seven Green Stars Movement and most recently by the Canarian Nationalist Congress. Delgado's paper had sufficient impact to spur a three-day battle for the control of La Laguna during a Canarian insurrection in 1909.

Delgado's main aim was that the islands should gain a degree of autonomy from Madrid so as to run their own affairs directly, though some of the successor parties that have used the *El Guanche* title have had more extreme aims.

One strange aspect of Canarian nationalism is the view—proposed with varying degrees of seriousness—that the Canaries would have been much better off if the Tenerife militia had let Nelson take Santa Cruz in 1797.

British and American interest: The reasoning behind this curious notion is that the British, who invested heavily in bunkering facilities

who invested heavily in bunkering facilities in the Canaries during Delgado's lifetime (1872 to 1912), were better administrators than the Spanish. The British built, as Canarios will proudly tell, most of the roads on the islands, set up the first public utility companies and they created *Ciudad Jardín* (Garden City), the only pleasant part of Las Palmas (Gran Canaria). They also built up Canarian agriculture, growing bananas, tomatoes and early potatoes, and they expanded the port of Las Palmas at a time when Canarian farmers had just gone through their worst crisis.

Indeed at one stage the possibility of annexation by Great Britain was taken so seriously that the Commander-in-Chief of the head of the Iberia section, who finally severed the connection.

The islands' strategic importance is now well understood by both NATO and the Warsaw Pact—the Canaries lie across the main shipping lanes from Europe to South America and the southern USA, as well as the routes from Europe to West and South Africa and beyond.

With Franco in charge, the Canary Islanders became loyal Spaniards, and the propaganda seems to have worked—the most Spanish Canarios are those aged between 35 and 60; those younger or older are Canarios first and Spaniards second, if they think of themselves as Spanish at all.

Spanish garrison in the islands informed Madrid, in 1873, that a separatist group "was proposing to take advantage of the right moment for England to annexe the islands".

The British were not the only ones interested in the rump of Spain's overseas possessions. The United States eyed the islands after throwing Spain out of the Philippines, Cuba and Puerto Rico in 1898, and Hitler had plans drawn up to take the Canaries over from France during World War II.

British military intelligence also had contacts with Canarian independence groups during the War, and it was probably the now infamous double-agent Kim Philby, former

Banned by Franco and spurned by Republicans in exile, the Canarian independence movement languished during the 1950s and early 1960s. But even before Franco and his regime showed signs of fading, MPAIAC (pronounced *emy-pie-ac*) was founded by Antonio Cubillo in 1963. MPAIAC's manifesto stated that, "opposition to Spain exists in our country not only because of historical reasons but also through ethnic, political, economic, geographic and cultural differences that make Canarios a self-contained unity distinct from Spaniards".

Tactics of terror: In 1976 and 1977, as Franco slipped into history, MPAIAC turned to terrorism, launching over a hundred bomb attacks against peninsula-based companies, military targets and, in an expression of solidarity with the Africans, the South African airline offices on the islands.

It was an MPAIAC bomb scare at Las Palmas airport which led to the world's worst air disaster in March 1977, when two jumbo jets were diverted to the inadequate Los Rodeos (now Tenerife North) airport where they collided. Street disturbances in the late 1970s were put down rigorously by the Spanish government; during a demonstration in December 1977 a student was killed, and after the funeral riot police from the peninsula ran amok.

election. But that does not mean that Canarios are disinterested in the independence issue—more moderate parties like AIC (a confederation of island parties) which was until November 1988 a major partner in a coalition regional government, take about 30 percent of the vote.

Unhappily for good government AIC is now dominated by ATI (the Tenerife island party) which has led to accusations of preferential treatment for Tenerife at the expense of the other islands. This has opened up the old wound of the *pleito insular*—is Tenerife or Gran Canaria to be the final seat of regional power?

The rivalry between the two islands—

Cubillo was eventually expelled and found temporary refuge in Algeria. Spanish political pressure and an assassination attempt, which left him unable to walk, curbed his influence at the UN and the OAU where he had managed to gain some acceptance of the Canarian case.

Since the return to democratic government, Cubillo has been able to return, and he now heads the Canarian Nationalist Congress party. The CNC gained a mere 1.3 percent of the vote at the last, and its first,

between the *canariones* of Gran Canaria and the *chicharreros* of Tenerife—makes a nonsense of regional government. There are two parliament buildings and two sets of offices. Government departments are split between the two islands, and if you want to find a particular official the chances are that he will be on the other island.

The marketing man might have liked the Canaries to a bridge between three continents and three cultures, but Canarios would sooner be at least two bridges—better still, seven independent ones—and Iberia and Trasmediterranean continue to ensure that the tolls on any bridge are exorbitant.

Left, Franco, on a rare visit to the islands. Above, moving bridges...frequent, but not cheap.

THE BRITISH PRESENCE

For the past 400 years the British have been inextricably involved in the history and economic development of the Canaries. The administrative capital, Las Palmas, even has several streets named after Britons, which must be a tribute to their influence. There were British traders in the Canaries during the 16th century, dealing in manufactured goods, fruit, slaves and wine; the Canary sack so praised by Shakespeare's Falstaff came mostly from Tenerife.

More unwelcome visitors were the privateers. Drake and Hawkins raided Las Palmas in 1595 and Raleigh landed in Lanzarote in 1617.

But it was in the 19th century, when the decline in Spain's fortunes coincided with the expansion of Britain's trade and colonial power, that the British presence in the islands began to be of greatest importance.

One of the streets in Las Palmas is named after one of the pioneers of the new era of trade between Britain and the Canaries, Thomas Miller. Miller arrived on Gran Canaria in 1824 to join his cousin James Swanston, who had come to the Canaries by accident. While sailing from impoverished Scotland to relatives in St Kitts, the ship on which Swantson was travelling was taken by pirates and he finally came ashore in Fuerteventura.

Swanston eventually set up in business in Las Palmas, doing so well that he sent for his brothers and then his cousin to help him. They exported agricultural products, and imported textiles and domestic goods. Every household in Las Palmas used to use hard blue-veined bars of Swanston soap for washing clothes.

In 1854 Thomas Miller separated from the Swanstons and set up his own business; he made a lot of money, exported cochineal and in 1870 built a fine house in Las Palmas (now number 40, Triana). The business on the ground floor included a bank (the first in Las Palmas) and the sale of agricultural tools, seeds, cloth etc. There was direct access to the sea for goods delivery.

At that time there was no breakwater and the ships had to anchor offshore. Loading and un-loading them was a risky task, especially in bad weather, and it was decided to build a new port five miles to the north, where the mountains of the *isleta* made a sheltered bay.

The planning and building of the port involved much co-operation between the Spanish authorities, including the engineer León y Castillo (whose name is given to an important road and the principal breakwater) and the British firms. The Santa Catalina mole, the first in the new port, was built by the next generation of Millers and Swanstons in 1881, and then began the great heyday of the British presence.

The Canaries were in a strategic position on the route from Europe to the new British colonies in Africa. The old sailing ships had given way to steam, and the steamers required large quantities of coal. Several firms were established to supply the ships, importing coal mainly from Cardiff. Dozens of Englishmen and their families came out to work in Las Palmas, creating a large British community.

The employees worked long hours as the ships were always in a hurry. Gerald Miller, a grandson of Thomas, recounted that he often had to walk home to Triana from the port in the dark, and could find his way only by following the tramlines which then ran all along the port road.

There were very few idle rich in this community and it was not a Gatsby-style existence. Most of the men worked hard as traders or in shipping offices, and although the wives did not go out to work and had plenty of local servants, housekeeping was not easy in the early years of this century. Only a limited range of food was available locally, and shopping had to be done every day as there were no refrigerators.

There were no dress shops in Las Palmas and all clothes had to be made by dressmakers or bought on the bi-annual home leaves. In accordance with the British custom of the time, the children were sent away to school in England at an early age, and communications with them and other relatives in the UK were slow.

But leisure hours were agreeable in the pleasant climate and the British set up various institutions for their own diversion. The Las Palmas Golf Club, founded in 1892, was the first to be established in Spain. The course was on the bare hilltop of Escaleritas, and the club-house had a corrugated iron roof held down by big stones; it has since moved to a new location at Bandama. There was a tennis club too, which still survives, and even a cricket club.

The British Club was founded in 1908 as a social and billiards club. It has been in its present location, a fine colonial-style mansion on León y Castillo, since 1912. Eighty years on it is still active, and is worth visiting for a glimpse of an earlier way of life.

Not far away is Holy Trinity Church, which was inaugurated in 1893, and is still used for regular worship by the British community. Strangely, by far the earliest non-commercial British institution was a cemetery, which dates from 1835, when there were only 31 British residents. A cemetery was a necessity as Protestants were refused burial in the Catholic graveyards.

With the increase in shipping, the need for a hospital arose, and so the Queen Victoria Hospital for Seamen was founded by the British firms in 1891. Its original building was by the Canteras beach but in 1966 it moved to Escaleritas.

Calle Alfredo L Jones is a street named after an Englishman. Sir Alfred Jones never lived in the islands but he was a great promoter of business, agriculture and tourism. He founded the Grand Canary Coaling Company, the very first to open in the new port; he introduced the cultivation of bananas, and he owned hotels and the shipping lines which brought in tourists.

GOD
BLESS OUR WORK

To begin with, these tourists were mostly invalids who spent several winter months in Las Palmas. In the 1890s the Hotel Santa Catalina had a resident English doctor. Later, in the inter-war years, a different kind of tourist came for shorter periods, and were deprecatingly known as "fifteen-pounders" by the British residents as this was the price of an all-in holiday! To the local Canarios, they were known as *chonis* (Johnnys).

The Tafira area used to be a favourite with holidaymakers and there were several British hotels there. Las Palmas was considered to be too hot and dusty, and of course the Maspalomas area was just a desert several hours' journey away.

The British also pioneered new services. Sunk into the pavements of Las Palmas are metal covers bearing the letters LPWW, the Las Palmas Water Works, a British company which installed the first water mains in the city. The electricity company too was British, and James Miller, Thomas' son, set up the first telephone exchange in 1912. A few years later he sold it to the Las Palmas Council, who immediately halved the tariffs! And the great fruit farms which sent bananas and tomatoes to England and the rest of Europe belonged to British firms.

The British lived mainly in the area between Las Palmas and the Port, known as "The Garden City". The original Hotel Metropole, next to the British Club, was a great haunt of the British community, who swam in its pool and then dined and danced in the restaurant. It now houses the Las Palmas Council offices.

The great days of the British in Las Palmas ended in 1930 when, due to the advent of oil-fired ships, the coaling companies had to amalgamate and dismiss a large number of staff. The unsettled world situation kept most tourists away, but one Englishman who came to Las Palmas in 1936 played a small part in an important event—he was Captain Bebb, the expert pilot contracted to fly General Franco from what was then a tiny airstrip at Gando, to Morocco to start the uprising which led to the Spanish Civil War.

After World War II, Spain's economic recovery and improved educational facilities meant that local people were able to take the jobs previously done by the British, though some British people with special knowledge are still employed. Today there is still quite a considerable British community, some of them working as teachers or in the catering business, but most of today's residents are retired people, content to enjoy the peace and sunshine of the Canaries.

There have been criticisms of the Britons' hard business methods and of the fact that they were almost an enclosed community, rarely mixing with Spanish society, and virtually never inter-marrying with Canarios. But they introduced a new way of living and working and most of the businesses and the clubs founded by the British are still in existence—but run by the Spanish.

PLACES

The islands of Gran Canaria, Fuerteventura and Lanzarote make up the eastern province of the autonomous region of the Canary Islands. On the whole, they are more barren islands than those in the western province, and, being closer to the African continent, have some of Africa's climate and landscape.

Gran Canaria, a continent in miniature, has a bit of everything. Industry, agriculture, tourism, forest, mountain, beach, capital city and deserted farmland. Las Palmas, the seat of Canary government, is the equal of any city on mainland Europe, thanks to the activities of its port, which is quite out of scale in comparison to the island it sits on. Las Palmas is also unusual in that it has a resort (Las Canteras) at its heart; otherwise the principal resort area—Maspalomas and surroundings—is on the southern coast of the island. The mountainous centre and the western coast are surprisingly remote.

Preceding pages: time moving slowly in Lanzarote; skin tanning quick on Playa Canteras, Gran Canaria; the flesh-like folds of Fuerteventura; the cathedral of Las Palmas.

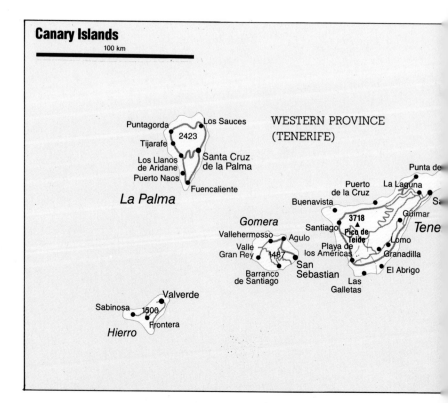

Canary Islands
100 km

Puntagorda
Los Sauces
2423
Tijarafe
Los Llanos de Aridane
Santa Cruz de la Palma
Puerto Naos
Fuencaliente
La Palma

WESTERN PROVINCE
(TENERIFE)

Punta de
Puerto de la Cruz
La Laguna
Buenavista
Sa
Güímar
Gomera
Santiago
3718
Pico de Teide
Tene
Vallehermosso
Agulo
Lomo
Valle
Gran Rey
1487
Playa de los Américas
Granadilla
San Sebastian
Barranco de Santiago
El Abrigo
Las Galletas

Valverde
Sabinosa
1500
Frontera
Hierro

Despite its size, Fuerteventura has a tiny population. With practically no rainfall and therefore no vegetation, the island offers little in the way of livelihood other than in tourism, which as yet is in its infancy on the island. The beaches are the best in the archipelago and some of the best in the world, but the water shortage is a major limiting factor. Nevertheless, a very substantial resort complex is planned for the island.

Lanzarote is a success story that other islands would like to emulate. In a harsh landscape, Lanzaroteños have managed to create successful agricultural methods and tourist urbanisations which are pleasing to the eye, partly thanks to the influence of resident artist César Manrique. Consequently the island attracts a better quality, higher-spending tourist, such as the two BBC executives who supposedly dreamed up the concept of the successful TV programme *Eastenders* while on a winter break.

These, then, are the eastern Canaries.

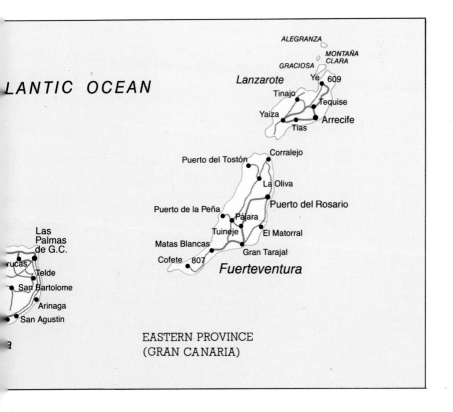

Gran Canaria

10 km

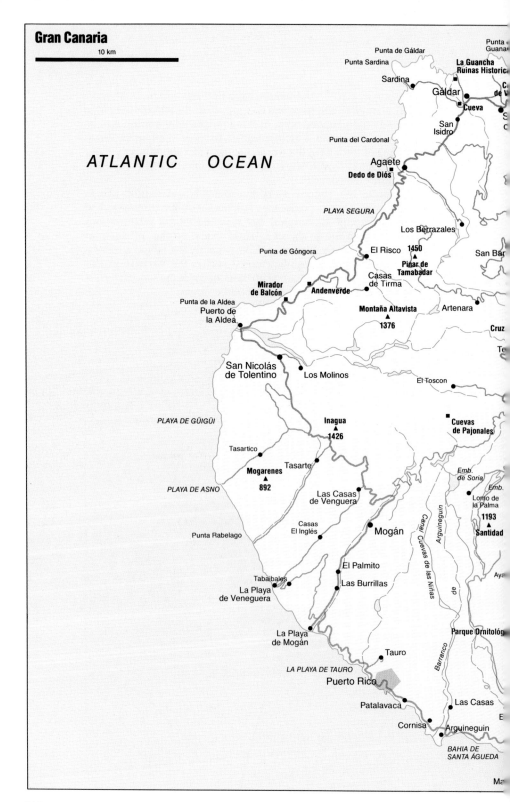

ATLANTIC OCEAN

Punta de Gáldar
Punta Sardina
Sardina
Punta del Cardonal

Punta
Guana
La Guancha
Ruinas Historic
C
de V
Gáldar
Cueva
San
Isidro
S
C

Agaete
Dedo de Diós

PLAYA SEGURA

Los Berrazales

Punta de Góngora
El Risco 1450
Pinar de
Tamabadar
Casas
de Tirma

San Bar

Mirador
de Balcón
Andenverde

Punta de la Aldea
Puerto de
la Aldea

Montaña Altavista
1376

Artenara

Cruz
Te

San Nicolás
de Tolentino
Los Molinos

El Toscon

PLAYA DE GÜIGÜI

Inagua
1426

Cuevas
de Pajonales

Tasartico
Tasarte

Mogarenes
892

PLAYA DE ASNO

Las Casas
de Venguera

Emb.
de Soria

Emb.
Lomo de
la Palma
1193
Santidad

Casas
El Inglés

Mogán

Punta Rabelago

El Palmito
Tabaibales
La Playa
de Veneguera

Las Burrillas

Aya

La Playa
de Mogán

Parque Ornitológ

Tauro

LA PLAYA DE TAURO

Puerto Rico

Patalavaca

Las Casas
E

Cornisa
Arguineguin

BAHIA DE
SANTA ÁGUEDA

Ma

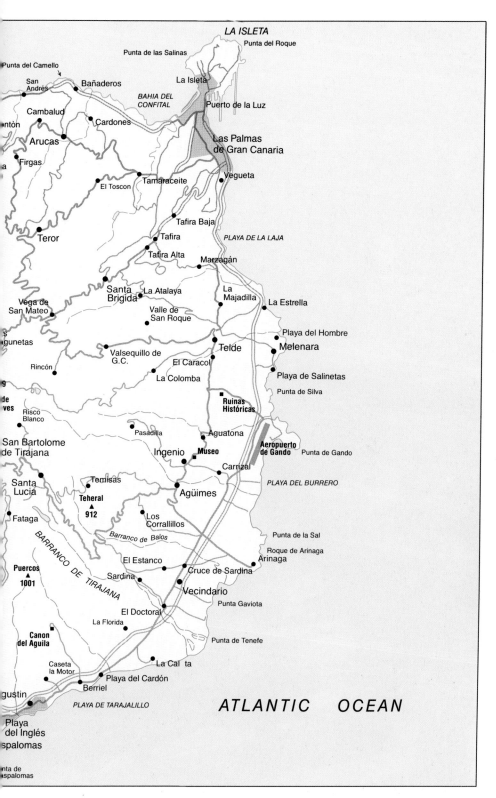

LA ISLETA

Punta del Roque

Punta de las Salinas

Punta del Camello

San Andrés

Bañaderos

La Isleta

BAHIA DEL CONFITAL

Cambalud

Cardones

Puerto de la Luz

ntòn

Arucas

Las Palmas de Gran Canaria

a

Firgas

El Toscon

Tamaraceite

Vegueta

Tafira Baja

Teror

Tafira

PLAYA DE LA LAJA

Tafira Alta

Marzagán

Santa Brigida

La Atalaya

La Majadilla

La Estrella

Vega de San Mateo

Valle de San Roque

Playa del Hombre

S gunetas

Valsequillo de G.C.

Telde

Melenara

Rincón

El Caracol

La Colomba

Playa de Salinetas

g

Punta de Silva

de ves

Risco Blanco

Ruinas Históricas

Pasadilla

Aguatona

San Bartolome de Tirajana

Ingenio

Museo

Aeropuerto de Gando

Punta de Gando

Carrizal

Santa Lucia

Temisas

Agüimes

PLAYA DEL BURRERO

Teheral
▲ 912

Fataga

Los Corrallillos

Barranco de Balos

Punta de la Sal

Roque de Arinaga

Arinaga

BARRANCO

Puercos
▲ 1001

El Estanco

Sardina

Cruce de Sardina

DE TIRAJANA

Vecindario

El Doctoral

Punta Gaviota

La Florida

Canon del Aguila

Punta de Tenefe

Caseta la Motor

La Cal ta

Berriel

Playa del Cardón

gustin

PLAYA DE TARAJALILLO

ATLANTIC   OCEAN

Playa del Inglés

spalomas

nta de spalomas

109

LAS PALMAS

The first view of Las Palmas from its southern approaches is quite breathtaking. As Ernest Hemingway said of the wide vista of Havana, "the city looks fine in the sun". Gleaming new hotels and office blocks along the sea-front are picked out against a permanently blue sky with hillside roofs and doors and island buses adding bright splashes of red, green and yellow.

In the harbour, and out in the ultramarine Atlantic swell, oil tankers, barges, container ships and tugs take on an almost toy-like quality in the sunlight. The four-mile (seven km) length of Las Palmas' coastline, from the beachside turret of San Cristóbal Fort to the Castle of Light at the tip of the port, displays a wealth of building styles, peopled by a mixture of races. Between the two ancient monuments every bend in the marina avenue reveals architectural variation, including glass-fronted *art nouveau* façades, Corinthian-style frontages, wooden balconied, red-tiled colonial homes and steel-framed, ultramodern skyscrapers. Three hundred and fifty thousand people live in this capital city of the Canaries.

Of the few early reflections on the seven Gardens of Hesperides, none fits Gran Canaria like that of the chronicler Richard Hakluyt in 1589: "To speake somewhat of these Ilands being called in olde time Insulae Fortunatae, by the means of the flourishing there of, the fruitfulnesse of them doeth surely exceed farre all other that I have heard of". Gran Canaria certainly has its share of tropical bounties and Las Palmas stands at its prow.

What nature started the authorities have finished, and Las Palmas harbour now has the status of a Free Port. The Puerto de la Luz is among the busiest in the world and boasts Spain's largest dock. Strategically located off the western coast of Africa yet just 700 miles (1,120 km) from the tip of Europe, the Canaries have enjoyed importance as a trading centre and Las Palmas has grown out of that trade into a city out of all proportion to the island it sits on.

Focal point: In the distant days of Gran Canaria's now extinct aborigines, the Guanches, this corner of the island was singled out for habitation. Evidence in caves suggests occupation by Neolithic people; the Phoenicians stopped here in their travels in the 12th century B.C. and a Carthagian, Hanno, stopped in 470 B.C. Later expeditions visiting this part of Gran Canaria included those of the Berber king, Juba II, and Arab venturers from North Africa.

Early maps like that of Beatus (1028-72) show the "Inslae Fortunatarum". The "continent in miniature", which is how Canarios refer to Gran Canaria, appeared in recognisable shape on 14th-century maps when Portugal claimed all seven islands in 1341.

After that, a constant stream of adventurers dropped in. Jean de Béthencourt made an abortive landing near today's airport site in 1402, and his contemporary, the Norman adventurer, Gadifer de la Salle, sailed past that part

Las
as
. Right,
was 80
ago.

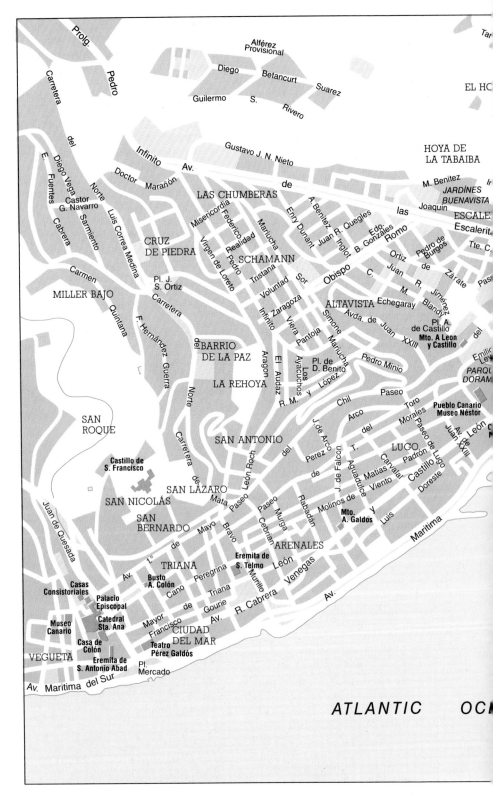

Prolg.

Alférez
Provisional

Diego Betancurt
Suarez

EL HC

Carretera

Pedro

Guilermo S. Rivero

HOYA DE
LA TABAIBA

del

Infinito

Gustavo J. N. Nieto

Av.

de

las

M. Benitez

Ir

JARDÍNES
BUENAVISTA

Joaquin

ESCALE

Escalerit

Tte. C.

E. Fuentes

Diego Vega

Norte

Doctor Marañón

Castor
G. Navarro

Sarmiento

Luis Correa Medina

LAS CHUMBERAS

Misericordia

Federico

Realidad

Virgen de Loreto

Pedro

Marucha

A. Benitez

Enry Dunant

Juan R. Quegles

Edo. Gonzáles

B. Gonzáles

Romo

Ortiz de

Pedro de
Burgos

Cabrera

Carmen

CRUZ
DE PIEDRA

Pl. J.
S. Ortiz

SCHAMANN

Tristana

Voluntad

Sor

Obispo

C.

Juan R.

Zárate

Pas

MILLER BAJO

Quintana

Carretera

F. Hernández

Guerra

Infinito

Zaragoza

Viera

Pantoja

Simone

ALTAVISTA

Avda. de

Echegaray

Mariucha

M.

Blandy

Jiménez

Pl. A.
de Castillo

Mto. A Leon
y Castillo

del

Juan XXIII

Emili

Le

PARQU

DORAM

BARRIO
DE LA PAZ

Aragon

El Audaz

LA REHOYA

Los
Ayacuchos

Pl. de
D. Benito
y López

R. M.

Pedro Minio

Paseo

Chil

Arco

del

Toro

Morales

Paseo de Lugo

Pueblo Canario
Museo Néstor

Av. de León

Juan XXIII

SAN
ROQUE

Carretera

de

SAN ANTONIO

León Roch

Perez

de

J. de Arco

J. de Falcon

T.

Aguadulce

Viento

LUGO

Carvajal

Matias

Padrón

Castillo

y

Doreste

Castillo de
S. Francisco

SAN LÁZARO

Mata

Paseo

SAN NICOLÁS

SAN
BERNARDO

Mayo

Bravo

Cebrian

Murga

Rabadan

Molinos de

Mto.
A. Galdos

Luis

Maritima

Juan de Quesada

de

Paseo

ARENALES

I.°

Av.

TRIANA

Busto
A. Colón

Peregrina

Cano

Eremita de
S. Telmo

León

Murillo

Venegas

Casas
Consistoriales

Palacio
Episcopal

Triana

de

Gourie

R. Cabrera

Av.

Museo
Canario

Catedral
Sta. Ana

Mayor

Francisco

Av.

Casa de
Colón

VEGUETA

Eremita de
S. Antonio Abad

Teatro
Pérez Galdós

CIUDAD
DEL MAR

Pl.
Mercado

Av. Maritima del Sur

ATLANTIC   OC

112

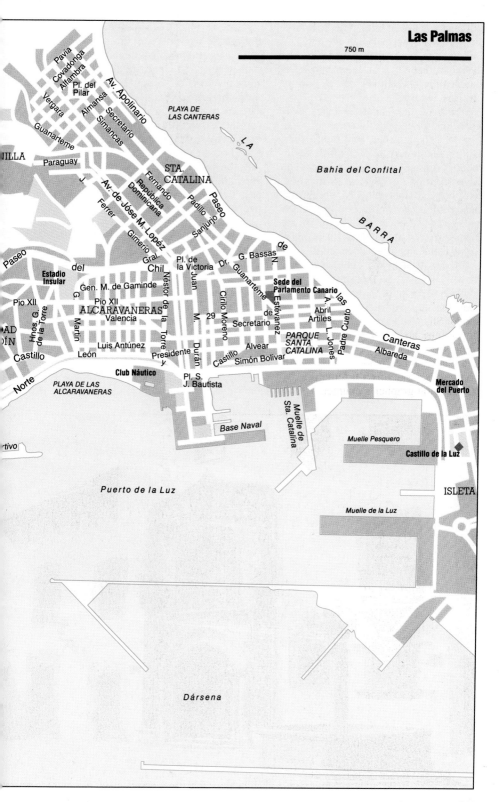

Las Palmas

750 m

Pavia
Covadonga
Alfambra
Pl. del Pilar
Vergara
Almansa
Secretario
Simancas
Guanarteme
Av. Apolinario

PLAYA DE
LAS CANTERAS

Paraguay

ILLA

STA.
CATALINA

Fernando
República
Dominicana
Padillo
Sanjurjo
Paseo

LA

Bahía del Confital

BARRA

J.
Ferrer
Av. de José M. López
Gimerio
Gral.
Chil
Néstor de la Torre
Pl. de
la Victoria
Juan
Dr.
G. Bassas
Guanarteme
de
N

Paseo
del
Estadio
Insular
Gen. M. de Gaminde
G.
Pío XII
ALCARAVANERAS
Valencia
29
M.
Cirilo Moreno
Estévanez
Secretario
Sede del
Parlamento Canario
A. L. Jones
Abril
Artiles
Padre Cueto
las

Pío XII
Hnos. G.
de la Torre
Martín
Luis Antúnez
León
Presidente
y
Durán
Castillo
Alvear
Simón Bolívar
PARQUE
SANTA
CATALINA
Canteras
Albareda

AD
ÍN
Castillo
Norte
Club Náutico
Pl. S.
J. Bautista

PLAYA DE LAS
ALCARAVANERAS

Base Naval

Muelle de
Sta. Catalina

Mercado
del Puerto

Muelle Pesquero

Castillo de la Luz

tivo

Puerto de la Luz

Muelle de la Luz

ISLETA

Dársena

113

of the island a year later. The Spaniard, Juan Rejón, landed near present-day Las Palmas, on La Isleta, in 1478. His soldiers constructed a camp known as the Real de las Palmas, and the future city was renamed.

Doramas, the Guanche chief, was killed in 1479 and the natives were finally defeated the following year. During the first years of Spanish settlement a miraculous event was said to have occurred; in 1481, when the town was but a hamlet, the Madonna appeared to a priest in a pine tree in the village of Teror in the centre of the island. Today the Blessed Virgin of Teror is the island's patron saint.

Old city: It is in the cobbled streets, narrow, gas-lit alleyways and tiny, shaded squares of **Vegueta** that the most classical building styles are to be found. Shuttered windows, ornate fan-lights, intricately carved balconies and impressive doorways, wrought-iron gates and arches leading to beautiful courtyards make this a fascinating district, a photographer's magnet.

Here are ornate brass door fittings, elaborately carved verandah supports, wrought-iron embellishments on street wall-lanterns and painted tiled street names; some buildings have corner shoes to protect the stonework from damage by early carriage wheels. This was the aristocratic quarter of Las Palmas, away from the dust formerly generated by the port.

South of the port area, along the Avenida Maritima del Sur, the oldest part of Las Palmas is situated around the overbuilt mouth of a river gorge known as the Barranco Guiniguada, which now carries a major road.

It is said that Christopher Columbus once prayed in the original church of **San Antonio Abad** before setting sail for the Americas. Set in a cobbled court-yard at the end of the street named after him—Calle Colón—this tiny church was rebuilt in 1892, exactly 400 years after he first set foot in the New World. The grand old mansion with its moulded gateway and latticed balconies at the beginning of Calle Colón is

The Casa Colon, La Palmas.

114

the **Casa de Colón**—supposedly Columbus's house.

Dating from the late 15th century and now a museum, this was once the residence of governors like Pedro de Vera, the island's first Spanish ruler from 1482. The building surrounds a cool, Renaissance *patio* and contains many nautical artefacts and weapons from the era of discovery, plus a grand collection of paintings. Columbus stayed here in 1492 and the Archives Museum, also housed here, details his early exploits.

At the other end of Calle Colón the **Cathedral of Santa Ana**, founded in 1497, but only finally finished in the 19th century, not only looms over the Plaza de Santa Ana, but dominates the skyline of the old district. A mixture of local, Gothic and neo-classical styles, the three naves are surmounted by pillars supporting bell-tower domes and linked by a rose window façade sporting a central arch.

A wealth of treasures are on display here, including a 1641 illuminated songbook, a gold and enamel *portapaz*

attributed to Benvenuto Cellini and figures carved by José Luján Pérez.

The cathedral also houses a gold-and-emerald chalice given by King Felipe IV and another presented by Cardinal Delgado, together with the 18th-century Bishop Verdugo's pectoral cross encrusted with diamonds and emeralds. A throne, also on display, contemporary with the Bishop's see, is of local importance because it was fashioned by the Canarian goldsmith José Eugenio.

Somewhere also in the Gothic depths of this massive building, is said to be the Pendon de la Conquista—the Banner of the Conquest—embroidered by Queen Isabella herself.

Of particular interest, is the **Museum of Religious Art**, connected to the main structure but entered from Calle Espiritu Santo. A fascinating collection of Spanish colonial art is represented here, including Aztec works, treasures from the Americas, 15th to 17th-century religious artefacts and tapestries, sculptures and early furniture.

Dogs of bronze: In the palm-lined

reet in
Vegueta
rict.

CANARIAN GOVERNMENT

Rivalry between the two major island capitals has always been a ruling reality of island government. Las Palmas and Santa Cruz (Tenerife) have vied for political prominence for hundreds of years. For years arbitration, apportionment, and appropriation decreed by the Popes and Spain bullied the government in the Canary Islands.

The death of General Franco in 1975 gave birth to a new era in government throughout Spain. A new constitution was drawn up and ratified. Demands for self-government for ethnic groups and regional entities were reiterated. All Spanish citizens over the age of 18 got the vote.

In 1977, the first general elections of this new era brought the Centre Democratic Union (UCD) to power, while the Spanish Socialist Labour Party (PSOE) became the major force in the opposition. In Tenerife, two high-water marks were reached in the wake of the UCD electoral victory: firstly Alfonso Soriano y Benítez de Lugo (UCD) presided over the first Council (Junta) of the Canaries, a pre-autonomous body constituted in Las Cañadas de Teide on 14 April 1987, and secondly the Institute of University Studies of Enterprise, an organ of the University of La Laguna, presented the draft of a statute of autonomy, a proposal of independent government for the Canary Islands.

The University of La Laguna in Tenerife has been witness to scores of socio-economic waves and political tide-turnings since 1701, when Pope Clement IX authorised the teaching of higher education by the order of Saint Augustine.

The royal decree of 1927 divided the Canary Archipelago into two provinces; the western province comprised the islands of Gomera, La Palma, Hierro and Tenerife, with its capital in Santa Cruz de Tenerife; the eastern province was made up of Fuerteventura, Lanzarote, and Gran Canaria with Las Palmas designated as its capital. With this act, General Primo de Rivero's government contrived to calm the controversy existing between the two capitals.

Many historians claim that the controversy dates back to 1812, when the parliament of Cadiz approved a new political organisation of Spain, proclaiming the entire Canary Archipelago one province, and Santa Cruz de Tenerife the capital of all the islands. The deputies from Gran Canaria declined to attend the sessions of the Provincial Chamber of Deputies in Santa Cruz.

Perhaps the more significant date is 1808, the year in which Tenerife activists convened the Supreme Council of the Canaries in La Laguna. Las Palmas responded to this by establishing the Permanent Island Council (*cabildo*) of Gran Canaria.

Cabildos, functioning like regional councils in each island, returned with a regulation approved by the National Parliament on 12 October 1912, to the approval of all the islands. The new *cabildos* assumed the administration of each island with jurisdiction comparable to, and in certain fields, exceeding that of the provincial deputations which were appointed from mainland Spain. They were a great success. Where alternative forms of administration had failed to understand and to act, each *cabildo* in each island was aware and efficient in a way that no central administration had been able to be.

In the elections of 1982, the socialist party (PSOE) scored a majority victory, not only in the Canaries, but throughout Spain. The Official State Bulletin published the Statute of Autonomy for the Canaries on 10 August 1982, and the seven islands, thus united, become one of the 17 Autonomous Communities of Spain. A Law of Transferences granted full jurisdiction (with the exception of the administration of justice, the military forces and the national police) to the Canary Parliament.

All the members of the new autonomous government are elected by popular vote every four years, at which point the seat of government shifts to the other of the two provincial capitals. Tax revenues, etc received from Madrid are apportioned to the island *cabildos* and thence to the municipal governments.

On 30 May 1984, the Day of the Canaries was celebrated for the first time as a holiday throughout all the islands. But the inter-island rivalry is still a reality.

square of **Santa Ana** bronze statues of the legendary giant Canary Island dogs guard the wide steps—dogs which have remained on the Las Palmas coat of arms since 1506. Looking from the cathedral, on the right, is the **Bishop's Palace**; at the end of the Plaza is the **Town Hall**, built in colonial style, and the other impressive building is the **Regent's House**, once the seat of the heads of the armed forces on the islands. The narrow square is a mass of colour at the annual Corpus Christi Festival when flower carpets deck the streets from the cathedral.

The **Museo Canario**, or Museum of the Canaries, is located on Calle Dr Chil. The collection includes relics from Guanche mummies and ceramics, clothing and jewellery, to items of geological interest and a library of more than 40,000 books. Skeletons and skulls of early Canary Island natives lend a macabre note. Not far from the museum, on the waterfront of the old quarter, is the grand Palace of Justice.

On the sea-front of the Vegueta area

is Las Palmas market, or the **"Market of the Forty Thieves"**, so called because of the number of stalls which sell anything from fruit, vegetables, fish and meat, to local cheese, leather goods and handicrafts. Around the market there are a number of excellent little restaurants serving local delicacies, bistros modelled on European cafés and tiny bars where one can enjoy a glass of wine and *tapas*, Canarian versions of Spanish side dishes.

Triana: On the other side of the dual carriageway which isolates Vegueta is **Plaza Colón**, where, in front of the church of San Francisco, there is an imposing bust of the explorer Columbus himself. Down the hill towards the sea is the Las Palmas theatre and opera house (1919), **Teatro Pérez Galdós**, named after the locally-born novelist Benito Pérez Galdós (1843-1920) who wrote prolifically about social injustice on the islands.

The theatre was decorated by Nestor Martin Fernandez de la Torre, in Modernist style, and is the gathering place of Las Palmas society. The novelist's house is on Calle Cano nearby, and is now a museum displaying a collection of his works and some of his personal belongings.

The granite-paved shopping precinct of **Calle Mayor de Triana**, the local equivalent of London's Bond Street or the Paris boulevards, stretches through the heart of Triana from the edge of Vegueta, ending at the southern corner of **San Telmo** park.

This was the site of Las Palmas' first pier, and the delightful little 15th-century chapel of San Telmo is in one corner. In the corner opposite stands a decaying Modernist coffee kiosk which would not look out of place in Paris, decorated with Manises ceramic tiling. At the back of the square is the old army headquarters building from where General Franco announced his *coup d'état* on 18 July 1936 and thus set in motion the Spanish Civil War; a plaque on the wall announces the fact.

At the sea-front end of the park is the main island bus station, from where *gua-guas* (buses) depart for almost

dernist
sk in San
mo park.

anywhere on Gran Canaria. From the flyover above are buses both south to the airport and north into the city: they are by far the most economical method of travel.

In the district behind San Telmo Park is part of the Canarian university, the source of much recent argument. The main university site is at La Laguna on Tenerife, but Gran Canarios believe that Las Palmas merits its own complete institution.

The city's largest park, **Parque Doramas**, lies some distance up Calle León y Castillo. It was named after the native island chief who resisted the Spanish conquest in the late 15th century. A model Canary Island village, **Pueblo Canario**, which stands in the park, was designed by Nestor de la Torre (1887-1938). The museum opposite shows the work of this painter and designer's life.

The zoo, botanical gardens, sports facilities and the Hotel Santa Catalina are located in the park, which really marks the boundary between the southern, old part of Las Palmas and the **Garden City**, a grand residential area, and port. Folk dance and song performances are held in the Pueblo Canaria on Sunday mornings and Thursday evenings.

City centre: Fronting the Parque Doramas, to one side of the wide marine boulevard, is the city's Nautical Club, just before the large Naval School and at the mouth of Spain's largest docks, the **Puerto de la Luz**. Here too is the small beach of **Playa de las Alcaravaneras**, once quite a popular resort itself.

Buses turn off the marina road at **Santa Catalina Park**. This is the edge of the centre of the city and is the site of the tourist office, a large souvenir and craft market and numerous street cafés with open-air tables, which make it a gathering point for tourists. From this park it is possible to hail a *tartana*, or horse-drawn taxi carriage. The main taxi rank is also located on Santa Catalina square.

Every street off this square is crammed with duty-free shops—radios, televisions, liquor and tobacco,

Santa Catalina park at dawn.

jewellery and clothes, particularly aimed at seamen shoppers from the harbour. At intervals are hotels, most of which seem to be facing away from the harbour area. There is good reason for the hotels to incline towards the west. Just a few steps away from Santa Catalina Park and the narrow shopping streets (which also function as the city's red-light district), is the beach of **Playa de las Canteras**. This two and a half mile (four km) stretch of fine, white-sanded beach, runs the length of the narrow isthmus between the main island of Gran Canaria and the little peninsula of La Isleta.

Las Canteras is not quite the fashionable resort it once was, although it is still popular with the Spanish themselves. Along the wide, constantly cleaned promenade, tourists mix with locals and visiting mariners. Bulgarian bistros rub shoulders with English pubs, Chinese restaurants are squashed between Italian ice-cream parlours and German beer cellars. Austrian bars compete with international night clubs and Japanese eating houses brush with Russian tea rooms, catering as much for sailors as tourists.

Deck chairs, pedal boats and a range of marine sports equipment can be hired at various points along the beach and life guards patrol the entire waterfront. To the north is the residential area known as **La Isleta** town. Built on steep slopes with stairways and narrow lanes, it is an area best avoided by the first-time visitor. However, the little local shops, like dried fish vendors and tiny bars, are worth browsing through when in a safe group.

Port quarter: The city's northern bus terminal is right at the end of the marina carriageway on the wharfside, which is why visitors leave the bus at Santa Catalina Park. This is a region of dockers and local labourers, being opposite the gates of the main harbour.

However, between the bend in the dual carriageway and the port entrance is one of Las Palmas' oldest structures, the **Castillo de la Luz**, or Castle of Light. Closed to visitors until it has been prepared as a Museum of the Sea, this well preserved 16th-century fortress was originally constructed in 1494. Not far from here, the giant oil storage tanks dominating the end of the road are part of the CEPSA refinery.

The **Puerto de la Luz** is a major fishing port, particularly for the Korean fleet, and merchant shipping base. The large bay also includes a pleasure yacht basin and a Naval Station. Five piers berth ships which fly flags from around the world; a far cry from the wallowing caravels of the Spanish founder, Juan Rejón, when he first landed on this coast in 1478, or the Arab sailing ships which put into this bay in A.D. 999.

For the best views of the beaches, the port and the spreading city of Las Palmas, take a taxi ride through La Isleta town onto the winding desert road beyond. Get the cab to stop at the foot of the steep track which leads to the summit of the rocky hill overlooking the entire area. Surmounted by a crude wooden cross, this precipitous, prickly-pear infested cliff looks down on what looks like a shanty town far below.

THE BIGGEST PORT IN EUROPE

If the lovely old cathedral of Santa Ana is the soul of Las Palmas, the magnificent port is surely its heart. Two enormous jetties thrust out into the Atlantic like gigantic arms protecting the city and the thousands of ships that call each year.

And what a strange and motley collection they are. Millionaires' yachts, luxury liners, tatty little fishing boats, massive container vessels, naval training ships under sail and huge floating oil platforms make this one of the busiest ports on the eastern Atlantic.

Across the bay lies the sporting marina, where each year yachts (in 1988 there were 180, 62 of them British), set off on the Canaries-Barbados race. Many more remain in the Marina, some owned by Canarios, who have a great love of the sea. Others belong to trans-Atlantic or round-the-world yachtsmen such as Dougal Robertson, the author of *Survive the Savage Sea*, who started his ill-fated voyage from Las Palmas in 1971. And there are quite a lot of transient visitors who mean to call for a week but stay for months, for Las Palmas lays its *mañana* spell on all, and why leave today if you can stay till tomorrow... or next month?

Situated as it is at the crossroads between three continents—Africa, Europe and the Americas, it is surprising that Puerto de la Luz—the Port of Light—only celebrated its 100th anniversary in 1983. At the start of this century it had one long wharf and some 358,000 sq yards (300,000 sq metres) of sheltered areas.

Today it boasts the longest jetty in the eastern seaboard, Muelle Reina Sofia, which is named after the Queen of Spain but is usually referred to as the Muelle Grande. It is more than two miles (3.5 km) in length and is being extended. There are six miles (10 km) of berthing wharves, about 2.4 million sq yards (two million sq metres) of floating zones and 1.8 million sq yards (1.5 million sq metres) of dockland.

But in spite of its modern facilities— massive bunkering tanks, container terminals and helicopter services, this great port has a sense of

history—and mystery.

We do not know when or where earlier travellers—Phoenicians, Romans, maybe Vikings—first set foot on the island. But it was on the sandy beach that is now the port that the Spanish conquistadors landed in 1478.

Many historians believe that Christopher Columbus stopped here too, in 1492 on his way to America, and Sir Francis Drake tried to but was repulsed. So were 10,000 Dutchmen in 1599.

In more recent times, Germany badly wanted to use this strategically-placed island during the Second World War. Hitler tried to make a deal with General Franco, offering him Gibraltar after victory if he could base his Stukas and anti-aircraft guns here. Franco said no, but the islands, Gran Canaria in particular, became a hotbed of conspiracy.

German submarines lurked round them, lying in wait for the US convoys bound for the Mediterranean and Britain. Ships slipped their moorings at night to surreptitiously refuel the "sharks" as they hunted their prey in a semi-circular route curving from the Irish Sea down to Freetown, West Africa.

In January and February 1941 the submarines sank 60 ships with a tonnage of 324,000 tons. And throughout the war, the German ship *Kersten Miles* was berthed in the port. Ostensibly she was collecting stores...for four and a half years. But possibly she was acting as a reserve tanker for two other German ships, the *Corrientes* and the *Charlotte Schliemann* who were definitely refuelling German submarines. (One of which, the U-37, was torpedoed and sunk in what is now the southern resort of San Agustin, in only 33 ft (10 metres) of water.

The Germans respected Spanish neutrality and there was a great hue and cry when a Canarian ship, the *San Carlos*, was torpedoed—luckily with no fatalities. Not long after this, a German ship in port, the *Corrientes*—one of the refuelling vessels—was rocked by a huge blast that shook the whole city.

The official version was that it had been torpedoed by a British submarine, but strange rumours swept the port that the missile had been fired from land (the *Corrientes* at the time of the blast was anchored in the bay of Al Caravaneras, midway between the port proper and the sporting marina). British Intelligence kept a vigilant watch on the port, the whole area was virtually teeming with spies for one side or the other, and the dock workers kept very quiet indeed.

No sooner had the war finished—and Germany paid compensation for the unfortunate *San Carlos*—then another drama began. Because of the war, shipping had come to a standstill. In 1945 only 45 foreign ships called at Las Palmas. But by 1948 the local fishing fleet suddenly became remarkably busy.

Boats would set out, presumably for the African coast, and then disappear completely. It was the start of the clandestine emigration to South America of thousands of Canarios who were fed up with the Franco regime and held out no great hopes for the future.

A great part of the fleet disappeared—some 90 ships in all. It started as a trickle and turned into a flood. Between 1948 and 1950 about 8,000 islanders vanished too. Heaven knows what they suffered, crammed 300 to a small ship and travelling under sail.

Writer Jose Ferrera Jimenez, who spent 30 years writing a history of the port, compares their adventures and hardships to those of the men in Homer's Odyssey. Later, in the early 1950s, Franco bowed to international pressure and legalised emigration. At least 150,000 Canarios opted to leave; their slogan was "Justice + Work = Venezuela." Today many islanders have relatives in Central America and many Venezuelan products are on the shelves of local shops.

In the 1960s and early 1970s Las Palmas saw days of glamour that will never be repeated. It was the era of the luxury liners and the weekly Royal Mail ships to South Africa. Every month dozens of floating hotels called at the port. Passages took four to six days from the UK, and a typical fare was £21 for third class and £62 for first.

The greatest ships in the world called regularly—the Cunard liners *Queen Mary* and *Queen Elizabeth*—and later the *QE 2*—the Union Castle ships, and liners from France, Italy and Greece. In February 1961 the *Leonardo de Vinci* called on her maiden voyage; among the passengers were Paul Newman, Zsa Zsa Gabor, Zachary Scott, Louella Parson and the writer Gore Vidal.

The peak years were from 1967 to 1971 when, with the Suez Canal closed, the P & O line also made Las Palmas a regular port of call. But it all stopped in 1973 when the price of petroleum soared. Only one ship, the *St Helena*, still makes a regular round-trip and accepts passengers.

Today the port is more prosaic but just as busy. Container ships and tankers are the main callers, and hundreds of fishing vessels are based here. Occasionally the old glamour briefly returns when the P & O liner *Canberra* is in port, or the Fred Olsen line's *Black Watch* and *Black Prince*. But gone are the days of leisurely cruises; now it's usually a weekly fly-and-sail package deal during the winter season.

In 1987, 9,106 ships called at Las Palmas, and 5,152,832 tons of goods were unloaded. Nearly half of that tonnage was oil or petroleum.

Goods weighing a total of 1,321,023 tons were embarked, about one-third being fruit, vegetables, fish and other foodstuffs.

Many ships, especially tankers, come to Las Palmas for cleaning, painting and repairs and there's often a queue of vessels right out into the open sea.

The airport: El Gando, 10.5 miles (17 kms) from Las Palmas, was rebuilt in the early 1970s to cope with the ever-growing flood of sun-seekers. It was badly needed. In 1970, 345,000 tourists visited the island. Ten years later the figure had doubled and in 1987 it was 1,971,891.

The airport terminal is spacious and built on two levels; in total some 2,500 people work there, and the two landing strips are each 3,600 yards (3,300 metres) long; they can cope with Concorde and almost daily Jumbo Jet landings. In 1987 a total of 6,500,000 passengers passed through the airport.

Like the port, El Gando has benefitted from a strategic position, and many flights bound for South America still stop at the airport for refuelling on their long journey.

It was a bomb scare at El Gando, provoked by Canary Island separatists, that was the indirect cause of the world's worst aircraft disaster when two diverted 747s collided on the tarmac of Los Rodeos airport, Tenerife, in 1977.

GRAN CANARIA: THE NORTH

They used to call it the "banana route". Perhaps it was 20 years ago, but now the banana industry is in decline many of the plantations have been left to run wild. Nevertheless the north of Gran Canaria is still the greenest and most attractive part of the island. The *barrancos* are as abrupt as elsewhere on the island but they are draped in a thick coat of tangled vegetation, even if some of it turns brown in summer.

The north coast: The northernmost route out of Las Palmas, through the crumbling working class housing and the warehouses of **Guanarteme** (Guanche word meaning "king"), is complicated, frustrating and frankly grim. As you join the main road out of town a fish-canning plant marks the end of Canteras Beach and a huddle of shanty houses lines the route on the inland side.

On the seaward side, the road has been landscaped with a jogging track and a pile of lava blocks forming a vaguely anthropomorphic bulk, a "Tribute to the Atlantic Ocean" the Atlantes monument, sculpted by Canario Tony Gallardo. The main road, now widened and improved, passes the foot of an enormous cliff of sedimentary deposits, former *barrancos* choked with their own rubbish, and ancient beaches which were formed as volcanic activity raised and lowered the island mass like an elevator in and out of the sea in past millennia.

The coast road passes through or by a series of uninspired, straggling villages. **Bañaderos** possesses natural rock swimming pools, an esplanade and tourist pretensions. It was here that a Canarian princess was captured by a Spanish raiding party shortly before the conquest while she was bathing in the rock pools.

The only other village of note is **El Roque**, a hamlet of square houses, "a cubist fantasy atop a single sea-surrounded rock". El Roque's main street is a winding alley at the end of which is a bar with views right along the coast.

The main road now climbs steeply to cross the *barrancos* of Moya and Calabozo via two high concrete bridges, known to the locals as "Salto del Canario" (Canarios' Leap). If you turn inland off the new road after the second bridge you pass **Cenobio de Valerón**, at the moment the only archaeological site in the Canaries still officially open to the public.

The Cenobio is first seen as a huge arc in the cliff-face opposite, apparently completely inaccessible. In fact a rather unsympathetic set of steps leads up to the monument, which is a mass of store-caves cut out of the living rock beneath the huge arched overhang. The specially cut sockets into which wooden covers for these caves fitted are still visible. The individual cubicles are now quite empty but the site is impressive— the equivalent of building a modern food superstore on a vertical cliff.

Down this cliff, the Cuesta de Silva, the *guanarteme* (Guanche king) of Gáldar led the captured Diego de Silva and his men after the Spaniards' unsuc-

cessful attack on the native capital. The native chief no doubt hoped that a demonstration of his magnanimity in victory would be repaid by an end to European landings—but he was to be sadly disappointed.

Back on the main road again is the town of **Guía**, a small town unremarkable except for its cheese, *queso de flor* (flower cheese) and its annual festival of the **Romeria de las Marias**. Guía is also the birth-place of the 18th-century sculptor, José Luján Pérez. A number of his works are to be found in his native parish church.

Guanche city: Cheek by jowl with Guía is **Gáldar**, the pre-Spanish capital of north-west Gran Canaria. Dominated by the naked Pico de Gáldar, a slag-heap of a volcano, the town huddles around the church, which also houses a collection of Luján Pérez's religious statuary. In the church is the *pila verde*, or green font, in which the natives of Gáldar were supposedly baptised after the conquest. When the present neo-classical church was built in the 18th century,

a number of buildings were unfortunately demolished including a small Spanish fort and the supposed "Palace of the Guanartemes".

Nearby is another testament to Gáldar's ancient history—the **Cueva Pintada**, Painted Cave. Shortly after its discovery in the last century, Olivia Stone, writer of one of the finest travelogues on the islands, "warmly urged the preservation of the cave and tried to make it so apparently feasible, that it should appeal to the pockets as well as the pride of the inhabitants".

The site was indeed preserved and opened up to the public, but the sensitive geometric paintings on the walls had deteriorated so much by 1970 that a programme of "restoration" was set up. The cave was enclosed by brick and concrete walling, which in fact stepped up the process of decomposition of the paintings. It is now closed to prevent humidity levels building up inside, whilst the autonomous government considers the problem—at length! Meanwhile there is a mock-up of the

A honeyco▶ of city suburbs.

cave in the Museo Canario in the Vegueta district of Las Palmas.

Gáldar's other great archaeological site, the **Tumulo de la Guancha**, (a Guanche necropolis) is reached by a narrow lane which leads out of the main plaza down between high, breeze-block walls enclosing banana plantations. As you near the coast, the site, an extensive group of burial cairns and stone houses, lies to the right. A few more rectangular houses are sandwiched between the road and the adjoining modern houses, all of which were built illegally after the Civil War.

The site was discovered in 1935 during agricultural works for the Leacock banana growing company; since then it has suffered from the building of holiday homes on the seaward edge and from unlimited access for vehicles to those houses.

Just west of Gáldar, beyond the bridge, the road forks. To the right is **Sardina**, a tiny fishing port crammed between the cliff and the sandy beach; the restaurant overlooking the bay or the crumbling hotel at the far end of the village serve freshly caught local fish. Well worth the stop.

The main road continues on to Agaete, passing another bare volcanic cone, **Montaña Almagro**, 1,643 ft (501 metres). On the lower slopes of Almagro is **Reptilandia**, a specialist zoo devoted mainly to lizards which live in craftily constructed enclosures that allow you to see them in almost natural conditions. The more unfriendly reptiles and poisonous frogs are kept behind glass in the small visitors' centre. From here there is a good view of the north-west corner of the island—the desert scrub, the pines on the inland heights, the wide Atlantic and, on a clear day, Tenerife and the peak of Mt Teide across the water.

Pastoral centre: The road to **Agaete** cuts through a group of prehistoric caves which have been reoccupied. The town is a jumble of narrow streets, white houses and impossible parking. The town council maintains the attractive **Huerto de las Flores**, a long estab-

CAVE LIVING

The Guanches were cavemen—some of them. The rest lived in houses, built of skilfully cut stone and roofed with sturdy well-shaped timbers. For long it has been presumed that the cave-dwelling Guanches were the lower orders—probably a relict population of palaeolithic savages driven into the islands' interiors by the more sophisticated house-dwellers.

But Europeans who visited the Canaries during and just after their conquest state quite clearly that the cave-dwellers were the rulers, not the ruled. "One part of these dwellings, built on the surface of the plateau above, was for the poor, and the other half, under-ground and worked with considerable skill...was for the nobles and the rich."

Torriani, a military engineer who gave us that description, also explained why the nobles and rich should have lived in such supposedly primitive homes. "The elders, the kings and the nobles lived in these cave-houses to protect themselves in winter with the warmth trapped in the rock pores, and in summer to take their ease in the freshness which finds refuge there from the sun's hot rays." Torriani was right. Cave houses *are* warmer in winter and cooler in summer.

Some of Gran Canaria's caves, like those in Acusa or in Atalaya, or those described by Torriani at Tara, (near Telde), have been lived in since before the conquest. Others have been re-occupied at various times—like those in the Barranco de Guayadeque. During the years immediately after the Civil War many islanders turned to cave squatting when house building, especially of working class housing, was at a standstill.

Many of the caves have become permanent homes, though in remote areas rural depopulation, since the tourist boom began in the 1960s, has seen whole cave villages—like Los Arbejas—abandoned.

Elsewhere, former cave dwellings, some of them important archaeological sites—Cuatro Puertes for example—have been turned into goat pens. Undoubtedly the goats appreciate the

warmth in winter, but the caves no longer retain their "freshness" in summer.

From time to time advertisements appear in the property columns of the two local papers, *Canarias 7* and *La Provincia*, offering for sale a *finca con cuevas* (farmland with caves). The idea of becoming a troglodyte is romantic and the spectacular setting of some of the caves is tempting for those looking for something unusual.

If you are interested, never pay the asking price. The land is invariably of little value, and it may well have been inherited by half a dozen brothers, each one of whom will be hoping to realise its full value. And as there is hardly any local market for this type of property the owners will look for a foreign buyer who can pay cash.

As with any other house in the islands check on the water, sewage, electricity and telephone services. Water is not supplied right round the clock and, if you are at the end of the pipeline, you might not get any for weeks on end. Putting in electricity is costly, and getting a phone installed in a country area (i.e. anywhere except the centre of Las Palmas and the tourist areas of the South) is virtually impossible in under two years.

Buying a cave-house is fraught with legal problems. The vendors rarely have the necessary papers and permissions—often you are buying what is technically a squat even though it may have been in existence for anything from 40 to 500 years. And trying to find a builder (a good one at least) is like banging your head against a cave wall—painful and pointless.

The best caves are not natural but are carved out of the native rock, usually compacted volcanic ash. This is easy to work and if you are so inclined, you can use a chain-saw to cut out seats, cupboards, shelves, tables or even beds—which saves on buying furniture.

A cave home need not be dark. If you need a window, just cut one. Many modern Canarian cave-dwellers have extended forward—where the cliff face allows—combining the features of a normal house and a cave-house. Often an enclosed courtyard is left between cave and brick—the original Spanish *patio*. If you have time, money and determination you could end up with a dream-home in a cave.

lished botanical garden, shady paths meandering among huge trees.

Agaete's other great attraction is the festival of the *Rama*, held during the summer, though never on a fixed date in order to control numbers. The *Rama* (branch) goes back to pre-Spanish days when the native islanders congregated in the mountains above the present town and, armed with green boughs, marched to the coast. There they beat the surface of the sea with the boughs as a culmination of a rain-making ritual. Nowadays the procession ends in the town itself, in a heaving throng of bobbing bodies, dancing and music.

Puerto de las Nieves—where the islanders used to end their ritual—was a small fishing harbour of considerable character. Now it is being developed for tourism—apartment blocks are sprouting up around the port and along the low coast to the north an esplanade is being built. Nevertheless it is still worth a visit for its fish restaurants, craft shops and traditional oared fishing boats. To the south is the **Dedo de Dios**, God's Finger, a tall slender pillar of rock just offshore, much photographed.

The local church, the **Ermita de las Nieves**, contains a recently restored 16th-century Flemish triptych dedicated to the Virgén de las Nieves. Suspended from the carved roof beams are several model sailing vessels and others are to be found in glass cases about the building—a reminder of the village's maritime heritage.

Inland: East of the town the Valle of Agaete climbs steadily up one of the most impressive *barrancos* in the island. The valley floor is a mixture of black lava—in which is an extensive prehistoric burial ground—and rich farmland full of orange trees, avocados, fig trees and almond trees. The road climbs up towards the dizzy heights of **Tamadaba**, 4,737 ft (1,444 metres) above the town, but tiring of the climb finally peters out above Los Berrezales.

Once a small spa, **Los Berrezales** boasts only a hotel, the only country hotel in north-west Gran Canaria, and superb views down the valley.

From Agaete you can follow the hair-raising coast road southwards to San Nicolás and Mogán, or take a winding inland route back to Las Palmas. For the latter turn inland opposite the Reptilandia junction, up to the village of **Hoya de Pineda**, where a handful of women potters still fashion clay by hand in their cave-homes.

The road spirals up to Caideros and swings northwards again to Montaña Alta. The fork here takes you past **Montaña Vergara**, a sacred mountain of the pre-Spanish inhabitants and the original starting point of the *Rama* of Guía before the festival was Christianised in the 18th century. The right fork heads more directly to Moya.

At the end of the **Barranco de Moya** you are on the edge of **Los Tilos**—one of the last redoubts of the laurel forest that once covered vast tracts of northern Gran Canaria.

Further up still, across country, is **Montaña Dorama**, the former centre of the forest which, like the mountain, took its name from Doramas, the last war-lord of the native islanders. Within a generation of the conquest these woods were being torn down to fuel the island's sugar mills, to build houses for the new settlers and to refurbish ships en route to the Americas.

A small and unpretentious market town, **Moya** is remarkable for its church which hangs tenaciously on the edge of a precipitous cliff.

From Moya the road leads on to **Firgas**, where the favourite mineral water on the island comes from and on to **Arucas**, a thriving small town with a cathedral-like church. Once important for sugar, then bananas and always for rum, Arucas began to build its gothic minster out of local stone towards the end of the last century. It took the craftsmen of the town—no one man designed it—a century to complete.

Potent virgin: But whether you get there from Arucas, Firgas, Moya or direct from Las Palmas, **Teror** is an essential call on an inland itinerary. Like all the small towns in the north, it is of pre-Spanish origin and possesses a fine wide street of colonial houses with traditional wooden balconies. At the end of the street is the basilican church dedicated to **Nuestra Señora del Pino**, patron saint of Gran Canaria. A church was in existence here by 1515 and was gradually enlarged until 1718 when it was destroyed by an explosion—caused by mixing gunpowder in the sacristy. The present building, financed by several important families and the *cabildo*, was not finished until the end of the 18th century.

Inside, the statue of Nuestra Señora del Pino dominates the church with a display of Marian *kitsch* more akin to the fantasia of a Las Palmas Carnival Queen than to a Virgin. Nevertheless she is a highly popular figure—every self-respecting taxi (or bus) driver has a faded postcard picture of the Virgen del Pino on the dash-board.

On the steps outside the church supplicants can buy not just postcards but a whole array of religious objects, including wax representations of any and every part of the human body—Nuestra Señora del Pino may not be as famous a

Moya Church, perching the cliff edge.

132

healer as Lourdes but she is just as effective for many Canarios, and much nearer to home.

But like so many others, the festival of Nuestra Señora del Pino is a Christian hijacking of an earlier tradition. Above the town is the ancient volcano and former crater lake of **Pino Santo**—the Holy Pine-tree. This was once a place of worship but with the conquest this changed. Until this century the image of the Virgin was taken down to the cathedral in Las Palmas when drought or plagues of locusts threatened.

On the other side of Teror, off the Teror to Arucas road, is **Osorio**, a Canarian-style country mansion, recently opened by the *cabildo* as an "Aula de la Naturaleza". The old house, a turn-of-the-century mansion, has been restored and is now used for teaching school groups, both day visitors and field-course students. The formal gardens have been replanted and the system of ponds and water-courses re-established. Part of the land associated with the house and garden is laurel for-est which is now being conserved—a series of forest walks are being set up within the grounds.

Green fingers: The conservation plan for Osorio was devised by the staff of the *cabildo's* Jardín Canario, (Canarian Garden), in **Tafira Baja**—follow signs for Tafira out of Las Palmas, up the hill past the Tropical brewery and the Tirma chocolate factory. This stretch of the Carretera del Centro, the Central Road, is known as the Scalextrix—the reason is obvious as cars hurtle round the hairpin bends.

The **Jardín Canario**—on the right going up the hill, after the turn to San Roque—was set up in 1952 and occupies a steep cliff and part of the valley of **Guiniguada** below. In the gardens a wide range of native Canarian plants grow in an almost natural setting, and a series of well-made paths take you down to a small visitors' centre. The restaurant, at the top by the entrance, offers views of the gardens and lava which oozed out of Monte Lentiscal to roll down the Guiniguada.

tocratic
dences
afira.

From the Jardín Canario, take the road to Tamaraceite—a Spanishisation of the Guanche place-name meaning "place of the palms"—but turn left soon into **La Calzada**. Beyond this long, winding village, where the favourite pastime seems to be congregating on blind corners, a bridge crosses the narrow gorge created by the volcano of Monte Lentiscal. It was in the caves on the other side of the gorge that two Spanish monks, emissaries to the native tribesmen, were murdered—the caves are known as **Cuevas de los Frailes**.

From the bridge and along the road through Angostura and Las Meleguinas, the whole panorama of the central mountains opens up. The valley itself, once occupied by a lake dammed up by Monte Lentiscal, is full of small market garden plots producing carnations, fruit and vegetables. By the bridge in **Las Xeleguinas** a goat-herd keeps his flock in prehistoric cave houses in the *barranco* side.

Across the bridge towards Santa Brigida is **Las Grutas de Artiles**, a restaurant-cum-country club with swimming pool and tennis courts. In the car park is an aged *lagar*, or wine-press. Opposite is one of the most impressive country houses in Gran Canaria, set among Babylonian hanging gardens (not open to the public).

Santa Brigida is an unpretentious market town which can also be reached from the Jardín Canario by the main road through **Tafira Alta**—where the really rich live, although from the narrow main street you might not realise it. At the foot of the hill through Tafira is **Los Frailes** hotel built by the British at the turn of the century and used by Franco's cronies as a rendezvous during the warm-up to civil war in 1936. The British connection with Tafira is still evident—the old Wood cinema and Mr Quincey's hotel still stand, though they are no longer used for their original purpose. Tafira and Monte are still the favourite places for resident foreigners to set up home.

Out of Tafira, a peculiarly Spanish roundabout leads off to **Bandama**, a vast volcanic crater and ash cone with views of all Las Palmas. The Peak of Bandama, 1,889 ft (574 metres), overlooks the **Golf Course**, the oldest in Spain. The road past the golf course leads to **Atalaya**, a village famous for its cave houses and its traditional potters—sadly new building on the main road obscures the original village and Panchito, doyen of Canarian craftsmen, died in 1985. Nevertheless the cave houses and craft pottery are still there.

Into Santa Brigida and out again towards San Mateo, is a turn to the right to Pino Santo. By the roadside is the only wild Dragon tree still growing in northern Gran Canaria—clinging grimly to a cliff face within a steep-walled *barranco*. Further up the main road are the **Mano de Hierro** restaurant and **Bar Martel**, for the best Canarian cuisine. Beyond is **San Mateo** with its **Cho'Zacarias** folk museum and excellent restaurant.

And beyond San Mateo—the long rambling climb to Tejeda, Artenara, the pines of Tamadaba and up to the roof of the world.

Left, an English country cottage? Right, a local resident.

134

CENTRAL SUMMITS, SOUTHERN BEACHES

All roads eventually lead to the mountains in Gran Canaria. You can reach **Tejeda**, the highest town at the heart of the island, from the capital in the north, from the east, from the south, and if you have nerves of iron, even from the west. But before starting an island tour at the weekend top up with petrol; most garages are closed on Sundays. Take a warm sweater for the chilly mountain air and a cool T-shirt for the extreme heat of the south and west. Finally, put not your faith in maps (though by all means use one to give you a general idea of where you are going) for even the most up-to-date ones are misleading. Fortunately signposts are clear and plentiful.

Into the heart: The second largest town in the island is **Telde**, 8.5 miles (14 km) from Las Palmas, which can be reached either direct from the main north-south highway, or by turning off this highway sooner, at the sign for Jinámar, a rather dreary dormitory suburb. Past it, the road is lined with magnificent palm trees, a fitting approach to the former court of the legendary Guanche king Doramas.

Telde is a prosperous bustling place with lots of one-way streets and terrible traffic problems so visitors are advised to take the frequent *Salcai* bus service from the capital. The town is divided into two parts, both old and picturesque. In the **San Juan** area the main attraction is the church of **St John the Baptist**, with an incredibly beautiful Flemish altar piece dating back nearly five centuries. The great golden screen dominates the church. It depicts six scenes from the Nativity; and there's also an interesting image of Christ made entirely from corn cobs, which were brought from Mexico at the end of the 15th century.

Just outside the church to the left is a secluded pavement cafe in a tiny *patio*, quite cut off from the bustle of traffic just yards away. In the narrow side streets are homes built by wealthy mer-

chants long ago, with intricate mosaic tiling and small balconies of wrought iron or carved wood. At the further end of the town is the church of **St Gregory**, beside a large plaza shaded by giant trees, with stone benches where old folk sit watching the new world go by.

Six miles (10 km) inland is **Valsequillo**, and though the land is cultivated there is some ugly construction work en route so keep your eyes on the great mountain ranges soaring ahead. Near Telde **Jeradore** is a tiny hamlet down in the valley. Stop at Balcon de Telde for a great view of the coastal plain; the island is dotted with these look-outs or *miradors* and every one of them is a photographer's dream.

Passing Montaña Las Palmas, the climbing road passes quarries signposted "Las Canteras". The famous beach in the capital Las Palmas is similarly named, because the reef that protects it is of a special rock which was extensively quarried last century. Today the reef is so weakened that the whole future of the beach is in danger

unless action is taken to strengthen it.

Just outside Valsequillo there is an artisan shop called **La Perrera** down a driveway lined with whitewashed pots crammed with brilliant geraniums. The owner is a weather-beaten elderly man who says that he, his wife and their off-spring (and judging by the enormous selection of handicrafts, a great army of cousins and grandchildren too) have made everything on show. Six rooms on two floors plus a huge basement contain ceramics, pottery, basketware, rush carpets and so on.

A bar-restaurant is opening on the flat roof with a panoramic view of the coast and mountains. But what the owner is most proud of is his strawberry field in the rich volcanic soil behind the carpark, and he'll be pleased to show you.

Valsequillo is a tranquil little place which was very popular in Guanche days. It has a tree-lined main street and although it has about 6,000 inhabitants you'll probably not see more than six or seven on a week-day. There's a *parador-cum-mirador* (closed at time of press) just outside the town called **El Helechal**, perched like a plate on a little peak on the right.

Cave quarters: From Valsequillo the road runs to **Tenteniguada** through the mountains and real Guanche territory. In the strange ridged volcanic formations are caves on the hills, amid cacti and bamboo. The road passes many more caves, an occasional house and a couple of picturesque restaurant-bars smothered with flowers and greenery. On both sides are lemon and almond trees and surprisingly green grass.

Tenteniguada is very small, built into the hillside and plunging down to a deep canyon. Here the land has been painstakingly terraced to utilise every available inch and giant cypress trees suddenly appear, like nature's sentries to the ancient caves. The road skirts the hills above **San Mateo**, offering splendid views of this lovely town in its fertile valley far below.

Climbing continuously, there is a sharp change in temperature as well as landscape. Here it is much cooler, and

Roadside
stall in th
mountain

the mountains are harsh, craggy grey or russet coloured, with huge cropped eucalyptus trees on their slopes. A crossroads shows left for Teror, right for Tejeda; go right, and pass several tiny hamlets and bar-restaurant El Patio. The evergreens are thicker now, touching overhead, and the occasional houses have vine-covered *patios*. They look small and cosy in contrast to the stark rockfaces behind them.

Some 13.5 miles (22 km) from San Mateo the road forks again; turn left to **Mirador Los Pechos**, the highest viewpoint on the island at 6,496 ft (1,980 metres). The view here is normally absolutely breathtaking, but do check the Tourist Radio in English, German and Scandinavian (750 mw, 8.30 to 9.30 a.m.) for the weather forecast or you might see nothing but pine trees!

Turn around and bear left for **Tejeda**, the mecca of most tourists. The **Parador** (a sort of castle) restaurant offers even more spectacular views along with a fairly pricey menu, although the menu of the day is a better bargain.

From here on, **Roque Nublo** (5,961 ft, 1,817 metres)—a strangely shaped spike of basalt rock—and **Roque Bentaiga** can always be seen. They were sacred mountains to the Guanches and they do have some magic to them— wherever you are, they seem to follow, like Mona Lisa's eyes.

The *Cruz* (Cross) of Tejeda is in the crater of an extinct volcano where almond trees are now grown—which is why marzipan and almond cakes predominate in the stalls around the *parador*. Here there are donkey-rides, souvenir shops and stalls selling lacewear and ethnic tops—from India!

Much more charming is **Artenara**, 7.4 miles (12 km) to the north-west. Bear right and follow the signposts, not the map. It's a wonderful drive through a pine forest with lots of cave houses, many with whitewashed façades and carved pine front doors leading straight into the mountain. Some of the unadorned caves are used by herdsmen to shelter goats.

Artenara is simple, tranquil and beau-

parador
ejeda.

tiful. It's one of the highest villages on the island and for some reason nearly always basking in the sun; perhaps because it's above cloud level. Whitewashed of course, with a small shady plaza beside the church in the centre of the village.

Look carefully for the sign **Meson la Silla**—it's a door in the side of the mountain marked number nine. Through this door—and through the mountain—is a magical mountain ledge where a restaurant and terrace have been carved out of the rocks. The sun shines more brightly here, the ledge is sheltered and the food is local and good (a three-course meal costs around 800 pesetas). The restaurant is open daily till sunset.

The island's back door: From Artenara the road goes through the fairytale pine forest of **Tamadaba**, past a camping ground, some weird and wonderful rocks amid the trees, and no sign of houses. Which is perhaps why it suddenly and infuriatingly ends at a forestry station. Return as far as a sign saying **Acusa**, turn right, and fasten your seat belts for the most magnificent, frightening and fantastic ride.

This is a secondary road (unmarked on some maps) and should be taken with great care, for it is a ledge on the mountain spiralling round hairpin bends through the island's own version of the Grand Canyon.

It's a wild, beautiful and rather intimidating route with little sign of civilisation and no crash barriers, either! There is a mini oasis deep in the canyon: here a sudden row of cave-houses by the road, white-façaded with flamboyant red geraniums on tiny front balconies. The afternoon sun gives the rocks a rosy hue but overall it is a harsh and lonely place, and the *mirador* comes as something of a relief. Other cars, other people, and far below, the Siberio dam and reservoir in the valley.

The road eventually runs down to this dam, with many a bend, and the *mirador* looks like a little saltcellar on the side of the mountain above. Those with a head for heights can walk along the huge dam

wall; but a Bathing Prohibited notice seems unnecessary, so dark and deep is the water.

The road, showing many signs of small but recent rockfalls, plummets down and down, mountains soaring on both sides, and pampas grass growing to head height. It is quite a relief when the terrain flattens out and cheerful little bar, complete with flags, friendly dogs and three waving young men—**El Colega**—suddenly appears, about 18 miles (30 km) from Artenara.

This "back door" approach to **San Nicolas of Tolentino** is really dramatic, and so is the sudden change in vegetation, which becomes lush and tropical, with orange and banana plantations, giant cacti and bamboo. It's also pleasantly warm. The road peters out into a dried river bed, a rubbish dump, and an unexpected sign saying "City Centre". You have arrived.

The unknown west: San Nicolas is the centre of the little visited western coast of the island, a land of windmills and women wearing straw hats and trousers under their skirts; the town is pleasant but not particularly interesting. There are *pensions* for the weary, and indifferent restaurants—one, **Las Cuevas**, is ready to catch the traveller with an unpriced menu and a startlingly large bill.

But beyond the town lies magic again, the headland of San Nicolas, known as **La Aldea** ("the village"). This place has been a rich source of ancient remains for archaeologists, and it is here that the fossilised bones of the Verdino dog dating back 2,120 years were found. To reach the sea, follow a wide lush valley, with palm trees and small white houses almost Moorish in appearance.

At the port, a new beautifully paved promenade overlooks the steep rocky beach. Behind it lies a small forest filled with giant slabs of rocks to be used as tables, with smaller rock stools surrounding them. Hundreds can and do gather here, especially in September, fiesta-time. At the end of the promenade is the *charco* or lagoon, which is small and slightly green. The pine-needled walk through the trees is delightful.

Roughly four miles (six km) on the road north of the port is the **Mirador del Balcon**, perched on the edge of a rugged cliff soaring 1,640 ft (500 metres) up from the sea. From here the whole north-western part of Gran Canaria can be clearly seen—Agaete and the point of Sardina del Norte; crane your neck for an almost close-up view of the houses in Guia. Out to sea lies Tenerife, sometimes partially hidden by a sea mist, but with the snowcapped mountain of Teide almost always visible.

South of San Nicolas on the road to Mogán is a layby three miles (five km) from the town which gives a magnificent view of the valley, the port and Tenerife. The road is well-surfaced, with guard rails and sign-posted hairpin bends, and there are lots of caves to the right. From here keen walkers can climb the mountain and reach the natural reserve and beach of **Güigüi**; the only other way is by boat.

The mountains soar above the road like cathedrals, and there is an amazing stretch where the rock face is as multi-coloured as an artist's palate, with a brilliant Wedgewood green strata predominating. This vivid green contrasts with rich russet red, sandy shades and even coral pink. The rockface is scored by frequent sharp gullies which become torrents when it rains. The rock formations are wild and weird.

After about 12 miles (20 km) an acute right turn (signposted) leads to **Veneguera**, a tiny Moorish-type village baking in the valley, hot and fertile with a poinsettia-filled roundabout—no Christmas plants these, but giants—and on the left there is a natural botanical garden at the bottom of the valley, filled with tropical plants and giant cacti. Although marked on the map, the road to the beach peters out after two miles (three km).

Mogán is a neat, pretty, and orderly town, though rather tame after the adventures of the mountains. Tourist-orientated, its restaurants are pricey; if approaching Mogán from the coast, take the left-hand fork just before the town to visit one of the island's best

In Mogán port.

restaurants, the **Acayma**, and a very large artisan workshop.

Mogán Port is perhaps the only tourist development that has really enhanced the charms of the South. An international yachting marina and rows of prim, pretty little houses complete with geranium window-boxes harmonise with the old town climbing up the hillside. This is an absolutely delightful resort, and the rocky beach has been covered by many layers of imported sand from Africa to make a wonderful swimming zone.

Land of concrete: The main coastal road from Mogán to Las Palmas runs southwards along the coast and is at times carved out of the cliff. This was once a fantastic drive but today, the developers have done their best to ruin it. Around a hairpin bend is the first development, **Taurito Tropical**, which is quite impressive and well-designed, though it lacks Mogán's charm. Giant arches of blue and white guard the entrance to the complex, or complexes rather; altogether 6,000 new tourist beds are planned.

The road passes several untouched tiny coves with ominous signs of urbanisation but no buildings as yet. Beyond, in a large bay renamed "Treasure of the Atlantic" a very large development is taking shape. Then the road runs round a headland, with craggy grey mountains to the left and a sheer fall to the sea on the right, and in front, a quite incredible sight: **Costa Paraiso**, where every rockface, every inch, seems to have been covered with tiny chalets, like crabs on the rock.

One or two blocks have a pleasant solid look about them, but many of the apartments and chalets creeping up the mountainside—they are white with yellow trim—look as flimsy as dolls' houses. The whole effect is that of a giant banana and vanilla ice-cream slick spilling down the mountains. Many homes don't have a sea view, and the beach itself can only accommodate maybe 10 percent of holiday makers in this area.

Lanzarote architect and artist César

st resorts
e deep
fishing
s.

Manrique mourned in *Der Spiegel* in December 1987, "My islands are being...killed", and referred to bunker-type dwellings "that even Hitler would not allow" now being put up everywhere. The German newspaper *Badische Zeitung*, in April 1987, commented, "The 'Fortunate Islands' are being covered with concrete". Here the evidence is clear.

Only in **Patalavaca** and **Arguineguin**—an enchanting fishing village with a horseshoe-shaped harbour—can any definite advantages be seen. Today the two are linked by a path on the rocks, a great improvement to the hazardous walk along the cliff road; and a new complex with an excellent restaurant has enhanced Arguineguin, which incidentally was the port where the conquistadores landed in their first fruitless attempts to colonise the island. A large and ugly cement factory rather spoils the overall view here, but where you have so much concrete, cement must also be needed.

Once the privileged resort and yachting marina of the south, **Puerto Rico** has been grotesquely overbuilt. On either side of the town new developments crawl up the mountains, impossibly far from the beach.

Only **Las Melenares** remains unspoilt—a charming little beach outside Maspalomas, near a nicely-designed caravan park (bring your own or rent one for 3,000 pesetas). In a guide book of 1963 the author writes of **Maspalomas** how "a new town of Lords will take away some of the wildness from this comparatively remote spot". It most certainly has. Maspalomas itself is now an unsightly sprawl of chalets as far as the eye can see, but no developer can spoil the magnificent sand dunes that run from here to **Playa del Inglés**.

The latter, not so long ago a raw-looking mass of hotels and apartments, is now positively olde-worlde! It has several commercial centres crammed with restaurants, bars and boutiques on three levels, an interesting Ecumenical Church, and some lovely trees and gar-

The dunes at Maspalom

dens round the various blocks. In all there are about 350 restaurants and 50 discos in this resort alone.

San Agustín is a pleasant beach resort with good swimming and a little further up the coast there's an attractive complex called **Bahia Feliz** (Happy Bay) which is quite charming; it has a hotel apartment blocks, shops and gardens, and a fine pool.

Back to the mountains: Inland from Maspalomas lies **El Tablero**, worth visiting if only because it is a typical Canarian village within easy reach of the coast, with relatively cheap *pensions* and restaurants.

Beyond is the **Los Palmitos Park**, a botanical and bird sanctuary, a German riding school and a go-kart track.

Inland, unmarked on any maps but signposted, is a most interesting place called **Monte Léon**. Not a village, but a collection of millionaires' villas, each with its high wall and huge gardens, it is the haunt of the extremely rich and powerful from all over the world—and very little is ever written about it. You can see one villa built on its own circular mountain top. Monte Léon has a musical tradition and even has its own private concert hall.

From the mundane world of **San Fernando**, dormitory suburb of Playa del Inglés, the road runs up to a lovely mountain village, **Fataga** (nine miles, 15 km). A *mirador* halfway up gives wonderful views of the mountains and the coast. The village is subtropical and very fertile, with many palms and fruit trees. Beyond it the road snakes round the mountains to **San Bartolome de Tirajana**, a further five miles (eight km), which is the administrative centre for most of the south.

San Bartolome is an exquisite mountain town with a brisk Sunday morning market outside the church. Here you can buy local liquors and fruit and be cheerfully overcharged for them by a man who proudly says he has seven children to feed. The Town Hall, the heart of the town, has a delightful gallery running round the first floor, and a *patio* in the centre, bursting with greenery. On a

mountain top within the town lies the cemetery, of great architectural interest—it's centuries old—with tombs on the ground; the usual Spanish custom is to bury their dead in cemetery walls. There are niches lovingly decorated with fresh flowers in little silver holders, flowering plants on the graves, and weather-beaten wooden crosses without inscriptions.

To the east of San Bartolome is **Santa Lucia** and the road connecting the two is shady and winding, with views of fertile valleys and dams far below, providing a great contrast to the harsh craggy red mountainside on the other side. Santa Lucia is a spread-out village of great beauty, with a church up on the hillside and clusters of whitewashed houses and flower-filled *patios*. Several artisan shops are worth visiting.

Las Fortaleza is actually a restaurant-cum-museum housed in a miniature castle (newly built), with several rooms devoted to archaeological exhibits. Here are pottery and leather garments, stone household implements

and other relics of Guanche days, as well as skeletons.

The restaurant **Jao** (part of the museum) is reached from the side turning on the right, and is huge. It serves typical Canarian food, including a *gofio* dish, on massive planked tables with wooden benches, and is very popular with local people as well as tourists, always a sign of good value; the restaurant is open-sided away from the kitchen, there's also a small garden and playground area for children.

The road to **Agüimes** (nine miles, 15 km) is chiselled through solid red rock and is very picturesque, curving from one valley to another. The striking mountain peak of **Teñeral** (2,992 ft, 912 metres) rises from the coastal plain to the north, and there are many caves on this stretch of road, formerly inhabited by Guanches. Agüimes itself is very old and attractive, despite the raw look of the buildings on its outskirts. The great towers of **San Sebastians'** church dominate the old sector, which is reached by tiny streets unsuitable for traffic. There's a museum here of interest to geologists and near Agüimes, in the **Barranco de Balos**, basalt rocks with mysterious inscriptions that have yet to be deciphered.

To the north **Ingenio** (with the Barranco Guayadeque nearby) can be translated several ways—"skill, talent, creative faculty" or even "sugar mill" which it once was. The first feature of the town is a modern distillery, and in olden days rum was distilled from molasses here. But the industry has declined and today it's principally an agricultural area, with tomatoes as the main crop.

The town has a very long main street, and just on the outskirts as one heads back to Las Palmas is the large **Museum of Rocks**, which has a display of ancient farm tools in the garden and a big collection of various rocks and stones as well as a large artisan workshop with particularly good pottery. Look out, too, for the openwork tablecloths, lace and shawls, evidence, perhaps, of that very same "creative faculty" that is implied by the town's name.

THE BARRANCO DE GUAYADEQUE

As you hammer down the *autopista* with a BMW up your exhaust-pipe and a clapped-out Seat 800 belching fumes in front, it stretches the imagination too much to think that there might be anything worth seeing on the east side of Gran Canaria. Yet just beyond the parched, abandoned tomato fields, where nothing now grows except billboards advertising mineral water and German beer, is the Barranco de Guayadeque.

The Guayadeque (a Guanche neame meaning "a place of running water," lies like a roughly axed trough hacked through the middle of the island. Just out of the town of Ingenio the road forks left and winds down the cliff to the bed of the ravine below.

In the hillside opposite is a small group of pre-historic cave dwellings, Las Haciendillas—long since looted—overlooking a series of cultivated terraces set with palm trees. By the roadside there is a pump-house which takes the water of Guayadeque to the towns of Ingenio and Agüimes.

Further up the ravine water flows in an open channel, but in the lower section it is enclosed in a concrete aqueduct. Reeds grow up to head height around leaking joints in the pipe—at one time in the past the watercourse within the gorge must have been lined by thick reed beds.

Opposite the cave-group of Las Haciendillas is another group of pre-historic caves known as Cuevas de la Guerra, though no-one knows which war it was that gave them their name. As this was the first native settlement the Spanish conquistadores would find as they explored the ancient principality of Agüimes, it is likely that the name does recall some ill-remembered battle.

A mile or so up the metalled road is a small side-valley almost completely blocked by a bank of scree. To the left, invisible from the road and a dangerous climb, is a group of ancient burial caves which were ransacked by some of the best-known antiquaries in the history of Canarian archaeology. To the right is a chaotic cliff-face of boulders and scree.

Among the scree a narrow path winds up the side-valley, losing its way occasionally among boulders and crumbling terraces. At the top lies a plateau of rough pasture and breath-taking—if you've any breath left—views of the gorge. Opposite is the pre-historic cave village of Risco de Vicentico, and below is a stream running through stands of cane. A tiny farmstead nestles in the mouth of Guayadeque's only major tributary, Barranco de la Sierra.

For the less adventurous, there is a good path which starts among the canes and leads up past an abandoned cave-byre and a gnarled palm to the triangular top of the bluff above the farmstead. On the bluff among the primordial *Aeonium* (primitive vegetation) is a small group of hut circles which almost certainly date from before the Spanish conquest.

Looking back across the gorge, you can see a vast arc of rock high on the cliff. Here, in the last century, mountaineering locals looted Guanche mummies to provide the core collections of the Museo Canario in Las Palmas. Even now, with the aid of field glasses, you can pick out the piles of bleached long bones they left behind.

Both the valley road and the upland plateau eventually lead to the cave village of Cueva Bermeja—a good path winds down the cliff to the village near a group of stone-built corrals.

The cave houses of Cueva Bermeja, the Scarlet Cave, are cut into a cliff of deep-red rock. Some of the caves were hacked out in pre-conquest times, but the rock-cut chapel and bars are modern—if the chapel is locked, ask for the key in the bar next door.

Excursions to the Guayadeque can be booked in most travel agents in Gran Canaria and part of the trip—from near the town of Agüimes to Cueva Bermeja—is a *burro* safari on mule back. The safari route usually follows a track in the bed of the gorge and affords a better view of the towering *barranco* walls, as well as the spindly *balos* bushes and chubby fingers of *Euphorbia* which grow in the lower part of the Guayadeque.

Beyond Cueva Bermeja is perhaps the most impressive archaeological site in Guayadeque—Cuevas Muchas, a vertical chain of artificial caves cut into a cliff of dark red rock. The upper caves, once used as grain stores by the native

152

islanders, are only accessible to good climbers and the lower ones are still used by the farmer who lives in a cave house at the bottom.

Unlike the three cave complexes between Barranco de la Sierra and Cueva Bermeja which contain dwellings, store-caves and burial caves, Cuevas Muchas was only used for storage, principally of food. A large room right at the top may have been used by the guardian of the granary—or perhaps for fertility rites, for here the peasants of Guayadeque used to perform an erotic dance, the *pámpano roto*.

The *pámpano roto* was still danced, secretly for fear of persecution by the Church (it was not the sort of display that the Inquisition approved of) until the early years of this century. The dance climaxed—literally and metaphorically—in the woman's protective skirt of yam-leaves being penetrated by a vine shoot *(pámpano)* carried by her male partner.

From Cuevas Muchas up to the two bars at Montaña de las Tierras, where the metalled road ends, the Guayadeque gropes its way between cliffs up to 1,000 ft (304 metres) high. In summer the sun beats blindingly on the rock walls of the canyon, but in winter the tops of the cliffs are wrapped in a blanket of grey cloud and the air is distinctly chilly.

The tiny terraced fields near the bottom of the ravine are much greener here, and almond trees and date palms soften the lower slopes. In spring the Guayadeque is a mass of almond blossom.

Montaña de las Tierras, perhaps the plug of an ancient volcano, dominates the central Guayadeque. From either of the two cave-bars you can watch the lower course of the ravine stumbling down to the coast. Behind is a dark orange cliff of compacted volcanic ash, and below knife-sharp ridges of solid lava cut their way uphill.

The cave-bars themselves are hacked out of the rock, and disorientating for those with an easily-confused sense of direction. This is a favourite spot for Canarios to take their Sunday lunch—the *vino tinto* is local, strong and served in tumblers; and the olives, steeped in green *mojo* sauce, come from Temisas, reputedly the best in Gran Canaria.

Beyond the cave-bars the road, now just a dirt-track, winds upwards through terraced fields bordered by almond and olive trees. The *barranco* walls are less precipitous—though no less impressive. Here, on the upper slopes, isolated Canary pines grow, left over from the substantial former forest that covered the centre of the island. Sometimes the clouds come down so low that this view is lost in mist, but even that can be a pleasant change from the unremitting heat of the crowded tourist beaches.

The track eventually turns up the north side of the *barranco* to meet the Cazadores road—a difficult stretch except for a four-wheel drive vehicle. But a footpath continues, more or less following the valley bottom, towards the Caldera de los Marteles, a volcanic crater. In the not so distant past the crater contained a lake which has since dried out leaving a flat, rich plain at the bottom of this natural basin.

The route from Montaña de las Tierras to the Caldera takes a full day on foot. Be sure to take plenty of water, particularly in the height of summer, when dehydration comes quickly.

The Guayadeque can be seen from other vantage points. Instead of taking the left fork into the *barranco* at Ingenio, take the right, signposted La Pasadilla. The road winds upwards to a sharp bend which overlooks Barranco de la Sierra and the Guayadeque beyond.

Behind, cut into the pink volcanic ash, are several artificial caves, now, like so many Canarian archaeological sites, used as a rubbish dump.

The road follows the edge of the northern branch of Barranco de la Sierra passing the village of La Pasadilla, where, every autumn, the *Baja del Macho* is held. The name—the "Descent of the Billy-goat"—parodies the various Bajadas (descents) de la Virgen celebrated throughout the islands. The herders of the Ingenio district choose the lustiest billy-goat in their flocks, deck him out with flowers and then escort him to the town square of Ingenio amid much merry-making.

Beyond La Pasadilla is El Roque with its cave-houses and striped Canarian pigs. Here the metalled road ends beside an ugly bomb-proof villa, although walkers can hike southwards across country to the cliff edge and look down on Cueva Bermeja. The view is startling—but there is no way down.

FUERTEVENTURA:
THE NORTH

The human "Giants of Fuerteventura" are now as legendary as its *verdinos*, or barkless dogs. Even the dromedary, obligatory transport on the long, inverted bottle-shaped island, is almost as scarce as its water. Ancients knew the isle as "Herbania"—a reference to its vegetation which has been reduced to that of a bald broom by rapacious goats, and its present name is thought to have been coined in a report to the French Crown by the adventurer and navigator, Gadifer de la Salle.

The Canary Islands' second largest land mass, this 63-mile (100-km) sliver so reminiscent of northwest African terrain, is certainly one of the less fortunate of what Herodotus described in the fifth century as the "Gardens of Hesperides".

Wizened mountain ranges and symmetrical volcanic cones ribbed by dried up *barrancos* are interspersed by large regions of *malpais*—cindered "badlands". These, and coastal features softened by Saharan sand dunes, give this island an inhospitable and moon-like prospect. Dust storms swirl across it and, although the greater part of the coastline sports beaches more typical to the Caribbean, cliffs of lava pose daunting barriers to their access.

The island is conveniently divided into six municipal regions from La Oliva in the far north, to Pájara in the southern peninsula. The central and northern part of the island is probably less exploited for its natural attributes than the extensive beach areas of the south. Almost central to the east coast is Puerto del Rosario, the capital of Fuerteventura, being its major port and possessing the island's only airport.

Village made good: Hardly a hamlet when it became the capital town in 1860, Puerto de Cabras (the Port of Goats) was founded as recently as 1797. Despite its name, the port was used to export locally produced soda and cereal products and became a separate municipality in 1835. Its name was changed to

Puerto del Rosario (Port of the Rosary) for aesthetic reasons in 1957.

It is at Fuerteventura's International Airport that most visitors' discovery of the island begins. The airport lies just four miles (six km) south of Rosario and, en route for the capital, the road passes the **Tourist Parador** (National-sponsored hotel). This is a split level, elegantly furnished inn, built on a point overlooking a crescent of white sand, **Playa Blanca**.

A number of gorges precede the outskirts of the neat, white-painted port, which is inhabited by around 7,500 townspeople. Beyond Puerto del Rosario's tree-shaded church square and tidy, cobbled older district, the imposing barracks and white walls of the military zone of the Spanish Foreign Legion accounts for an extra 3,000 people. It is said that one mayor of the town, who dictated that no structure in Puerto del Rosario should be high-rise, himself built the capital's only skyscraper, dominating the harbour.

Puerto del Rosario is the commercial

Fuerteventura

15 km

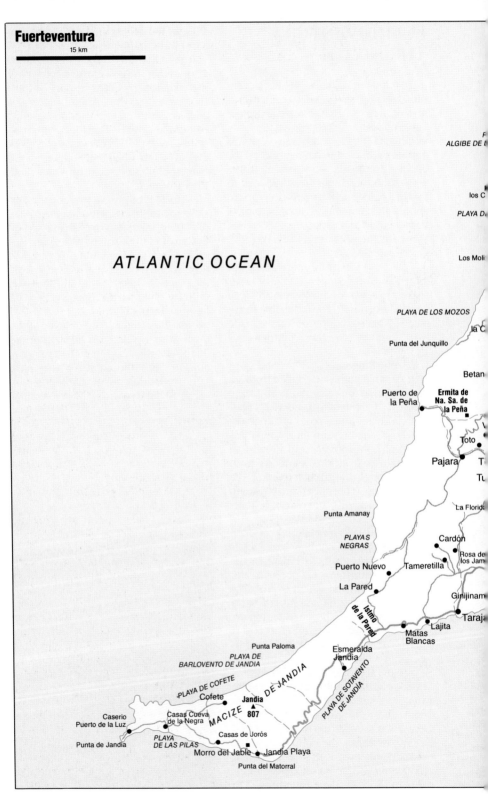

ATLANTIC OCEAN

F
ALGIBE DE E

los C

PLAYA D

Los Moli

PLAYA DE LOS MOZOS

la C

Punta del Junquillo

Betan

Puerto de
la Peña

**Ermita de
Na. Sa. de
la Peña**

Toto

Pajara   T

Tu

Punta Amanay

La Florid

PLAYAS
NEGRAS

Cardón

Rosa de
los Jam

Puerto Nuevo   Tameretilla

La Pared

Ginijinam

Istmo
de la Pared

Taraj

Lajita

Matas
Blancas

Punta Paloma

Esmeralda
Jandia

PLAYA DE
BARLOVENTO DE JANDIA

DE JANDIA

PLAYA DE COFETE

PLAYA DE SOTAVENTO
DE JANDIA

Cofete   **Jandia**

MACIZE   **807**

Caserio
Puerto de la Luz

Casas Cueva
de la Negra

PLAYA
DE LAS PILAS

Casas de Jorós

Punta de Jandia

Morro del Jable   Jandia Playa

Punta del Matorral

ATLANTIC OCEAN

and administrative centre of Fuerteventura and the seat of the island's government. Inter-island ferries use the tiny port which supports a lively fishing industry. The capital's long jetty arm was built in 1837.

Two roads lead out of Puerto del Rosario towards the north. From the dockside boulevard the shorter, comparatively uninteresting coastal route of about 16 miles (29 km) leads to **Corralejo**. Lava fields, rock-strewn *malpais* and craggy cliffs overhang peacock-blue waters, which are popular diving locations. Abandoned stone dwellings dot the arid hillsides.

Suddenly, further north, small volcanic mountains and dark lava give way to swirling sand dunes so similar to those of Saharan Morocco just 60 miles (95 km) to the east. Towards Corralejo the dunes become hills, fortifying sea strands of coral white beaches which themselves support new resorts.

The other northern route is more rewarding. Although a couple of *guaguas*, or local buses leave for La Oliva every day, it is really essential to have independent transport as the public service is infrequent and erratic. Signposting is scarce but the first real landmark is an abandoned airfield, Los Estancos, crossing the broad tarmac'd road, and almost impossible to trace on the rocky desert terrain.

Beyond the airport, the fang-like mountain to the right is the **Devil's Claw**. A narrow lane leads around the peak to the old hermitage of Las Mercedes at **El Time** village. Some distance beyond the hamlets of Tetir and La Matilla the flank of **Montaña Quemada** (Burnt Mountain) is broken by a white monument commemorating the exiled Spanish writer, Miguel de Unamuno (1864-1936). He it was who enthused on the island with the words, "A rock thirsting in the sun, Fuerteventura, a treasure of health and honesty..." Even in the desolation of the brown-green landscape the winding black road gives the suddenly isolated motorist a secure feeling of civilisation in the near-moonscape. At the junction an archaeological site reveals Neolithic occupation and it is at this point that the vista of **La Oliva** plain opens up. Like cast dice on a khaki cloth, the tiny town itself, with its whitewashed houses, windmills and little church, invites the traveller to explore.

Past grandeur: In the main thoroughfare of La Oliva the **Casa de los Coroneles**, the 18th-century Colonels' House, is one of the island's most celebrated antiquities. The sweeping approach, grandiose façade, red tiled roof and ornate balconies seem incongruously placed in the volcanic wilderness. Count the doors and windows of the main building, now restored, and your total should number the days in a year. From 1708 the military colonels governed Fuerteventura after the Lords of the Island had departed for Tenerife.

Two aristocratic families, the Sánchez Dumpiérrez and Cabreras, ran La Oliva through to 1808. Today the carved, stone coat of arms above the magnificent door looks out over agave fields and fronts an oasis-like, palm-surrounded farm. The cone of Montaña de Escantraga (1,735 ft, 529 metres) dominates the countryside. Set alongside the imposing manor are the ruined buildings of a smallholding and the **Casa del Capellan** (Chaplain's House) with its strange door decorated with a triangular design of Aztec origin.

La Oliva's church, **Iglesia de Nuestra Señora de Candelaria**, looks more like a fort than a place of worship, with buttressed walls and a stone bell-tower built in the 18th century. Many carvings of saints and paintings by Juan de Miranda adorn its three naves but the focal point is the image of the Virgin. On 2 February, La Oliva's fiesta is celebrated for four days, during which the holy relic is paraded through the small town. Much of past La Oliva has crumbled into ruins.

A straggle of houses clustered around the road junction with the route to **El Cotillo** on the west coast, a few bars, a working men's club and a small restaurant comprise the former ancient capital of "Maxorata"—the seat of Guanche King Guixe 500 years ago.

Sand dun
at Corral

On the side road to El Cotillo, the hamlet of **Lajares** boasts a peculiar form of windmill, a school of local embroidery and a tourist shop. Needlework is an important home industry on Fuerteventura and the examples produced at Lajares are excellent. From here the road links with that which goes to Corralejo.

Approaching El Cotillo itself the two dominant features are the sea and the round defence tower. Constructed in 1740 by Claude de Lisle, the Torre is the double of that in the tourist resort of Caleta Fuste, near the airport. These forts were built to repel English, Moorish and Arab pirates—not to mention Lord Nelson who passed the island in 1797. **La Torre de Rico Roque** now overlooks little fishing boats bobbing in the small harbour of **Puerto del Tostón**. Cliffs and sandy beaches stretch both north and south along this coastline.

Returning to the main La Oliva to Corralejo road, there is a worthwhile small detour on foot to be made across the *malpais*, or badlands, to the peak of Bayuyo. The 882 ft (269 metres) peak provides an excellent viewpoint for a vista across dunes and volcanic cinders to the sea, to the island of **Lobos**, to distant Lanzarote and of course to the white-buildinged town of Corralejo.

Fish and fine weather: Famed throughout the Canary Islands for its fabulous beaches and prolific fishing grounds, **Corralejo** is the northernmost town on Fuerteventura. Although its peaceful tranquility has been disrupted by the tourism invasion, and a shopping mall reminiscent of European suburbia has been erected in its heart, the quayside and the older parts of the town still retain their naive quality.

A one-way traffic system includes tiny back streets and circles a pedestrian precinct with tourist shops and French-type bars and street cafés. The main thoroughfare is a broad boulevard running parallel to the harbourside, its main building, the **Corralejo Beach Hotel** rubbing shoulders with little, beachside restaurants and private seaside villas.

Nearer the jetty, where a ferry plies three times a day to Playa Blanca, Lanzarote, a 40-minute sail away, is a quayside bar frequented by the fishermen whose tiny barques add colour to the minute beach alongside.

Fishing has been the mainstay of this fast expanding port for eons, although this is rapidly being superceded by the more novel industry of tourism. Fisherwives sit in doorways wrapped in voluminous black dresses while, on the dune-fringed miles of white beaches, nude and semi-nude bathers surf, sail, stroll or just bronze under the near-African sun.

To reach these beaches and the larger shoreside hotels, take the turning off the Corralejo to La Oliva road, south, at the Canary Island Bank on the outskirts of town. This road also leads back to Puerto del Rosario.

Everywhere around this port there is evidence of development and new apartments, hotel complexes and villas being built—a phenomenon common to most of Fuerteventura's coastline.

Hired camels or dromedaries add a touch of extra surrealism to the land-

scape of endless sand. One hotel has defied the natural order of parched wastes by constructing an immense, freshwater pool alongside the sea shore. Deepwater fishing and diving are big attractions in this northern resort and a half-hour boat trip can take the sportsfisherman or skin diver out, past the ever-present silhouette of Lobos Island, to some of the best fishing grounds in the Atlantic.

Two miles across the narrow strait named El Rio (the river), is the National Park island of **Isla de Los Lobos**. Once called Vegi Marina, Lobos is now named after the seals, or sea-wolves, which were prolific on its sandy shores at one time. On the island the tiny hamlet of **El Puertito** plays host to numerous vacationing visitors from both Lanzarote and Fuerteventura. Historians relate how, in 1402, the French adventurer, La Salle, survived being marooned on the island by devouring seal meat.

Today Lobos has become a picnic isle, idyllic and peaceful, still existing in a sort of cocoon-state. Modern-day brushes, apart from the ever-present outlines of booming Lanzarote and the expanding skyline of Corralejo, are those with boatloads of day trippers and the regular passing of *Yaiza*, the Alisur inter-island car ferry.

The central route: From the modern capital of Puerto del Rosario the central tour of the island not only reveals the variety of landscapes on Fuerteventura, but follows a route through its most historic places. The best itinerary is to take the airport road, turning sharply away from the coastline just before the airport's gates, after passing the *Parador*. Soon the road returns to follow the shore whilst, behind low hills to the right, is the Sahara Armed Forces' encampment of the Spanish Foreign Legion. A little further on down the same road, the octagonal building on a hill heralds the entrance to the extensive **Castillo Beach** bungalow, chalet and apartment development.

Constructed around a lovely gold sand beach and incorporating the round

A calm da at Castill de Fuste.

164

stone-built **Castillo de Fustes**, Castillo complex is served by a small yacht basin. It is entered by long avenues of palm and bougainvillea, prickly pear and agave, and is one of the island's more tastefully designed resorts. The tower dates from the days of English pirate attack, around 1740, and, although locked and drawbridged, contains a spiral of small rooms, surmounted by battlements and little else. It is the twin of the fort at Cotillo.

Incongruously, the ancient watchtower is now surrounded by several bright blue swimming pools and a kiddies' playground, peopled daily by mixed vacationers including some from the old enemy, England.

Back on the coastal road, just after **Casa de las Salinas**, the salt house, the road turns inland and passes, on the left, an important ancient site, including ruins of Guanche origin. Five miles (eight km) further on, the road is joined by that from the beach resort of Pozo Negro. A similar distance past the Hermitage of San Francisco on the right, is the main highway which runs the length of the island. This spot, a centre of agriculture as the mills testify, is approximately the middle point of the island of Fuerteventura.

Turn to the right here, and, a few metres away is the pleasantly peaceful township of **Antigua**. This is the administrative town for Antigua Municipality, set up in 1812.

Between 1834 and 1835 Antigua was the island's capital; nearby Betancuria took over this mantle from 1836. Originally, Antigua was thought to have been founded by French and Spanish settlers and parish records date back before the 1760s. Its low, whitewashed houses betray the distinct Moorish-African traditions of some of the town's earliest inhabitants. Other architectural styles, like that used in the building of the **Town Hall** and the design of the attractive little church, reflect mainland Spanish influence.

The lovely, peaceful town square to one side of Antigua's church is shaded by mature trees and its flower beds are constantly watered to combat the heat on this parched plain. The little bar on the square is the menfolk's meeting place at most hours of the day.

At the far north end of the town, on a low hill, the round restaurant **El Molino** is actually built in the reconstructed granary store of the beautifully restored mill in the same grounds. The stark, white, 200-year-old mill is typical of most of Fuerteventura's mills, many of which are currently under a programme of preservation.

This at Antigua, together with its handsomely repaired wooden ceilinged granary is perhaps the best preserved example on the island. It is paradoxically the town's most recent, yet one of its oldest, attractions.

Several windmills break the skyline of the direct route to Betancuria as it winds around La Florida hamlet and into **Betancuria** itself. Surrounded by high mountain slopes and bisected by numerous gullies, Betancuria's monuments are among the most unusual in the entire Canary Islands. The town is indeed an oasis, not only of historic

cal
mill on
teven-

treasures, but of lush vegetation, due to its accessible water table.

Pirate sanctuary: In the early years of the 15th century, the Norman conqueror, Juan de Béthencourt, after whom Betancuria is named, constructed a fort, the legendary Richeroque, on Fuerteventura's west coast. In this tower, long since reduced to ruins, the adventurer and his relations sought refuge from frequent pirate attacks. Exasperated by coastal harrassment, de Béthencourt moved to a more remote location which also offered adequate fresh water, thus establishing the town of Betancuria.

Today, the National Monument is home to many interesting relics such as those dating back to Guanche times, items contemporary with de Béthencourt's Lordship over the region, and more modern artefacts all housed in the **Museo Arqueologico**. The town's cathedral, **Iglesia Santa Maria de Betancuria**, destroyed by fire in 1539, is a gem in itself and contains many ancient treasures. A Norman image of St Catherine in the cathedral is said to be the oldest relic in the Canary Isles and its statue of the Virgen de la Peña is the centre of the town's annual fiesta on 14 June, as well as being the patron saint of Fuerteventura.

Other interesting sights are the ruins of the Franciscan Convent and the Hermitage of **San Diego de Alcala**, constructed over the Spanish monk's cave. This is a short walk from the town and its well, nearby, which has long been a place of pilgrimage, is wreathed in tales of miracles.

Surrounding Betancuria are several points of interest: the **Cruz de la Vieja**; **Castillo de Lava** and the stunning **Valley of Palms** at Vega de Rio de Palmas near the Hermitage of the **Virgen de la Peña** (Virgin of Sorrow).

South towards the town of **Pájara**, the brilliant greenery of the canyon of Rio Palma is a blaze of colour against the browns of the Barranco of Betancuria. The "Tiny Hen" (Pájara) is as pretty as the local species of canary, which are hung in little wooden cages from window frames. Locals gather in the shade of the square around the town's 1687 parish church, **Virgen de la Regla**. Blending into its leafy surroundings the church was initially built in 1645. Thought to be part of the earlier structure the huge entrance with its Aztec-influenced carved stone doorway is famous for its unusual design.

Two small bars on the main street offer a chance of refreshment in Pájara as, similarly, does the bar opposite the church in the next town, **Tuineje**, six miles (10 km) further on. Tuineje lies on the crossroads of five routes. The road north, back to Antigua, passes tomato enclaves, each fenced in with tall bamboo stakes in order to keep out the voracious goats.

The land surrounding **Agua de Bueyes**, "Oxen's Water", is intensely farmed in the traditional terraced way, with every small plot sucking its moisture from the air each morning by means of its black, cinder topsoil. The tiny village is little more than a group of North African low, white buildings leading onto the Valley of Ortega.

Left, ruine convent a Betancuria Right, Betancuria and surroundi

166

DESERT LIFE

"An oasis in the middle of civilisation's desert", wrote Miguel de Unamuno, exiled on Fuerteventura during 1924. Undoubtedly the Spanish poet was impressed by the isolation of the island and its people from the busy world outside.

Despite a harsh climate, persistent invasions and barren aspect, this desolate outcrop of volcanic rock and sand has its endearing qualities and its special surprises. Like Sir Richard Burton's obsession with Saudi Arabia's "Empty Quarter", or Wilfred Thesiger's enthusiasm for deserts, Fuerteventura's wastes conceal secrets inviting discovery by the discerning traveller who has a taste for something unusual.

Some say the island's magic lies in its chameleon-like quality of subtly changing colour. Mountains blush from pink to vivid vermilion under stunning sunsets and the flatness of its plains widen an egg-blue sky to broader horizons of immense proportions. Purple hills and violet volcanoes drift like water-coloured backcloths behind long slivers of silver beach.

Surf-white wave crests are the only actions which disturb the shot-silk emerald and indigo of coastal waters and sea breezes change the khaki drab of withered, scree-side grasses to autumn gold or corn-yellow. It is under this painter's palette of surface colour that one finds the real call of this inhospitable isle.

Dig under the shallow soil of the island and dry rock will be your only reward. Scratch the surface for curiosities and peculiarities and a surprising wealth of unusual delights come to light.

Nature has been frugal in dispensing gifts here. The weird dragon tree *(Dracaena draco)*, is a primitive, wizened trunk with contorted branches topped by shocks of spiky leaves. This throwback to fossil times was once the source of wood for native shields and produces a sap which turns blood-red in the air. Greatly sought after for its resinous juice in ancient times, the tree is said to live for many thousands of years, a true curiosity and quite rare on the island.

Agave, or century plants, are grown for rope-

making sisal. Said to flower once every 100 years, the agave is better known probably than the prickly pear or tuna (grown as fencing). Among the great variety of palms on Fuerteventura are groves of date palm, palmetto and stubby fan palms, used in decoration. The island's palms still provide raw material for locally-produced woven fish traps, camel and donkey baskets and even cheese moulds.

Succulents and cacti abound on the island in the most desolate terrain, none more fascinating than the euphorbia whose growth is based on divisions of five (five new fingers from each new shoot, etc.) and the sap of which is the milky-white poison once used by native Gaunches to stun fish caught in fish traps.

Few exotically colourful flowers bloom on the island; some yellows, reds and violet splashes dot the mountainsides but the prickly pear or raquet cactus, covering acres of rocky soil, is not grown for its brilliant flower. Instead the plant was cultivated for the cochineal beetle which grows fat on its spiny leaves. Until synthetic dyes were produced the beetle gave work and prosperity to many islanders who picked the minute insects for their precious crimson and orange dye, so important to colour the silks and satins of Europe.

Early colonists sought to starve the local *majoreros* into submission, but the hardy race discovered the grain-like value of certain grasses which swelled when immersed in water. It was from this substitute to maize that the indigenous tribes made the original *gofio* or native meal. These glasswort plants later became a source of another economic benefit when it was found that the leaves produced soda, an essential ingredient in glass-making, when burnt. Most surviving plants are those which have escaped cropping by the island's omnivorous and rapacious goats.

Where water is more plentiful, in the town squares and the holiday resorts, the Fuerteventuran soil demonstrates its richness in a profusion of cultivated vegetation. Bright hibiscus, oleander, poinsettia, bougainvillea, camellias and giant geraniums splash primary colours across the greens of palm and pine fronds.

Nurtured plots raise rare banana plants and

exotic flora like the amazing bird of paradise flowers, the strelitzia. On the coast, where there is even the smell of fresh water, thrift-like grasses cling to sand dunes and the odd conifer makes a valiant attempt to brace itself against the wild onshore wind.

However it is really offshore that the island's flora and fauna become its saving grace. Surrounded by beaches and vast stretches of rocky coastline, Fuerteventura's shores conceal a multitude of underwater miracles, surprising when the dry land above it is seemingly so unrewarding to the eye.

So important are the submarine formations and underwater life in parts of the island's coast that two areas have been designated as National Parks. A triangular region in the far north, between the town of Corralejo, the Isle of Lobos and the Dunes National Park has been set aside for preservation.

In the southern peninsula of Jandia, a large area of the Sotavento beachline has also been made a National Underwater Park. Internationally, these, and several other regions which could soon come under the conservation laws, are recognized as the finest natural marine park waters in all of Spain.

The shallow seas offer diving down to a maximum of around 65 feet (20 metres) and the clear waters are host to a remarkable range of tropical and sub-tropical marine life. Sea water temperatures off the island range from 17°C to 22°C and provide an ideal environment for a wide range of fish from barracuda to moray eels, from parrot fish to wrasse, and from trumpet fish to rays.

Fish more familiar at the table can also be encountered along the island's reefs. Sea bass, haddock, mackerel and grouper are plentiful, and, in some stretches of unprotected coast, can be fished relatively easily with harpoon-guns.

Much of the island's waters remain virgin and undiscovered. Volcanic activity has left a strange mixture of contorted rock, great underwater deserts and steep drop-offs. The continental shelf supports some of the best and most sought-after commercial fish.

Four large areas off the coast are set aside as fishing zones. These include the entire Barlov-ento shoreline; the easternmost heel of the island from Gran Tarajal almost to Pozo Negro; a small area off Los Molinos in the northwest, and another zone just north of the capital and port, Puerto del Rosario.

A fisherman's catch can be made up of a silver shower of cabrillas (a little sea perch), eels, mackerel and sea bass. Depending on the tackle used one might see tunny, tuna, swordfish, dorado, cod, hake, dogfish, a mixture of squid and octopus and even a shark. The cold Canary current also brings albacore, bigeye, bluefin, skipjack and yellowfin to the waters off Fuerteventura. More exotic fish are also taken, such as the lion or scorpion fish, oar fish or horse fish.

In the folklore of Fuerteventura there are tales of legendary birds once making their home on this island, but no real evidence to support those tales. Nevertheless the island gives sanctuary to nearly 100 varieties of birds.

The larger birds, such as the Canarian buzzard, the peregrine, the osprey and the Egyptian vulture, are worth an expedition. On the mountain slopes and hillsides, quail, partridge and sand grouse are so common that areas have been allotted for hunting them. The rare Fuerteventura houbara bustard, the ruff, snipe and curlew which choose similar habitats are not so easily spotted.

At least 40 different varieties of birds actually breed on the island. Perhaps the most attractive, visually, is the hoopoe, with its large crest and striking attempt at camouflage. Doves, finches and waders, like sandpipers, turnstones, whimbrels, dunlins and plover are common. Flamingo and spoonbills have been seen on the island's shores and stork, razorbill, gannet and oystercatcher are frequent visitors.

The dun-coloured little bird with the sweet voice haunting village square or woodland grove is the male canary. The tiny finch seems to turn a remarkable yellow or orange colour once caged! In its natural state the *Serinus canaria* is no more flashy than the average sparrow but it makes up for its dull plumage with its song.

The canary, heard singing in the wilds of the Fuerteventuran landscape, is one of the jewels that make this desert island a place of hidden treasures.

FUERTEVENTURA: THE SOUTH

The southern peninsula of Fuerteventura contrasts with the historic central region of the island. It has a more scenic backdrop than the desert views along Fuerteventura's northern routes, with jagged peaks, cliff-edge precipices and vistas of fabulous beaches on either side of the tortuous southern highway.

In ancient times, two Lords of the Isle, the Kings of Maxorata in the north and Jandia in the south, erected a dividing wall across the narrow neck of Fuerteventura. Little trace is left of this mini Hadrian's Wall, but a secondary road running from Pájara traces the approximate boundary line. This way of entering the Jandia Peninsula, on the road through **La Pared** village, is one of the island's most isolated routes. Crossing steep mountains and winding across deep gorges with empty wastes on either side, one can appreciate the island's nickname of "Solitude Isle".

Fuerteventura's thin southern extremity has its windward and leeward sides—its **Sotavento** and **Barlovento**. Beaches on the Barlovento coast are visible as the road south nears the tiny village of La Pared, "The Wall". The new tourist development nearby is known as Club Atlantid.

After the village the scenery reverts from khaki mountains to black lava humps coated with deep, windswept sand dunes. It is almost a relief to emerge from the desolate landscape on to the main road on the Sotavento side of the long peninsula, turning immediately right at the junction towards the town of Morro. Below, as the isthmus road links with the highway, a brilliant turquoise gash in the deep, ultramarine sea reveals the waters of **Matas Blancas** beach.

Mills and mountains: It is at least 46 miles (75 km) drive from Puerto del Rosario to Playa Matas Blancas. This is the scenic route most holidaymakers take as they head for the tourist traps all along the 16 miles (25 km) of southern beaches from the international airport.

A good number of Fuerteventura's major points of interest and several old mills are passed along the way; **Antigua**, in particular, is famous for its windmills, several of which are still standing together with their rotund granaries. Many have lost their outbuildings as the stone blocks have been cannibalised to construct houses or walls. Only one or two are in working order but there are plans to renovate some and work them for the benefit of interested visitors.

Mills worth visiting are those at **Tuineje**; the three-storey mill at **Tiscamanita**, a similar one with six sails at **Llanos de la Concepcíon**, another typically with four sails, several mills at **Villaverde**, a famous one at **Lajares**, a few mills at **El Cotillo** and one in the middle of **Corralejo**. Lime kilns, like that at **Caleta de Fuste**, should not be mistaken for the ruins of windmills although, with the state of disrepair of many mills, it is difficult to distinguish which is which from a distance. Lime is still produced at a factory in Puerto del

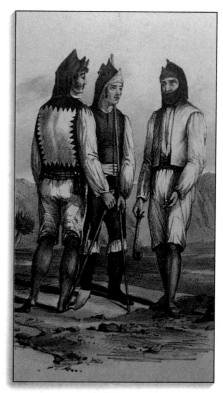

THE FOREIGN LEGION

Supported by models of olden-day halberds, highway signs on Fuerteventura announce the presence of the military. The Spanish Foreign Legion detachment comprises an estimated total of over 3,000 troops based on the island, not 50 miles (80 km) from the turbulent Sahara region of northwest Africa.

The headquarters of this colourful, yet spurned legion, is located in the island capital of Puerto del Rosario, near the port area on the northern side of town. Most imposing of all civil edifices on Fuerteventura, the garrison building, with wide-doored archway and pristine battlements, looks out over the harbour across Calle Almirante Lallemand. Tassel-hatted sentries guard the comings and goings from the main compound on Calle Dominguez Peña and watch-towers punctuate the long, high white-washed perimeter wall stretching the full breadth of the town.

A large territorial strip between Morocco and Mauritania on the African coastline had long been the scene of disputes between the two countries and Spain, which claimed its part of the Sahara. After King Hassan II of Morocco mobilised several hundred thousand people to a peaceful invasion of Spanish Sahara, Spain finally relinquished its hold on the territory in the mid-1970s.

However, ever since the region was handed over, there have been squabbles and guerrilla skirmishes between claimants to the land. The Spanish Sahara Armed Forces, the Spanish Foreign Legion, was entrenched on Spain's nearest island, Fuerteventura, to keep an eye on the whole confused business.

The force has been on the island since 1975, when the population of around 15,000 was suddenly increased to 25,000 by the advent of the legionnaires. On the palm-shaded levels below the garrison gates, a shrine-like collection of memorials and militaria celebrates the heroic actions of past legions. Dramatic bronze statues, early cannon, and an aeroplane propellor, painted shell cases and carved totem poles, stand carefully positioned around the statue of a 16th-century adventurer.

A strange building resembling a cross between church and fort, just opposite the the adorned steps, houses further military personnel and, a little way along from the headquarter's façade is the house of the Colonels-in-Chief. From the road, this verandahed building looks more like a tavern or bistro, with blue and white awnings and metal sign suspended from a miniature halberd.

In a nearby plaza, a plaque commemorates the establishment of the army barracks as the seat of the Captain General of the archipelago. A date on the ceramic plaque, in an expression of the animosity of the islanders towards the legionnaires, has been chipped from the tiling.

The Legion's presence is just another in a long series of invasions, since the Berbers first settled to establish the original population. King Juba II's expedition from Mauritania in the early years of this millennium was shortly followed by Genoese and French visits. Later the Frenchman, de Béthencourt, settled, and called himself the "king of the Canaries". This period, up to 1405, was known as "The Conquest"—yet the persecution of the Guanches continued until they were eliminated.

Moorish pirate raids persuaded Spanish settlers to dig-in on the island and subsequent English sorties between 1596 and 1740 promoted the consolidation of settlements. In the 1930s General Franco split the island by presenting half to a German entrepreneur. The first waves of a half-hearted tourist invasion began in the 1950s and the mid-1970s migration of thousands of Foreign Legion troops represented the final relinquishment of the islanders to a near-minority.

There have been clashes between elated troops on leave and the local *majoreros*, but the troops try to keep a low profile on the island. The visitor may fleetingly notice the khaki lorries, battle-dress-clad infantry and crossed halberd or double-eagle signs of the military. On the airport road out of town stands the Spanish Sahara Forces hospital building. Traffic control and general civil maintenance duties, including a certain amount of policing, are among the services performed by the locally-shunned forces.

Rosario. *Gofio*, the olden-day staple diet, once ground from cereals by the disappearing windmills, is now an island delicacy.

The mountain of Tamacite and the magnificent view of the Caldera de la Laguna and Caldera de los Arrabales, are typical volcanic skylines in the green-brown plain south of Tuineje. Goat paddocks and tomato plots edge the roadside. **Gran Tarajal**, due south, is the island's second port and it is from here that the tomato exports are shipped. The town's black sand beach holds little attraction for the visitor hurrying to get to the golden stretches of Sotavento.

Little more than 14 miles (20 km) from Gran Tarajal is the first of a series of Jandia resorts developed next to the little seaside village of **Tarajalejo**. Most visitors speed on through Tarajalejo as the coast becomes more rugged and the route begins to skirt bay after bay, cliff after cliff. Magnificent marine views and beaches like **Lajita** tempt the passer-by who might stop-over at the

beauty spot just before **Playa Puerto Rico**; here the popular Aussichtspunkt Restaurant offers both local and European dishes.

Sand, sand, sand: From Matas Blancas and its extensive hillside development to the right of the main road, it appears that every other bend in the road, apart from cliffside screes and one or two quarries, has been earmarked for tourist accommodation. From Gran Tarajal to La Lajita the apartments and hotel rooms are comparatively inexpensive, but from Matas Blancas—the beginning of the legendary 16-mile (25-km) beach—resorts vary from luxury villas to tiny cabins, multi-stacked up hillsides facing the sea.

Some little dwellings have been purchased for restructuring into seaside chalets but others just appear to be abandoned. Few isolated farmsteads or fishermen's homes seem to have escaped the almost relentless spread of tourism developments along the southeast coastline.

Cañada del Rio and **Costa Calma**

A CHIP OF SAHARA

Atlantic clouds drift tauntingly across a dry, desert isle, but they never break. Few places on earth compare to the total aridity found in the Saharan wastes. A chip off the old block of Africa, Fuerteventura inherits much of the characteristics of that vast desert and has the unfortunate accolade of being the driest of the seven Canary Islands. Less than 150mm of rain falls on the low mountain peaks and wide, fertile plains of the island.

Brackish water is found in a few precious locations and tiny springs have been found in the extreme south of the island. Several hundred wells have been dug in the countryside, many of which produce undrinkable water.

However, the water table of Fuerteventura is sinking out of reach of most water-drawing methods. The few ancient mills on the island were only used to grind maize for *gofio* but, in some regions, Chicago-built metal windmills now reach deep down to tap into the disappearing aqueous stratas.

Voracious goats, indiscriminate felling of trees and shrubs and natural erosion by wind and scouring sand have reduced the terrain to that of a barren waste. Locust plagues and the work of small mammals on the roots and low vegetation, has further denuded the landscape. Early attempts at water conservation proved futile.

Over the years the islanders have resorted to numerous methods of supporting both themselves and their crops and herds on whatever water became available. Most successful of these was the system of terracing, the most rewarding cultivation scheme yet developed. Terrace farming consists of sectioning hillside slopes by stone walls into four or more levels.

In many areas the volcanic soil is rich—yet, without water, as unproductive as desert dust. This fertile earth is underlined by a special type of impervious soil on which any moisture will collect. A peculiar variety of cinder, mined in northern areas, has been found to have an unusual property, that of collecting moisture from early morning and evening mists and dews. Spread thinly over the surface of good soil, the water thus collected filters through the black volcanic cinders and finds its level on the terrace lining. Only the lowest of the terraces is first cultivated, whether with potatoes, alfalfa, maize, tomatoes, or, as garden plots, with perhaps a few cabbages and onions.

The government has constructed several reservoirs in suitable ravines. Every farmstead has its shallow, lined depression where each available drop of rare rain and infrequent dews are collected—often only to evaporate in the intense heat of the sub-tropics. But loans for sink wells have not been taken advantage of because of the doubtful repayment ability of the homesteaders.

Water tankers, many operated by the Saharan Armed Forces, are a common sight on the roads. These are generally carrying drinking water from the ports, shipped in cistern ships from mainland Spain by the Navy.

From a carpet of green-yellow khaki scrub, the sudden torrential rain that does fall (usually only once a year and overnight) turns the hillsides of Fuerteventura a bright emerald green. The island becomes almost unrecognisable for a few days, and the locals furiously attend their collection pools and repair any cracks in dams or walls. Wheat, barley, chick peas and local grasses and cereals like vetch, *cosco* and glasswort thrive after the annual downpour.

There is an island optimism that, as global weather patterns swing around, Fuerteventura may soon be on the receiving end of damper winds than those of the disastrous years experienced over the past centuries.

Blame for drought lies with the squat nature of the island's mountains which fail to break even the most threatening clouds. Paradoxically, it is the evaporating rays of the fierce sun which may eventually be the economy's saving grace.

The increasing financial influx from growing numbers of tourists visiting Fuerteventura for its beaches and year-long sunshine is being diverted into improving the island's efforts to trap, extract, conserve and even produce (by means of desalination) water. It's a commodity that islanders have almost learned to live without.

face vast beaches of picture-postcard sand. Between each *urbanization* are typical tourist establishments like **Bar Costa Calad** and **Club Soliventura**. Further along, a road leads down to **Playa Esmeralda Jandia**, not far from the giant Sol Group hotel of **Los Goriones** with numerous bars, cafés, restaurants, pools and entertainments—including a bowling alley and camels on the beach.

Most of the more popular complexes are located on the Sotavento side of the Jandia Peninsula—houses, apartments, hotels and aparthotels—even though the northwest coast has its share of golden sandy beaches.

By the time one reaches the port town of **Morro de Jable**, having followed numerous trucks piled with building materials and construction equipment along the Sotavento Strip, the sea and sand does not run out but tourist developments tend to tail off. Beyond Morro the road narrows and winds more, keeping inland from sheer cliffs under which shelter secluded crescents of sandy

beaches like the popular **Juan Gomez** and **Playa de las Pillas**. Little villages are also passed along this secondary road—Casa de Joros and, between road and shore, **Casas Cueva de la Negra**, a recent tourist complex.

More than two-thirds of El Jandia's coastline is beach, comprising half of the total beach area of the entire island. Of 152 named beaches on Fuerteventura, at least 30 are in the Pájara district in which the peninsula lies. As with the beach vistas, the mountain scenery in the south is similar to that in parts of Morocco. Ever-present are the sawtoothed mountain ranges sheltering the beaches of the Sotavento from the prevailing northwest winds which drift the sand along the great expanses of the Barlovento shores.

On the Sotavento beaches there are opportunities for all kinds of watersports, but it is to the Barlovento that the serious divers head when in search of some of the island's most exquisite sites for undersea exploration and underwater spearfishing.

ya de
dia.

Food and tourism: Fishing off both coasts is excellent. Morro Jable, the tiny fishing town expanding rapidly through tourism development, is a leading island centre for commercial fishing, and some of the best traditional fish recipes can be tasted in its local restaurants. Try **Casa Andres** or **Café Restaurant Jandia**, **Rayo del Sol**, **Rodrigues** or **Los Guanches** on Carmen, the town's main street. Taverns, like that at Caosta Calma and **Taberna del Pescador** at Matorral Beach, both serve the famous *majorero*, Fuerteventura's goat milk cheese and fresh fish from *cherne*, sea bass, to *espada*, swordfish. *Cazuela* is a local fish casserole and *grabanzo compuesto* a chick-pea dish with *papas*, potatoes, and *gofio*.

Both these dishes are popular on the island but, in the upper class, western-type restaurants such as **Casa Juan** and **Casa Luis**, the **Deutsches Café** and **El Méson**, all at Matorral, more sophisticated, European-type dishes are the order of the day. There are more than 30 varied restaurants along the Sotavento beaches, most in Morro Jable itself, but some adjoining the hotel complexes. At Tarajalejo there is the **Molino Azul** and Gran Tarajal's **Roma** is well known.

There are about 7,000 beds available in more than 20 tourist establishments in Pájara Municipality (El Jandia) itself. Considering that the total number of rooms available to visitors in the entire 666 sq miles (1,725 sq km) of Fuerteventura numbers 14,000 beds, the importance of the beaches of the region is self-evident.

However as a contribution to the overall economy of the island, and as an opportunity for work in the tourist sector for local islanders, the region's developments fall short in the benefits they are expected to bring. A fair number of workers in hotels and apartments come from other islands in the Canaries or elsewhere, and their salaries are generally sent out of the island to families back home.

Few restrictions or conservation laws have interfered with the boom of tourist development in areas like Playa de

The dese
beach of
Cofete.

180

Sotavento and there is a real threat to the islanders' identity in the exposure to mainland European gimmickry and gadgetry. The very thing that brings a little prosperity and the chance of self-sufficiency, even in the case of fresh water, might itself be responsible for wiping away ancient traditions and island customs as effectively as the French and Spanish eliminated the native Gaunches.

Concern for the environment is now flouted as cars and jeeps career across sand dunes and beaches; litter piles up until a dust-devil sweeps it high into the sand-ladened air; and plants and birds cling tenuously to life in the arid wastes.

With all the resort construction along the Sotavento beaches (which are among the best in the Canary Islands) and the stream of visitors, it is hard to imagine that an almost empty beach of 13 miles (20 km) is three miles away across the peninsula.

The spine of the Jandia is a ridge of mountains with no roads linking one coast with the other. Peak after gullied peak act as a barrier to the prevailing winds off the Atlantic. Fuerteventura's highest mountain, **Jandia** itself, or Pico de Zarza, 2,646 ft (807 metres), is set in the cordillera's centre. Tracks, possible to navigate with the popular four-wheel drive jeeps cramming tourist resorts, lead across some of the less high passes to the **Playa de Barlovento de Jandia** and **Playa de Cofete** (near an abandoned hamlet), but so deserted are these coasts that naturism seems to be almost a necessity.

Relics of war: Right at the tip of the Jandia Peninsula, 87 miles (140 km) from Puerto del Rosario, there is a lighthouse near **Caserio Puerto de la Luz**. Crossing the road on the town's outskirts is a small airstrip said to have been used by a German entrepreneur, Winter, who was presented with the entire peninsula by General Franco. Rumours are still circulating about what exactly it was that went on there.

Certainly, the deserted village of Cofete has dubious connections with World War II and, some say, subsequent political movements. Underground bunkers and stories of nocturnal landings from submarines near the ruined church by the beach, all have the ring of a rather dated thriller.

The terrain at this end of Fuerteventura is full of surprises. The rocks which form the peaks in Jandia are the oldest in the entire Canary archipelago. There are geologists who consider that the mountain ridge is just a tiny portion of an immense volcanic crater rim which could have extended more than 30 miles (50 km) into the Atlantic to the north of Barlovento.

Along this northerly part of the Jandia extension the dunes are flanked by crumbling cliffs of sandstone covered by tamarisk and sea spurge. Little wildlife except stray goats inhabit these bleak regions although one place is named Deer Valley, and another The Deer House.

Snipe and sand grouse—both favoured by hunters, especially on the shoot belonging to the Los Goriones Hotel—are some of the few birds in this part of the island.

ist ur-
sations
ne
dia
t.

LANZAROTE: THE CITY AND THE SOUTH

Ask a bored timeshare seller, wearily plying his or her trade in the southern resort of Puerto del Carmen, for his or her opinion on Lanzarote and you're likely to get a stream of invective in return. One Geordie (an Englishman from Newcastle) who'd stopped off in Lanzarote hoping to make a fast buck compared the surrounding volcanic landscape to the industrial slag heaps in his birth-place. He was not impressed, and he expressed his opinion in not the best of language.

Few people in Lanzarote—residents or tourists—have time for the opinions of fly-by-night timeshare itinerants. In any case, that kind of comparison is as ungenerous as it is unimaginative. To Europeans used to greener and more fertile landscapes, Lanzarote's stark volcanic slopes might seem to harbour little of real interest. Yet the island is a beautiful combination of vulcanicity and aridity.

Even those who come with only beaches and beer in mind should take time to explore inland. Given the massive tourist developments at various points around the coast, it's a credit to Lanzarote's government that further inland its many small, quiet villages have remained small and quiet. You can do no worse than rent a car—they say that in the course of his or her lifetime every *conejo* (Lanzarote islander) will have worked for a time in the car hire industry—and take to the road for a day or two, one day for the north, and one day for the south.

Don't expect to find tailormade "sights"; the drive to develop the island economy stops at building hotels and apartments. Nobody has yet seen fit to create additional tacky tourist attractions. Many of the places that can be visited owe their charisma to nature— or the way Lanzarote's islanders have tamed nature.

Capital heap: Lanzarote's principal town, **Arrecife**, is not a good advertisement for the island. It's modern, it's messy and has a surfeit of potholes.

With the exception of Valverde on El Hierro, all the Canary capitals are the ports of their respective islands. But, until a little over 200 years ago, Arrecife was *just* the port. The capital was Teguise, seven miles (11 km) inland, and out of reach of hit-and-run raids by the Moors. It's this lack of history that means there's only limited interest here for tourists (go to Teguise), and what it lacks in interest it tries to make up for in construction sights: Arrecife's northern outskirts are a sprawl of gleaming white townhouses and small concrete apartment blocks.

In the centre of town cracked pavements, badly surfaced roads and some tired looking buildings make some corners of Arrecife look war-torn. Half-finished roads have been a fact of life for several years and, as the town continues to grow, bulldozers, freshly-laid tarmac and traffic diversions will remain familiar sights.

César Manrique, a celebrated artist, a landscape conservationist and one of

ᵉceding
ᵍes:
ᵑsport in
ᵃanfaya
ᵢonal
ᵏ;
ᵣking the
a. Left,
ᵃzarote
ᵣ Yaiza.
ht,
htseeing.

15 km

ATLANTIC   OCEAN

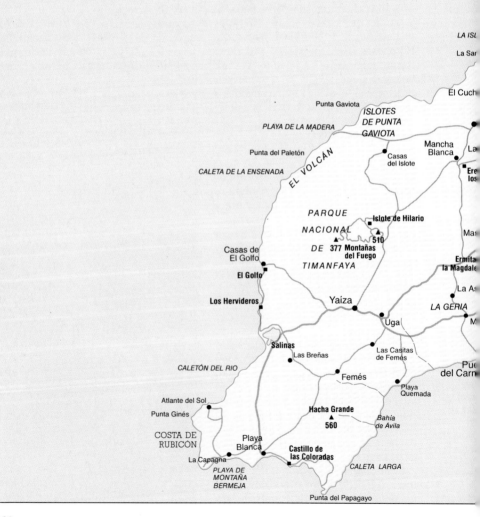

LA ISL

La Sar

El Cuch

Punta Gaviota

PLAYA DE LA MADERA

ISLOTES DE PUNTA GAVIOTA

Punta del Paletón

Mancha Blanca   La

Casas del Islote

CALETA DE LA ENSENADA

EL VOLCÁN

Ere los

PARQUE

Islote de Hilario

NACIONAL

▲ 510

Ma:

Casas de El Golfo

DE 377 **Montañas del Fuego**

Ermita la Magdal

TIMANFAYA

El Golfo

La A:

Los Hervideros

Yaiza

LA GERIA

Uga

M

Salinas

Las Casitas de Femés

CALETÓN DEL RIO

Las Breñas

Pu del Carn

Femés

Playa Quemada

Atlante del Sol

Punta Ginés

Hacha Grande

▲ 560

Bahía de Avila

COSTA DE RUBICON

Playa Blanca

La Capagna

Castillo de las Coloradas

CALETA LARGA

PLAYA DE MONTAÑA BERMEJA

Punta del Papagayo

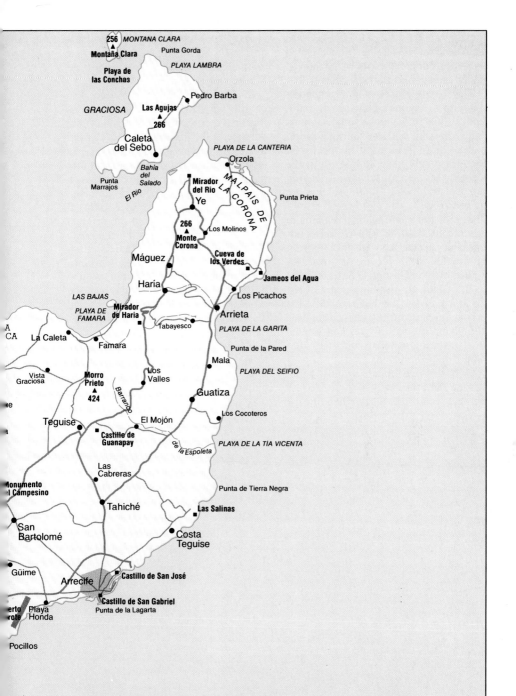

256 MONTANA CLARA
Montaña Clara
Punta Gorda

Playa de
las Conchas

PLAYA LAMBRA

Pedro Barba

GRACIOSA   Las Agujas
▲
266

Caleta
del Sebo

PLAYA DE LA CANTERIA

Orzola

Bahia
del
Salado

Punta
Marrajos

El Rio

Mirador
del Rio

Ye

Punta Prieta

266
▲
Monte
Corona

Los Molinos

Máguez

Cueva de
los Verdes

Haría

Jameos del Agua

LAS BAJAS

Los Picachos

PLAYA DE
FAMARA

Mirador
de Haria

Tabayesco

Arrieta

PLAYA DE LA GARITA

A
CA

La Caleta

Famara

Punta de la Pared

Mala

PLAYA DEL SEIFIO

Vista
Graciosa

Morro
Prieto
▲
424

Los
Valles

Guatiza

Barranco

El Mojón

Los Cocoteros

Teguise

Castillo de
Guanapay

de la Espoleta

PLAYA DE LA TÍA VICENTA

Las
Cabreras

Monumento
l Campesino

Punta de Tierra Negra

Tahiché

Las Salinas

San
Bartolomé

Costa
Teguise

Güime

Arrecife

Castillo de San José

erto
rote

Playa
Honda

Castillo de San Gabriel

Punta de la Lagarta

Pocillos

ATLANTIC   OCEAN

189

Lanzarote's best-known citizens, has little time for the capital. "It is crushed by cruel concrete blocks and buried under asphalt and traffic," he says.

The **Gran Hotel**, still dominating Arrecife's skyline, was, when built, Lanzarote's brave new symbol of tourism, complete with a Manrique mural made out of lava rock in the foyer. Smarter hotels have sprung up in the resorts elsewhere on the island, leaving the isolated Gran Hotel looking not quite so *gran*.

One of the most historic remains in Arrecife is **Castillo San Gabriel**, unmissable at the end of the seafront promontory in the centre of town. Designed by Don Gaspar de Salcedo (sent to the island by the high court of the Canaries to be the head of the first prison on Lanzarote), the castle was completed in 1573. It was constructed to a quadrangular plan with four diamond-shaped bastions.

Only 13 years later, in July 1586, Arraez Amurat attacked Arrecife and burnt the castle down, later invading the island. The Moorish commander withdrew at the end of August that same year after signing a peace treaty with the Marquis of Lanzarote.

In 1590, an Italian engineer, Leonardo Torriani, was commissioned by Phillip II of Spain to reorganise the defence of the Canary Islands. The old fortress was rebuilt and external walls were added to the corners of the diamond shapes and the spaces in between were filled with rubble. Today, the rubble has been removed so as to reveal the passageways between the original outside wall and the later Torriani one.

Reading about the castle's past, however, is more interesting than actually visiting it. Inside, on a hot day, the building feels like a sauna and the modest displays of pottery, coins and jewellery tell you little about Lanzarote's past.

If César Manrique has not been able to leave his mark on the way Arrecife looks, he has at least given it two art galleries. The **Castillo San José**, on the way out of Arrecife along the road to

The Casti▶
San Gabri▶
and Arrec▶

190

Costa Teguise, is the home of the **Museum of Contemporary Art**. This collection of abstract art, which includes several works by Manrique as well as Picasso and Miró, occupies what was once the cellar of this castle, built in the reign of Charles III of Spain, in 1799. If this spacious and elegant art gallery isn't reason enough for visiting Castillo San José, you should try its excellent restaurant and bar—a quiet and uncommercial alternative to the razamattaz of the wide variety of eating places in the southern resorts.

Manrique's second major contribution to Arrecife is **El Almacen**, a small but very chic art gallery that sells high-quality (though expensive) prints of the artist's works. El Almacen is on Calle José Betancort.

Star resort: Beyond the sprawl of Arrecife the island thankfully improves. Its southern half comprises the municipalities of San Bartolome, Tias, Yaiza and Tinajo, and has the best-known of the resorts.

The star attraction of the municipality of Tias is **Puerto del Carmen**. During the day the long beach glows with good health as the tanned bodies insatiably lap up the sun, and at night Puerto del Carmen glitters with neon as those healthy bodies do their damnedest to get unhealthy again by whatever means available.

Restaurants, bars, shops and apartments line a promenade which stretches more than two miles (three kms) from Hotel San Antonio (to the northeast) to Hotel Los Ferriones (to the southwest). Lanzarote's main resort caters for the tastes of the different nationalities of tourists: watering holes such as the London Pub provide succour to the Brits while the Germans are mollified by restaurants which are more likely to serve weinerschnitzel than paella.

Such a modest streak of commercialism is excusable—for Puerto del Carmen has not yet gone over the top. While a few discos energetically pump their beat out into the night, this resort is relatively quiet. It was here that two BBC executives on a winter break sup-

posedly dreamed up the British television soap *Eastenders*.

Pueto del Carmen is also very well behaved. Well-dressed holidaymakers amble up and down **Avenida de las Playas** inspecting the menus and the brightly lit shopfronts as they go. It's all very innocent and very relaxed.

The Waikiki Bar, overlooking the long uninterrupted stretch of beach, provides a more laid-back alternative where, once your suntan is firmly in place, you can spend an evening or two projecting cool.

Puerto del Carmen is Lanzarote at its most affluent. In the 1970s, the Avenida de las Playas was just a track. Local retailers and hotels paid for the road all the way from Playa Grande to Hotel Los Ferriones. Never widened or re-laid, this narrow route has already had more than its fair share of traffic.

Since that all-important road was built the rapid development has not been without its hitches. A large development just before Playa de los Pocillos has been left to fall apart at the seams. It is said that a foreign owner who was selling holidays in this complex failed to forward funds to pay for local bills. Workers were not paid and unions boycotted the buildings. Today the site is urgently in need of redevelopment, but Spanish law says that any new owner must collect the debts when buying the land.

There was more than a little controversy too when a new wing was built onto the Hotel Los Ferriones. The new structure, which backs onto the Avenida de las Playas, blocked the beach views of a complex that had been built some time before on the other side of this road, although the court action that followed was unsuccessful.

A more recent dispute concerned the hotel next to the San Antonio. Local residents were angered because this development sits on the beach itself. A demonstration led by César Manrique failed to stop construction work.

Inland attractions: Also part of Tias municipality, but in another world a few miles inland, is the valley of **La Geria**,

Country v
in the Ger
valley.

Lanzarote's wine-producing area. The small semi-circular walls of volcanic stone, patterning the apparently barren fields either side of the main road from Masdache to Uga are called *zocos*, and provide an ingenious method of cultivation in this otherwise arid landscape. Inside the *zocos*, vines grow in earth covered by *picon*—porous lava granules which absorb the dew at night and drip-feed it down to the roots below.

These vines yield a fresh, golden wine called Malvasia, and its delicious taste has earned it a good reputation. Tour guides make much of the fact that Canary Island wine is mentioned by Shakespeare. One such reference is to be found in the play *The Merry Wives Of Windsor* (Act III) when the host of the Garter Inn says: "Farewell my hearts, I will drink to my honest knight Falstaff and drink Canary with him".

Driving in Lanzarote can be as memorable as the places that are visited. Many of the roads have still to be surfaced and there's an element of suspense on some routes as to the staying power of the shock absorbers of the hired cars. The road to the tiny village of **Femes** is a welcome exception. Leaving the main route near Uga, a small side-road winds up a narrow cultivated valley to a small bar overlooking this village's marketplace.

Femes has the oldest church on the island which, instead of religious pictures, houses a collection of model sailing boats. Dedicated to the island's patron saint, San Marcos, the church is only open for services or during festivals. You can drive on through Femes—though the road definitely deteriorates from here on down to the plain of Los Ajaches.

The island's sight of sights—even for those who seldom abandon the beach—is **Timanfaya National Park**. One of the nine national parks in Spain, Timanfaya's keepers are acutely aware of the need to keep this geologically young and therefore pristine volcanic landscape in good shape. The restrictions in Timanfaya are clearly stated (and should be welcomed): you cannot walk

ing the
icult
.

over lava or any pyroclastic (fire-created) materials; you cannot get out of your car; you can't camp or stay out overnight.

If Timanfaya National Park—spectacular though it is—still leaves you with the urge to clamber among volcanic debris, then take the first right off the Playa Blanca road after you have passed through Yaiza. Here an unsurfaced road leads through some spectacular *malpais* (badlands) to the village of **El Golfo**. There are no restrictions here; you can get out of your car and marvel at how the lava twisted and turned as it crept towards the sea.

At the end of the road El Golfo is a small bay, a half-collapsed volcano, a crescent-shaped lagoon and a small, unspoilt fishing village—all at the same time. Turn right at the first junction on the unsurfaced road and you'll reach the village. Turn left at this junction and, in another minute, you reach some boulders placed across the road that lead toward the beach.

It's tempting to turn back without taking a look at what lies beyond those boulders. But the walk to the beach is worth the effort. A few hundred feet down a wide track the forces of erosion have conspired with volcanic sculpture to create an enormous natural amphitheatre, formed out of one half of a volcanic cone (the other half having been washed into the sea).

Wind has sculpted the cliff face into a series of jagged terraces below which a lagoon seems to glow luminous green. This, too, is El Golfo. The sound of the sea collects here and is amplified by the cliff wall. There are few places in the Canary Islands more inspiring.

The village of El Golfo can be reached on foot from the beach but cars need to drive back round the headland to get to it. The village's restaurants (one of which sits right at the water's edge) serve fresh fish and Malvasia wine. Facing directly west, El Golfo is an excellent place to eat as you watch the sunset over the sea.

To the tip: The surfaced road follows the coast for a mile or two before swing-

El Golfo, emerald lagoon.

ing inland again to join the main road to Playa Blanca. The sea batters this jagged coast with full force. Just a mile or two south of El Golfo the tides have carved out a small inlet where waves collide in a cauldron of currents. A short flight of steps allows you to descend nearer to sea level to study the surf at **Los Hervideros** (the name of this inlet) more closely.

As you turn inland you pass the natural lagoon of **Janubio** and the grid-shaped terraces of **Las Salinas de Janubio**, from which salt is extracted by evaporation. There are several such *salinas* throughout the island, for salt is one of the oldest industries in the Canaries. The coarse salt which Janubio yields is not intended for domestic use, but for preserving fish in Arrecife's five fish factories.

Like the rocks off El Golfo, this is a wild and rocky stretch of coast—no port was ever built on the western side of Lanzarote. The black sands of Playa de Janubio, running along the edge of Las Salinas, seem an appropriate ingredient

in this uncompromising coastline.

"The standard excursion to the south," said one 1960s guidebook, "goes no further than Janubio, but all who can should push on across the desolate plain of Rubicon to Playa Blanca, the poverty-stricken village of the far south, with its magnificent views across the straits called the Bocaina towards the islet of Lobos and the equally poverty-stricken northern tip of Fuerteventura. Prosperity of a sort may be on the way in Playa Blanca…"

In those days, package tours had no reason to herd Europeans any further than Las Salinas de Janubio. Today it's a very different story. Almost at Lanzarote's southern tip, **Playa Blanca** is another of the island's fast-growing communities, though it's very much a place for passing through.

The ferry for Fuerteventura leaves from Playa Blanca's small quayside and tourists stop here for lunch on their way to or from the isolated beaches of Papagayo. This southern tip of the island is still sometimes referred to by the his-

salt
s at
ubio.

toric name of Rubicon.

It was in this vicinity that the Norman invader Jean de Béthencourt chose to build the first European settlement. Here stood the "castle of Rubicon," a fortification referred to by Pierre Boutier and John le Verrier, two chaplains who accompanied de Béthencourt on his first expedition and whose diaries form the first major document of Canary history.

Finding your way to the beaches of **Papagayo** is almost more memorable than arriving. The surfaced road comes to an abrupt end just east of Playa Blanca and it's up to you to follow the maze of dirt tracks that head seaward. Better still, follow a four-wheel drive full of tanned Germans.

In Lanzarote, there are those who know how good the Papagayo beaches are (and how to get to them), and there are those who don't. It's as simple as that. The most crowded beach is just beyond where the cars park—you can stretch out with or without your cherished swimming trunks or bikini; no-

body will worry either way.

A little further up the coast are numerous secluded coves where it seems unnatural to sunbathe anything but *au naturel*. While deliberating on whether you are going to adopt a modest or brazen sunbathing strategy, you might miss the circular watch-tower on the first beach by the car park. Erroneously attributed to de Béthencourt, it actually boasts a less ancient pedigree and was constructed in 1778.

The Heartlands: In the rush to head for the panorama of Timanfaya or the pleasures of Papagayo, it's possible to forget the centre of the island. If you want to be certain just where the centre is, then visit the stark, modern, white sculpture of **Monumento al Campesino**, which rises proudly from the fields a short distance north of **San Bartolome** on the road to Mozaga.

Beside it is a rural museum with a restaurant serving typical dishes. Created in 1968 by César Manrique, the monument is situated deliberately and symbolically in the geographical centre

Manrique Monumer al Campesi

of the island and pays tribute to Lanzarote's peasants and their ingenious methods of cultivation.

To the northwest of San Bartolome, **Mancha Blanca** has a more ancient monument. Here, a cross marks the very edge of the lava field. It was placed here by residents as a symbol of what they considered to be divine intervention in the face of advancing lava flows; the molten stream miraculously changed direction at this point. In recognition of this divine intervention the festival of the Virgin of the Volcanoes is held on 15 September in the hermitage of Mancha Blanca.

Just beyond La Santa, **La Isleta** is occasionally what its name suggests: an island. When tides permit, the inlet connects with the ocean at both ends. A travel writer who came to Lanzarote in the 1960s told of a curious fishing method employed in this narrow neck of water. As the tide ebbed, so the story goes, fishermen dammed both ends of the inlet and placed in the water the milky sap of a plant they found on the hillsides. This made the fish float unconscious to the surface ready to be harvested.

By the time the road reaches **Club La Santa**, the volcanoes of Timanfaya have receded into the distance. Suddenly sport—and lots of it—looms large. Club La Santa bills itself as "Europe's best-kept secret." Whether this "secret" refers to La Santa's exhaustive facilities or the fact that it is really a timeshare complex in disguise is not clear.

What is beyond dispute is its determination to exhaust its guests—the facilities include squash, basketball, badminton, handball, swimming, mini-golf, volleyball, windsurfing, scuba diving, discus, high-jump and soccer. And that's only the half of it. Reading their exhaustive brochure is enough to leave you out of breath.

Of course, if your idea of a demanding day out is to play dead on a sun-soaked beach you'd do well to give La Santa a miss and stay down in the vicinity of Puerto del Carmen.

romptu
market
the west
st.

TIMANFAYA: BADLANDS MADE GOOD

If Puerto del Carmen shows Lanzarote developing itself for all it's worth, then **Parque Nacional Timanfaya** shows the island leaving well alone. This is one of the youngest major volcanic landscapes on the planet, the product in the early 18th century of six years of frequent volcanic eruptions that altered the face of more than a third of the island.

It is said that eleven villages still lie buried beneath the lava fields, their names no more than folklore memories: Vegas de Timanfaya, Maretas, Tingafa, Santa Catalina, Jaritas, Masdache… Twenty-five years ago Italian film director Paolo Pasolini used this undiscovered, surreal landscape for settings in some of his films.

Eye witnesses and a few official communications from the Lanzarote *cabildo* (local government) to the authorities (then in Tenerife) have left a fascinating account of what happened. The most interesting document is the manuscript of the Priest of Yaiza, Don Andres Lorenzo Curbelo. He witnessed the whole process from close quarters and told how the villagers, terrified by what was happening, gave up hope that the eruptions would ever stop and emigrated to Gran Canaria.

The main entry to the park is from the south at **Yaiza**. A long straight road cuts north from the main road to Playa Blanca and leads quickly into another world. For anybody who has not before seen a volcanic landscape close up, it's a memorable experience. Your first instinct is to get out of your car and walk on the lava, pick it up and touch it. But you'd be breaking the National Park's regulations if you did. Even this seemingly indestructible rock needs protection from human erosion.

There are just two opportunities to get close to the earth in Timanfaya. A mile or two into the park, you can take a camel ride up the slopes of a volcanic cone. There are dozens of camels continually being herded up to the starting point and the groups of nervous waiting tourists. Two people at a time are carried in seats suspended over the camel's hump.

It may look a little too commercialised, but it's a fact that camels, with their big splayed feet, offer the best way of climbing slopes covered in volcanic ash, and the view from the top over dozens of spent volcanoes should not be missed. At the boarding point, the **Rock Museum and Information Centre** is a modest underground display of rocks, minerals and maps relating to the eruptions that created the landforms. All the exhibits are in Spanish.

One map shows how far the various volcanic materials spread; present-day Yaiza marks the southern edge of Timanfaya's lava fields. A table of dates listing the major eruptions, which occurred over a period of six years, makes awesome reading. Individual eruptions were of considerable duration: the one which started on 3 February 1731 lasted for no less than 25 days.

Better still is a spot called **Islote de Hilario**. You need to buy a ticket at a small stone hut (look for a red-and-white barrier gate) situated about a mile further on from the camel rides. You can drive right up into one of the craters, park your car and then take a tour bus on an eight-mile (13 km) circular route through the very heart of Timanfaya's volcanoes.

Any verbal account of the landscape inevitably involves the word "lunar". Viewed from an armchair, descriptions of Timanfaya's volcanic horizons might seem clichéd—yet mere terrestrial vocabulary can't do Timanfaya justice. It really is out of this world and you've got to see it to believe it.

Perhaps the best word picture comes from Curbelo, whose account of the eruptions enumerates the upheavals as they happened. "On 1 September, between nine and ten o'clock in the afternoon, the earth suddenly opened near Timanfaya, two miles away from Yaiza. The first night an enormous mountain rose up from the depths of the earth, and from its point issued flames which continued to burn for 19 days.

"A few days later, a new gulf was formed and a torrent of lava hurled down onto Timanfaya, Los Roques and part of Mancha Blanca. The lava spread over the estates to the North, at first as quickly as water, but its speed soon diminished, so that it did not go faster than honey. But on 7

September, a rock of considerable size surged from the earth, with a noise similar to that of thunder, and by its pressure forced the lava, which from the first had been flowing toward the North, to change its course, veering to the Northwest and West-Northwest. The mass of lava arrived at, and speedily destroyed the villages of Maretas and Santa Catalina, in the valley.

"The volcanic action continued like this for ten whole days, until 28 October when suddenly the cattle of the whole area fell dead, suffocated by the development of pestilent vapours, which condensed and fell in the form of rain. On 30 October all was quiet.

"On 16 December, the lava which up until then had veered towards the sea, changed direction, bearing to the Southwest, reaching Chupadero, which soon after, on the 17th, was no more than a vast fire. After this, it ruined the fertile valley of Uga, but did not go any further.

"On 7 January 1731, new eruptions came, which surpassed all precedent ones. Incandescent flows, together with thick smoke, issued from the openings which had formed on the mountain. The clouds of smoke were often pierced through with lightning of blinding blue and red light, followed by violent claps of thunder, as in storms. This sight was both frightening and new to the inhabitants of this region, who had never experienced storms.

"On the 13th, two mountains collapsed amid incredible noise and on 1 May, this volcanic fire seemed to be extinguished, only to rise again on the 2nd, quarter of a mile away. A new hill emerged and a lava flow threatened to reach the village of Yaiza. On 6 May, these events had stopped, and during the rest of the month it seemed that this enormous eruption had come to an end.

"On the 18th, a new cone arose between those which had already risen on the ruins of Mato, Santa Catalina and Timanfaya. A crater which had opened on the side of this cone threw out ash and lightning, and another mountain let out a white steam.

"About the end of June 1731 all the beaches and the coast of the West was covered in an incredible quantity of dead fish of all kinds, some

of which had never been seen before on the Northwest.

"In October and November, other eruptions came to renew the distress of the inhabitants of the island. On 25 December 1731, the island was shaken by the most violent earthquakes which had been felt in the last two disastrous years. On 28 December a lava flow came out of an already active cone, towards Jaretas burning down the village and destroying the chapel of St John the Baptist, near Yaiza."

The **Montañas del Fuego** (mountains of fire), as these created mountains are called, are not solely the product of this era of eruptions. A new phase of volcanic activity followed in 1834. The eruptions were shorter and less important on this occasion, lasting only from 31 July to 21 October.

Despite the wasteland that has been created, Timanfaya National Park can boast a handful of plant species. One of the most common is a type of wild geranium which grows on the slopes. There are also over a dozen species of lichen. Timanfaya's fauna is more limited. Only one vertebrate inhabits the lava fields: the Haria lizard (*Lacerta Atlantica*), which grows to about eight inches (20 cms) in length.

The silence and solitude of Timanfaya makes it difficult to imagine the vast eruptions that took place here; they seem to belong very much to the past. Nevertheless the land is still boiling and bubbling just beneath visitors' feet.

At Islote de Hilario every crowd of tourists is treated to curious thermal demonstrations. Water poured into a metal tube inserted just a few feet into the ground explodes into the air forming a momentary geyser. Bushes held over a shallow hole take just a minute or two to smoulder and then suddenly burst into flames. Potatoes can be baked by burying them just a few inches in the soil.

These are partly tourism gimmicks, but they show that Canary Island vulcanicity is not necessarily a thing of the past, and if Lanzarote's volcanoes were ever to erupt again there would be more at stake in terms of lives and investment than just a few villages. Meanwhile, however, you as visitors are unlikely to be blown up.

LANZAROTE: THE NORTH

A convenient dividing line can be drawn across Lanzarote above Arrecife. The result, geometrically speaking at least, is what could be termed "the north" of the island: the three municipalities of Teguise, Haria and La Graciosa. This half of Lanzarote boasts the best views, its most fertile valley, a nightclub for troglodytes, Lanzarote's historic capital, and a 16th-century hilltop castle.

It will also one day come out on top in Lanzarote's unofficial seaside development contest. Just a few miles up the coast from Arrecife, **Costa Teguise** is clear proof that Lanzarote's tourist boom shows few signs of stopping. The brain-child of Union Explosivos Rio Tinto, one of Spain's largest industrial firms, the development is classified as a Residential and Touristic Urbanization and will eventually provide 11 million sq metres of hotels, apartments and holiday complexes.

Costa marketing: Among the many developments along this stretch of coast are the British-owned **Los Zocos Aparthotel**, which opened in 1988, and the **Lanzarote Garden Aparthotel**, adjoining Los Zocos. Requirements for roadways, street lighting, telephone lines, electricity, sewerage, desalination plants and water re-cycling plants mean that Costa Teguise is about much more than throwing up a few hotels. Even some of the beaches have been extended.

Costa Teguise attracted residents long before the construction programmes had been completed. This stretch of coast scored a marketing success when King Hussein of Jordan, whose house was designed by César Manrique, purchased an additional large amount of land.

When it comes to marketing Costa Teguise, **Lanzarote Beach Club**, one of the best-known developments here, has really got its act together. Not content with the leaflet-tucked-under-the-windscreen-wiper method adopted by other holiday complexes on Lanzarote, Lanzarote Beach Club has gone in for a 20-page full-colour newspaper called the *European Islander*, in which hard-sell suddenly takes on the guise of important news, thus: "A growing number of holidaymakers who take their vacations on Lanzarote go home richer than they came. This startling conclusion is now fast emerging from a look at the benefits of holiday ownership with the Lanzarote Beach Club, the island's exclusive five-star holiday ownership resort."

The qualities that make the club the "world's most exclusive" resort (according to their own publicity) are swimming pools with jacuzzis surrounded by astroturf, UK and US satellite television piped to every room, and the 10,000 sq ft (900 sq metres) of white Italian marble that makes the Clubhouse "one of the most dazzling and magnificent buildings in the whole of the Canary Islands".

Lanzarote Beach Club is, of course, just another timeshare complex and, in

FARMERS IN LAVA

The moisture-laden trade winds have little influence on an island with such relatively low mountains. The clouds rarely deliver, and rainfall has always been minimal. When the southern part of Lanzarote fell victim to the Timanfaya eruptions in the 18th century, agriculture could have died forever under the lava. Ironically, the island's volcanic legacy has yielded a sophisticated method of farming that has left a characteristic mark on the landscape.

As if to mimic the surrounding volcanoes, Lanzarote's vineyards take the form of fields of man-made ash-filled craters. Each about eight ft (2.5 metres) in diameter, these are protected by a low wall of lava rocks. At the centre of each circle of stones is a single vine.

On first sight, the vine appears to be growing straight from the dark volcanic dust. In fact, it has been planted in enough soil to cover its roots. The black lava cinders (*picon*) are the key to growth: they distil the dew each night and provide the plant with the only moisture it receives.

The vineyards exploit soils that would otherwise serve no purpose. The walls and side of the crater protect the plant from wind and sand and the half-buried position of the vine reduces the sun's angle of incidence. Thus the vine is in shadow for a longer period than if it were growing out in the open. It's been calculated that one more hour of direct exposure to the sun each day would be enough to kill the Lanzarote vines, but the climate takes its toll despite careful landscaping.

There are vineyards throughout the island. From the region of La Geria comes Lanzarote's well-known Malvasia wine. One of the oldest vineyards on the island is called Mozaga, after the village near which it is located. The fields produce a red, a white and a rosé, all of which carry the Mozaga label on the bottle.

Picon is put to extensive use throughout the island. Whole fields of perfectly good but virtually waterless soil are covered with about an inch of volcanic ash so that crops can be grown. Lanzarote's produce includes onions, tomatoes,

watermelon, squash, potatoes, garlic, wheat, barley, rye, beans, peas, corn and tobacco.

The island's northern tip is a good area for a closer look at the island's agriculture. The slopes around Ye, just south of Mirador del Rio, are heavily planted with vines. The Tabayesco valley is not given over to viticulture but grows a variety of vegetables and cereals.

Enter this valley by turning left as you approach Arrieta from the the south. On the climb up towards the Famara Massif it becomes clear just how much dedication has been required to force growth out of Lanzarote's soil. The Tabayesco valley is carefully manicured, terraced along its entire length with up to 40 low stone walls ascending any slope.

Plantations of cacti are all over Lanzarote. These plants are extensively cultivated, but not for their own sake; they are a specific strain of cactus that attracts the cochineal beetle, a parasite which feeds on the flesh of the plant. The beetle is white but when crushed produces a valuable purple dye called carmine. The nopal cactus, which has become an integral part of the island's landscape, was imported especially to nourish this insect.

From 1825 to the mid-1870s, fortunes were made in a mounting speculative fever which eventually burst with a catastrophic drop in cochineal prices. The cochineal "blood" was used to dye lipsticks and Campari, but the discovery of substitute substances brought about a decline in this part of Lanzarote's agricultural economy. There are still enough buyers for the island's much reduced cochineal yield.

April is harvest time in Lanzarote, especially for the onion crop, today the island's main export. However, failed harvests, which follow winter months with more heat than rain, come as no surprise. Farming has never been easy or lucrative on Lanzarote and the growth of tourism means that one or more sons or daughters of families who make a living from farming will inevitably be drawn to the securer incomes of the island's growth industry. More and more young people are moving into tourism. The sight of crops growing in black *picon* fields could one day be reserved for the pages of old guide books.

common with other island developments, is sold on the Club/Trustee system and finds it difficult to live up to the hyperbole of its promotional literature.

Local newspapers and expatriate magazines ask if this continuing timeshare boom is good for the island and grudgingly reach the conclusion that it is a necessary part of promoting tourism. But Lanzarote is all too aware of the bad publicity surrounding the timeshare touts along the seafront in Puerto del Carmen and, when construction has finished and this new seaside resort is in full swing, Costa Teguise will attract a new crew of sweet-talking marketeers.

The municipality of **Teguise**, with its 20 villages and the island of La Graciosa, is the largest governed area of Lanzarote. The contrast between commercial forward-looking Costa Teguise and the quiet backwater of Teguise itself, Lanzarote's former capital, couldn't be more stark.

From the 16th-century castle of **Guanapay**, you can see how Teguise sits out of reach in the middle of the island, midway between the oceans to the northeast and the southwest. Built by Phillip II of Spain against the hit-and-run raids of the Moors, Guanapay Castle (unfortunately, no access is allowed to the building itself) provides commanding views over the sea-approach to Arrecife.

Yet despite the past importance of this community, Teguise is today small and quiet. Nevertheless, to *conejos* (natives of Lanzarote), it remains La Villa, the royal town, whereas Arrecife is just *el puerto*, the port.

Teguise ceased to be the capital in 1852 and many of the original buildings and monuments were destroyed during repeated attacks by pirates. The town has been smartened up in recent years and its cobble-stone lanes and hidden workshops give it that feeling of old-world charm that tourists are supposed to love.

Teguise isn't just for tourists, though. Every Sunday and Feast Day there is a market in the square, in front of the

UNDERGROUND LANDSCAPES

If the main course of Lanzarote's gourmet scenic dinner is above ground in the National Park of Timanfaya to the south, the dessert is below ground in the north. Here Lanzarote conceals its most spectacular volcanic landscapes below the earth's surface in the cave complexes of Cueva de los Verdes and Jameos del Agua.

These two natural curiosities lie close together near the east coast and are the products of much older volcanic eruptions than those that shaped Timanfaya National Park.

Cueva de los Verdes was formed by explosive gases which, trying to escape from beneath the lava filling a dry river bed, forced their way through a mile-long tunnel. The spectacular caverns that resulted were put to good use by the islanders.

These caves provided a refuge from Barbary raids more than 300 years ago. In the 20th century, Lanzarote has found an even better use for them having turned them into a premiere tourist attraction. The volcanic conduits of this group of caves are well worth seeing. With more than four miles (six km) of galleries, it is the longest known volcanic cave in the world.

Exploration of the main passageways is only in the company of a guide. Down underground the route has been imaginatively lit so as to bring out the full effect of the colourful and eccentric rock formations. The tour includes an unnerving and memorable optical illusion.

Cueva de los Verdes has unfortunately become the victim of its own success—the tour groups can be so large midway through the day as to become unmanageable in the narrow passageways. Check first for opening times and aim to arrive as soon as the caves open or just before they shut so as to miss the crowds.

Jameos del Agua, a much shorter cavern nearer the sea, was formed in a slightly different way. Sea water rushing into a white-hot molten fissure built up such a head of steam that it blew off the stone "cork", opening the cavern to daylight. The salt water remained as a still lagoon.

Unlike Cueva de los Verdes, Jameos del Agua bears the unmistakable mark of César Manrique's work. Between 1965 and 1968 he turned the lava grotto of Jameos into a friendly oasis. In 1976 he added to his good work by designing the auditorium, which is used to stage concerts. It can seat 800 people and combines excellent acoustics with unique natural surroundings.

Jameos Del Agua is guaranteed to bring out the troglodyte in visitors. Don't be put off by the uninspiring surroundings and presentation; even after you pay your entry fee the wooden door next to the ticket booth doesn't give anything away, but once through that door you will find that your mood will change.

During the day, subterranean music provides an eerie and ethereal greeting on the descent down into a gaping cavern. Above, a red canopy stretches across this unlikely hole in the ground to keep out the invading sunlight. As you descend into the half light, you pass through a neatly arranged bar and restaurant. Nothing unusual about that. Then four more short flights of steps take you down still further to a lower gallery and a deep, crystal clear lagoon. The trapped water glints—thanks to the many pesetas that have been thrown into it over the years. Cut off from the sea, small crabs (a distinct species called *Munidopsis polimorpha*), have made this watery cavern their home and over the passing centuries, away from daylight have become blind albinos.

Nature laid the foundations for Jameos del Agua and César Manrique enhanced its charm with some imaginative and understated interior design. A few well-positioned lights and some lush tropical plants make all the difference. More than 650 ft (200 metres) long, this volcanic gallery now provides a quiet, cool sanctuary from the heat outside.

The intention of the Jameos design—to create a feeling of magic and the supernatural—has worked. For proof, sit at the far end of the cave and watch the expressions of reverence as people descend the steps and catch their first glimpse of the shimmering lagoon. Even at night, when Jameos del Agua metamorphoses and becomes a disco, it's still a unique place.

church and the Palace of Spinola, where between 9 a.m. and about 3 p.m. a variety of offerings from fruit, jewellery and clothes to dried fish, paintings and crafts are on sale. You'll also see examples of Teguise's most famous product, the *timple*, a musical instrument like a ukelele.

Teguise gets its name from that of the daughter of the last native king of the island. She became the wife of Maciot de Béthencourt, nephew and successor to the conqueror. This small community marks the start of Lanzarote's Spanish colonial heritage—and there are still some distinctly colonial-style buildings left standing—though they are in a sorry state of repair.

On the southern edge of the town, for example, is the **Church of Santo Domingo**. In 1988 its exterior plaster was in need of renewal, its windows were smashed and an exterior stone carving above its eastern door was missing. Fortunately it has been earmarked for a 22 million peseta (£2 million) renovation programme.

Near the main square, the church of **Nuestra Señora de Guadalupe**, one of the oldest in the Canaries, is in much better condition. You can also visit the convents of **San Francisco** and **Vera Cruz**. All these buildings are usually locked and only opened on request.

El Meson de Paco, also near the square, illustrates how attractive the older buildings of Teguise can be when restored. This townhouse is said to be 250 years old; its owners have restored it to its original style. Downstairs there is a small art gallery, upstairs an excellent restaurant.

Northern palms: A line drawn across Lanzarote where it begins to narrow out into its northwest tip would roughly mark out the southern boundary of the municipality of Haria. Rising up from the northwestern shore is the **Famara Massif** and **Peñas del Chache**—at 2,198 ft (670 metres), Lanzarote's highest point. Drive around in this vicinity and you might well be up in the clouds—a reminder that, while it doesn't rain very often in Lanzarote,

ya
nara and
Famara
ssif.

there's nevertheless no shortage of moisture in the air.

One of the best viewpoints of these highlands is at **Ermita Las Nieves**, a neat and tidy whitewashed hermitage near the cliffs overlooking **Playa Famara**, the long, sandy beach below. If you prefer to experience Playa Famara from sea-level, double back to the Tiagua-Teguise road, from where Famara is signposted.

There is a wreck in the sea directly in front of the village of **Caleta**; the ill-fated ship was carrying a cargo of cement. The beaches here are much less crowded than elsewhere on the island and the sea here can be very rough, with severe undercurrents that can make swimming dangerous.

Another viewpoint is **Los Helechos**, a purpose-built restaurant overlooking the long valley of Tabayesco. From here the patchwork effect of the terraced fields sprinkled with volcanic ash is clearly visible, the working fields being a quite different shade of grey to those that are idle. The road forks here: you can follow the valley down past the small village of **Tabayesco** on to the main coast road from Guatiza to Arrieta; or you can stay in the highlands and drive on to **Haria**.

Much is made of Haria's "valley of 1,000 palms". Don't come here expecting suddenly to stumble onto a forest, though. Thanks to its elevation, this sprawling village can inject welcome splashes of green among its crisp white-washed houses, even in the driest parts of the year. It is said that the palm trees that spread out on the slopes of Haria's valley sides were once much more densely packed and that many were burnt down during Arraez Amurat's invasion of 1586.

In this island's bare and arid countryside, trees are worth making a fuss about. When Lanzarote's celebrated artist César Manrique is ready to open his house, Taro de Tahiche, to the public, he plans to make his new home in Haria, away from the worst excesses of the construction boom.

Tourist coaches conducting guided tours inevitably include Haria on their itineraries, but despite those attentions, this village perched up in Lanzarote's northwest corner is still unspoilt—a pristine symbol of how successfully the islanders can add beauty to their arid environment.

Crumbled giant: The volcanoes in this vicinity are more ancient than those of Timanfaya. Unlike the lava north of Yaiza, which geologically speaking belongs to yesterday, the *malpais* here has experienced erosion and is covered by thin mosses. The subtle change this brings to the landscape helps to make Lanzarote's northern tip look and feel substantially different to the southern part of the island.

The east coast road which runs from Orzola to Jameos del Agua crosses a great mass of this older lava which spewed forth from **Volcan de la Corona**. If you want to see La Corona close up you should continue on the road north out of Haria. At first sight from this side the mountain appears to be a perfect cone.

Just before the village of **Guinate**, park your car and, if you are wearing tough shoes or boots and have time and strength on your side, climb right up to the lip of the crater. From here you'll discover what is plain to anyone viewing the mountain from anywhere along the east coast above Jameos del Agua: La Corona is only half a cone—most of the eastern bulk of the mountain was lost long ago in its last almighty eruption. This exhausted giant, an awesome sight, accounts for the shape of much of the northeastern tip of the island.

Both Jameos del Agua and Cueva de los Verdes (see panel) are also the work of volcanic activity, tempered by the creative flair of César Manrique. The Jameos has been specially adapted and has an auditorium for 1,000 people.

On the other side of the island to these underground attractions is another example of Manrique's hand at work, this time high on the mountainside in the **Mirador del Rio**. This observation gallery is built into the cliffs overlooking the island of La Graciosa and the lesser islands beyond it. Wide and un-obstructed open space to view almost limitless horizons—this is the interior design message that Manrique has delivered. The bold interior of this lofty bar and restaurant is an appropriate response to the challenge of the splendid surroundings.

Up in the mountains, Mirador del Rio is the end of the road. Down below, however, Lanzarote's northernmost point is **Orzola**, a quiet and compact fishing village sitting in the shadow of the northern slopes. Journey's end is amply rewarded here with excellent seafood that includes prawns, octopus, mussels, lobster, grilled limpets, crab, grouper, sea bream, sea bass and even parrot fish. There are even quieter locations to be enjoyed still further north.

Island escape: If you really want to "get away from it all" in Lanzarote, you can leave the island altogether and spend a restful day on **La Graciosa**, which is part of the municipality of Teguise. A small boat will ferry you across from Orzola in the morning and bring you back in the evening.

The mile-wide channel separating this small island from Lanzarote is called **El Rio** (the river) and it was here that de Béthencourt first cast anchor. La Graciosa was the setting for a number of minor incidents during the early months of the conquest, and in the centuries that followed, it has been an outpost of Canarian life offering both visitors and residents sand, silence and solitude.

At one time the people of La Graciosa lived from fish alone and it wasn't until a philanthropic Captain-General of the Canaries named Garcia divided the land up among the people (he also gave them a dozen camels) that La Graciosa's peasants were allowed to profitably farm their island.

La Graciosa seems a thousand miles from Costa Teguise, though in reality it's barely a 30-minute drive away. The island's relatively undisturbed existence is a measure of how rampant the developers are on Lanzarote. If one day you spy a hotel or a timeshare complex on La Graciosa from the distant heights of Mirador del Rio, it will be a sad turning point.

*ciosa
*nd and
*io.

TENERIFE AND THE WESTERN ISLES

The Western province of the autonomous region of the Canary Islands, comprising the islands of Tenerife, La Palma, Gomera and Hierro, boasts a greener and more hospitable landscape than in the eastern islands as described elsewhere in this book.

At one time these islands were the last outpost of the known world, and it is for that reason that the island of Hierro was used by geographers as the axis of the first meridian, since relocated to run through Greenwich. From these islands the explorer Christopher Columbus stepped off into the unknown and discovered America.

Inter-island rivalry in the Canaries is intense, but nowhere is it more intense than between the two leader-islands, Gran Canaria and Tenerife. These two have fought over the captaincy of the archipelago for centuries, with Tenerife having the better of the past couple of centuries, although Gran Canaria is currently in the ascendancy as the seat of the autonomous government.

Such is the rivalry that residents of each island will often go out of their way to avoid having to go to the other, and agencies that function in one province often do not in the other. Government offices are in Gran Canaria, shipping business is in Gran Canaria, and regional television is in Gran Canaria, but the university is in Tenerife; the latter became such a subject of debate (Las Palmas wants its own university) that it caused the collapse of the autonomous government in 1988.

The islanders know instinctively whether a newcomer is a pure outsider or from a rival island. One resident tells the story of the Tinerfeño (Tenerife islander) barber who travelled over to Gran Canaria only once, a decade ago, and went into a barber's shop for a haircut to see how it was done there. Just as he was preparing to sit down he overheard the barber mutter something about the smell of sardines (Tenerife has a festival featuring the mock burial of a sardine). The Tinerfeño stormed out, and hasn't been back to Gran Canaria since that day.

Tenerife: The largest of the islands (794 sq miles, 2,057 sq km), Tenerife has a population of 600,000, and a significant number of foreign residents, particularly English, Germans and Indians. Perhaps it is because of this, and because the island's mountain, Teide (12,188 ft/3,715 metres) is the highest point in the whole of Spain, that Tenerife is the most widely known of all the Canary Islands.

Certainly it was a combination of expatriate residents and the lure of the mountain that drew the earliest tourists, and climbing expeditions arrived to conquer the European Everest as early at the 17th century. The Orotava valley and Puerto de la Cruz (or Puerto Orotava, as it was known then) was the centre of this early tourism. The Hotel Taoro (now a casino) was Spain's largest when it was built in 1892.

Although the town of Orotava itself has remained much the same, and is one

of the most attractive on the whole Canary Islands, the valley has much changed since the day in 1799 when the German naturalist Alexander von Humboldt turned the corner to be greeted by "the most enchanting view that eyes have ever seen." Humboldt's corner is now a viewpoint, but the former carpet of careful agriculture that he must have looked down upon is now covered in a netting of roads and urbanisations that are spreading and spreading through the banana plantations.

The sea of this northern coast is rough and wild, and Puerto is not the ideal place for a sea-resort; consequently the town has built a complex of swimming pools known as the Lido Martianez, designed by Lanzarote artist César Manrique, which juts out into the sea. Despite this, and despite warning notices, the sea regularly sweeps tourists off the mole at the fishing harbour.

There is so much greenery and mist in the northern part of the island that it would be natural to expect the *barrancos* (ravines) to flow with water as they once must have done. However these days the water is syphoned off for man's use far higher up the mountainside, and the demands on it are extreme: new resort towns such as Los Cristianos and Playa de las Américas (1.6 million tourists a year, giving the island an annual turnover of £80,000 per metre of beach) on the otherwise uninteresting southern coast demand great quantities of fresh water, most of which has to be piped from the north. As yet there are no desalination plants on Tenerife as there are on Gran Canaria.

Tenerife's main town, Santa Cruz, is a far more friendly and pleasant place than the city of Las Palmas on Gran Canaria, although it is far smaller and quieter. Its port, although extensive and well-protected, was always in the shadow of that on Gran Canaria, and the shopping centres do not have such a wealth of goods as in Las Palmas.

Santa Cruz is also in the shadow of the Anaga mountains, a rugged ridge that completes the northern tip of the island. Excellent for walking, the Anaga vil-

Los Cristianos, Tenerife's beach resort.

lages are still very traditional, complete with cave houses. The Anaga is mirrored on the western end of the island in the Teno hills, which also look inhospitable but conceal tiny villages.

The high-point, literally and metaphorically, of Tenerife is of course Mount Teide, whose peak is now easily reached by way of good roads, a cable-car, and a 20-minute scramble. Teide is a volcano which has been dormant since 1798. It is surrounded by an enormous crater-bowl called Las Cañadas, which forms the main part of Teide's National Park. Las Cañadas contains some unusual rock forms, rock colourations and plants and a government-run *parador* and visitors' centre.

La Palma: The fifth largest island in the Canaries (281 sq miles, 728 sq km), La Palma has retained much of its population (now 72,000), largely because of its continued suitability for agriculture. It is the greenest and the most varied of the islands, and its principal town, Santa Cruz de la Palma, is particularly attractive, with long streets of Canarian balconies and colonial architecture. It also has a massive cement model of the *Santa Maria*, a ship in the fleet led by Columbus, who never set foot on La Palma.

The island is very steep, rising to a high-point of 7,959 ft (2,426 metres) at the **Roque de los Muchachos**, but falling sharply to the sea most of the way around the coast. Here there are bays of black sand, particularly at Puerto Naos on the western coast.

Much of the northern part of the island is occupied by the **Caldera de Taburiente**, one of the largest volcanic craters in the world at 5.5 miles (nine km) in diameter. The Caldera is a national park administered by ICONA, and is excellent for walking. On the crater rim near the Roque de los Muchachos is the **Observatorio de Astrofisica**, an observatory shared by several European countries, here because of the particularly clear skies. On a good night it is possible to distinguish car headlights moving along the coast of Tenerife, 60 miles (96 km) away.

Palma's
dera de
uriente.

La Palma was the scene of the most recent volcanic activity in the Canaries, when in 1971 an eruption in the side of the old volcano of San Antonio formed a new cone, the Volcan de Teneguia, which still smokes gently to this day. Postcards depicting volcanic eruptions on the Canaries are usually from photographs taken of this explosion.

Gomera: Distinguished by being Columbus's chosen stepping off point for the New World in 1492, things have changed little in Gomera since then; the sixth largest island is the only one not to have its own airport. Gomera (146 sq miles/378 sq km) has a population of 20,000, unfairly derided by other Canarios as being stupid. Like the smaller island of Hierro, Gomera has been the scene of massive depopulation in the last centuries thanks to lack of work opportunities, and it is the most traditional and less ambitious who stay behind, thus the jokes.

The Gomeran must have a curious impression of tourists, who divide into two categories; those who come over in fast-moving bus-loads on the ferry from Los Cristianos (Tenerife), the only frequent transport link with the outside world, and those who come over with packs on their backs and a few pesetas in their pockets. The former are daytrippers who come over on the morning ferry, whirl around the island, buy up the handicrafts, and disappear back over the 20 miles (32 km) of water to Tenerife on the last ferry of the evening. The backpackers (principally German-speaking) drift off any old ferry, sit on their packs in the main square of San Sebastian (the principal town and port) for a couple of hours and debate their next move.

Many of these tourists stay for periods of months at a time, particularly in the winter. Traditionally they congregate in the Valle Gran Rey, a deep and luxuriant valley on the south-eastern corner of the island, where every house seems to be for rent. They are also beginning to spread to Santiago, the sunniest spot on the island and the site of Gomera's only resort hotel, the up-

Traveller about to embark fo **Gomera.**

market Hotel Tecina.

The island rises to its highest point (Mount Garajonay, 4,879 ft/1,487 metres) almost at its centre. Six principal valleys or *barrancos* descend from this high ground to the sea. Most of the southern slopes, particularly around San Sebastian and Santiago, are depressingly barren, but the central high ground and the northern valleys, particularly that of Hermigua, are green, damp and lush.

In the centre of the island is the Garajonay National Park, a large area composed mainly of ancient tertiary era forest, with moss-cloaked laurel and cedar trees. The forest (declared a heritage of mankind by UNESCO) is threaded by many forest tracks, excellent for walking.

The *parador* (state-run hotel) in San Sebastian is one of the most atmospheric in the Canaries, and its gardens are the most likely place to hear *Silbo*, an ancient whistling language exclusive to the island, practiced by Gomerans to communicate across the *barrancos*.

Silbo has all but died out, but the *parador's* gardeners still maintain the tradition as they go about their work.

Hierro: The smallest of the Canaries (107 sq miles/277 sq km) Hierro is also the most backward and the least populated (6,000 inhabitants). On the map it looks like the clumsily chipped flint of an aboriginal tool, which is appropriate enough. Cattle and livestock farming are the mainstay of the community, with excellent walled pastures of the Nisdafe tableland near San Andrés in the centre of the island.

Like La Palma, Hierro also had its own massive crater of which the bay of El Golfo was part; the remainder of the rim has since disappeared under the sea. El Golfo remains a sheltered, calm spot, and is the centre of the island's wine-growing industry. Wine from Hierro is reckoned the best in the islands.

The island's principal town, Valverder (literally "green valley"), is now the only Canary Island capital inland, indicative of the fact that Hierro has always had greater stress on its agriculture than on seaborne trade. The second town, Frontera, has an unusual church with the bell-tower some distance from the church building on top of a small hill, so that its chimes could be clearly heard far and wide.

Hierro has its own peculiar trees to match the dragon trees on Tenerife; for decades great mythology surrounded a *garoe* or water tree north of San Andres, said to rain down water from its leaves. The myth was probably due to the island's many mists condensing on the tree and dripping down; it has since been replaced by a very ordinary looking lime. By contrast, the trees at Sabinosa, *Juniperus sabina*, have been much battered, twisted and wizened by the wind and barely look like trees at all.

Hierro's beaches are along the southern, inaccessible coastline of El Julan. Here too are the inscriptions known as Los Letreros, a primitive script carved into a rock face.

Tourism on the island is still very limited, so limited in fact that Hierro has a tiny hotel on the quay at Las Puntas, with only four rooms.

GOING TO AFRICA

Although politically part of Spain since the early 16th century, the Canary Islands are geographically part of northwest Africa. This is particularly true of Fuerteventura, the second island of the archipelago in size and the closest to the African coast—just 60 miles (100 km) away. It and, to a lesser extent, the other islands are geologically similar to the desert regions and Atlas mountains of the north and west of Africa.

Unsurprisingly, therefore, many of the customs and even the physique of the islands' first inhabitants, the Guanches, are closely related to the indigenous inhabitants of what is nowadays Morocco, Algeria and Mauritania. Theories abound concerning the original settlers, but it is believed that a Berber tribe, possibly one known as the Canarii, came to the islands from North Africa 6,000 years ago following the decay of local regions of forest and vegetation.

This belief is supported by the appearance of the Guanches and the Canarii, (tall and with a fair complexion), the similarity of language and symbols, worship and burial habits, animal and crop husbandry, tools and weapons.

However, the Canarian Stone Age ended in 1496, with the conquest of Guanche Tenerife by the Spanish under Alonso Fernández de Lugo (the latter's first attempt to subdue the natives of Tenerife failed at the village of La Matanza, "the massacre", but succeeded three years later at what is now appropriately called La Victoria).

With the Canaries firmly under Spanish control—the vanquished Guanches were even baptised and given Christian names—contact with Africa largely disappeared as the axis shifted 700 miles (1,100 km) northwards to Cadiz and Seville in southern Spain. It was not long, however, before the conquistadores were annexing parts of Africa for the Spanish Empire; Ceuta and Melilla, enclaves on the north coast of Morocco

still governed today from Madrid as well as Spanish Sahara, a vast area of desert over 100,000 sq miles (160,000 sq km), ceded by Spain to Morocco in the mid-1970s.

Since then Morocco, Mauritania and the Polisario Front have been arguing about—among other things—who should have the right to mine the rich phosphate deposits near El Aiún, the former capital of the Spanish Sahara.

Hopefully, gone are the days when Moroccan gunboats machine-gunned Spanish (especially Canarian) fishing boats which strayed too close to the Moroccan coastline. Only recently have relations improved sufficiently between Spain and Morocco for official regular sea and air communications to be re-established.

Getting there: Royal Air Maroc and Iberia are the main air carriers. From Las Palmas de Gran Canaria (Gando Airport) RAM has flights to Agadir (Wednesdays), Casablanca (Mondays, Wednesdays and Fridays), Marrakesh (Wednesdays), Oujda (Wednesdays) and Tan Tan (Fridays).

The Spanish state airline, Iberia, operates to Abidjan on the Ivory Coast on Sundays, to Dakar in Senegal every Monday and Friday and to Melilla each Monday, Friday, Saturday and Sunday. All these flights operate from Tenerife South (Reina Sofía Airport).

From Las Palmas de Gran Canaria Iberia has departures to Dakar on Mondays, Wednesdays and Fridays; to Abidjan on Sundays; to Melilla every day of the week except Tuesdays and Wednesdays; to Nouakchott in Mauritania each Tuesday, Thursday and Saturday; and to Noudhibou in Mauritania, on Tuesdays and Saturdays. Royal Air Maroc also operates flights to Abidjan, to Libreville in Gabon and Malabo in Equatorial Guinea, all on a Sunday and all departing from Gando Airport in Gran Canaria.

So much for flying there. The only regular passenger boat service (some cargo boats have limited passenger accommodation but are infrequent) is by Compañía Marroquí de Navegación with its car ferry *Rif* sailing weekly Las

Palmas-Agadir-Las Palmas, the one-way journey taking 18 hours. The company hopes that it will be able to extend this service to other ports on the Moroccan coast soon.

Further information on this can be obtained in Las Palmas from Guillermo Sintes Reyes SA Calle Artemi Semidan N. 11, 3rd floor (Tel. 277153/277208/ 274114); in Agadir—Comanav, Boulevard Mohamed V, BP 201 (Tel. (8) 20446/20452/20646); in Casablanca—Comanav Casablanca, 7 Boulevard de la Résistance (Tel. 302412/301825); in Paris—SNCM Paris, 12 rue Godot de Mauroy 75009 (Tel. (1) 4266-6019); or through Viajes Martin Travel Las Palmas Tel. 222500/04/08; Puerto de la Cruz, Tenerife Tel. 387209/387112/ 387197; Puerto del Carmen, Lanzarote Tel. 825925/826527; and finally in Fuerteventura Tel. 876326/876349.

Travel wisdom: Briefly, the places mentioned have something to recommend to those wanting a holiday with a difference, but take care with money and valuables (as always) especially in potentially dangerous places such as the densely crowded alleys and the markets or *souks*.

Geographically the nearest to the Canaries, Morocco is probably the likeliest destination with Marrakesh, Casablanca, Agadir and El Aiún on travel agents' lists for short package holidays. But further afield, Dakar in Senegal, Libreville in Gabon, Abidjan on the Ivory Coast and Malabo in Equatorial Guinea are worth visiting and can easily be reached by air either from Tenerife or Las Palmas.

Coming from northwest Africa to the Canaries are three unwelcome visitors. Locusts, fortunately, are infrequent and short-lived, although recent years have seen an increase in their numbers; the *Scirocco* (fine wind-borne sand and dust) which covers everything, even indoors, and which visits the islands four or five times a year, and lasts between a day and a week; the *Calina*, sand in suspension, is also an African export and hangs heavily over the islands for periods of up to several days, seriously limiting visibility.

227

The late 1980s have been untypical in so far as items in the news are concerned. Politics are not the islanders' favourite topic in the press or in conversation, but in the late 1980s political issues surfaced more often in newspapers than usual because of a resurgence of inter-province rivalry. The debate was prompted by Gran Canaria's intention to have its own university rather than share the Universidad de la Laguna, established in Tenerife in 1774.

Tinerfeños believe that a second university in such a small region is not only unnecessary but detrimental, as the cost of two universities in the Canary Islands will impoverish both. The issue caused a change of presidents in the Canary Islands Autonomous Government and a major political crisis. This issue might yet cause a split of the present single Canary Islands Government into two separate Autonomous Governments—a really ridiculous situation.

Media: The average islander does not read the newspapers at all. Literacy is not all that high and perhaps only 38 percent of the population reads a newspaper, and even less a book.

How many of the population watch television and listen to the radio is difficult to assess, but almost certainly the vast majority gather news from those media alone. The island newspapers do not attempt to compete for international news with the mainland press. Those interested enough in the latter subject buy *El Pais*, a bulky daily flown in from Madrid and even so costing less than the local papers.

Major international events are reported in the local press, but in succinct form usually on an inner page. All papers devote more space to local sports—wrestling, basketball and especially soccer. Bullfighting is not included for the simple reason that it no longer takes place on these islands, having given way to soccer, and being too expensive to arrange.

Festivals of every sort and kind, be they

village or town affairs or the hugely important *Carnaval* are a favourite topic of conversation, covered extensively by the press. *Carnaval* exceeds all else in terms of column-inches, in daily reports and special supplements, before, during and after the annual event. The time, effort and money spent on Carnaval in these islands is enormous. If the same effort was expended on business or industrial activity the Canaries would probably be top of the EEC's economic league.

Bar talk: The topics of conversations in bars depend on the type of bar and its location. In the wine shops or *ventas* in the country districts it is probable that the potato crop will be the most frequent topic. Potatoes of many excellent varieties are grown here and harvested up to four times a year, and the subject comes up in conversations in unexpected places, such as ladies' hairdressing salons, elegant dinner tables and cocktail parties. *Papas* and their prices are discussed in the latter places as ardently as stock prices in the City of London.

In more sophisticated places such as *tapas* bars in Santa Cruz or Las Palmas you might

Preceding pages: dancing in the Pueblo Canario; crowded café in Lanzarote. Left and right, agriculture is still a prime topic of conversation.

hear the latest jokes about Gomerans, the undeserved butt of jokes, rather as the Irish are in the UK and the Belgians in Europe. "Why does a Gomeran keep an empty bottle in his fridge? To cater for visitors who do not drink." Or, "Why is cold milk not available on Gomera? Because the Gomeran cannot fit his cow into his refrigerator".

The name of a recent cabinet minister gave rise to a constant string of Moronic/Moranic jokes told amongst the more educated society. One concerned his reply to a journalist's question about the Israeli position at an international conference in Madrid; the minister said it gave his wife hiccups.

One might expect tourism to be a frequent

The break-down of nationalities visiting the islands is often reported in the press. It may surprise many British visitors who feel themselves heavily outnumbered by Germans, (the latter somehow manage to get into the hotel lifts and swimming pool sunbeds first) that they, the Brits, outnumber the Germans and other nationalities by a considerable margin in all the islands except Fuerteventura, where the Germans win.

Crime: Drugs, robberies and traffic accidents are frequent, if not daily issues in the newspapers. These islands, because of their Free Port status and their strategic position are naturally attractive to the drug dealers. The large number of foreign visitors and

subject of conversation or press comment amongst the inhabitants of these tourist-supported islands. Travel agents, hotel managers and car-hire operators may discuss the matter, but the general public seldom bothers with the topic unless it is to comment upon the latest barbarity committed by the lager louts in Playa de las Americas or Playa del Inglés. The newspapers carry occasional statistics on visitors to the islands—a continual breaking of records. Timeshare, which seems to be considered to have negative effects on the tourist trade because all payments are made outside the islands, is a fairly frequent topic.

Spain's very lenient anti-drug laws are other attractions for the dealers—almost amounting to an invitation. In one court case in Tenerife a young English heroin addict called the islands "Heroin Paradise" which, thank God, it is not.

Theft is commonplace here, especially in those urbanisations with numerous temporarily absent foreign residents. The police tend to get bored with so many reports and with catching the same delinquents at regular intervals.

There has been a very steep rise in the

Above, discussing the latest—in the shade.

WATER

The so-called Fortunate Isles (an early name for the Canaries) have their problems, not least of which is water. Nearly 2,000 years ago, Plutarch wrote that the islands "enjoy a fortunate climate in consequence of the mingling and the barely perceptible change of the seasons." This predictable climate may be good for tourism, but it isn't for agriculture. Blessed with sunshine the islands may be throughout the year, but blessed with water they are not.

It was not always thus. One of the characteristics of the islands, the deep, gorged, *barrancos* or ravines which cut through the volcanic rock were originally carved out by millions upon millions of tons of water crashing down to the sea, and stones which have been polished by thousands of years of water are aplenty at the foot of *barranco* walls. But since then the world's climate has changed, and is still changing.

The eastern islands— particularly Fuerteventura and Lanzarote—bear the brunt of the water shortage, with the more mountainous western islands receiving triple their amount of rainfall.

Puerto de la Cruz on Tenerife has an annual average of 75 days of rain; Maspalomas on Gran Canaria has only 15. The island of La Palma has the most rainfall, and that of Fuerteventura the least. Being considerably lower than the other islands, Fuerteventura cannot provoke the passing clouds to get rid of their rain, and there are places on all three islands in the eastern province where evidence of the existence of water is scant, other than in resort swimming pools.

Ground water, much of which condenses in the form of dew rather than falling as rain, is extracted by means of wells and *galerías*, the latter being tunnels bored into the rock to tap underground sources where the water has soaked through the porous volcanic rock and come to rest on an impermeable shelf of stone below. Few of the islands' dried-up river beds ever run, and when they do the water sometimes only flows a few hundred yards before disappearing back into the dry and stony ground.

There is only limited state involvement in the supply of water. Unlike mainland Spain, where a nationalised water industry operates, most of this precious liquid on the islands is privately owned by the landowners who operate their own wells or *galerías* and sell to farmers or industry on a basis of the number of hours of supply.

Pipelines run the length of the islands, delivering water from the north, where rain falls infrequently, to the south, where it hardly falls at all.

This cottage industry, where the water is largely in the hands of small farmers, has always been a contentious issue, and in 1985 it caused the toppling of the socialist party in power in the autonomous government: the socialists had supported an unpopular Water Law passed on mainland Spain, which may well have been appropriate to that society where services are nationalised, but was not appropriate to the Canaries where the industry is privatised.

The quality of the water supply is also problematic. With the constant lowering of the water table to below sea-level the supply is beginning to be brackish and salty, unpleasant to taste. Tourism has taken a heavy toll on the supply. The cost of water is a major factor in the realisation of many tourist developments, some of which ensure their own supply through purification and desalination plants.

Much of the Gran Canaria tap supply comes from the massive seawater desalination plant on the shore just south of Las Palmas; it's hard to believe, passing this monster, pumping out soot and smoke through day and night, that visitors and residents alike are meant to drink its product. Desalinated water does not lather well with soap, is unpleasant to taste, and is generally a poor substitute for the real thing.

For drinking purposes islanders and visitors would do best to stick to bottled water, such as the popular Firgas which comes from a natural spring in the mountains of Gran Canaria.

Until a couple of centuries ago the islanders of Hierro, an island in the western province, believed that their sacred Garoe tree was able to produce water, but the tree in question has since blown down and it took its secret with it.

number of fatal traffic accidents over the last two or three years as also in the number of vehicles on the road (7,000 new cars every month). The roads themselves are quite good; it is speed, inexperience, drink or drugs that causes most of these fatal accidents, occurring usually during the early hours of weekend mornings. In Tenerife alone, 140 people, most of them under 25, died in car and motorcycle accidents in 1988, a frightful figure for a small population.

Environment: The poorly-understood subject of ecology comes up when new urbanisations or hotel buildings begin—a pretty frequent occurrence in the south of Tenerife and Gran Canaria these days. It is also a topic

when, with unwelcome regularity each summer, forest fires break out in the lovely forests of Gomera, La Palma, Tenerife or Gran Canaria. Many hundreds of hectares of pine forest have been ravaged by fires in the last few years, and a big one in Gomera in 1984 claimed the lives of 21 people, including the newly appointed Civil Governor of Tenerife Province who, tragically, put politics before safety.

The only satisfactory outcome of these disastrous fires is that they increase membership in the ecological groups.

While the development of a barren, arid wasteland in the south of an island might cause an uproar of protest, nothing is said, and far less is done to stop the uncontrolled, unplanned and unlicensed construction of cement-block houses on the fringes of towns and villages on all the islands. Politics is the reason why a blind eye is turned to these real eyesores on the landscape, as more residents mean more votes for the councillor who looks the other way.

Separatism: Independence is a word appearing often in the newspapers and in graffiti messages sprayed on walls. Its meaning is often misunderstood by visitors who see it as a desire on the part of the islanders to separate from Mother Spain. There does exist a small group of radicals who desire complete independence from Spain on ethnic grounds. This group was originally represented by MPAIC established in 1963, today calling itself AWANAK, whose initials translate roughly as "The Canary Islands Popular Front" written in the ancient Guanche language.

The symbol or logo-type displayed by this party is the spiral labyrinth, and this can sometimes be seen accompanying a written invitation to *godos* (the nickname for the Peninsular Spaniard) to go back to the mainland. The uninitiated visitor who thinks he's in Spain is completely bewildered when he sees an occasional message written in English which says "Spanish Go Home".

The other meaning of independence, used in the title of some local political parties, is independence from any of the main peninsula-based parties such as the Spanish Labour Party (PSOE), the Alliance of Conservative parties (AP), the Liberal Party, or the left-of-centre Social Democrat party (CDS).

The Association of Independents of Tenerife (ATI), of Canary Independents (ACI), and of the independents from Hierro, are not separatists. They want to establish their own identities in the same way as the Catalans, Basques, and Andalucians.

A final warning to innocent visitors to these islands (and to mainland Spain for that matter): beware of the newspapers and stories you may read or hear on 28 December, the day of the Holy Innocents. This is Spain's April Fools Day, when the newspapers publish elaborate hoaxes.

Left, the roads are improving, but the drivers may not be. Right, an islander on Lanzarote.

FLORA AND FAUNA

At first sight, to the casual observer, the Canarian flora is one of large-flowered spectacular shrubs of hibiscus, bougainvillea, lantana and acacia. All these, however, are exotic species introduced to the archipelago from other tropical and subtropical regions of the world. They are the plants and flowers of public parks and hotel gardens in tourist areas, a domain into which only a very few indigenous Canarian plants such as the statice or siempreviva (*Limonium arborescens*) and the Paris daisy or margaritas (*Argyranthemum winteri*) are able to penetrate.

A second flora of unique and interesting native species also exists. This is mainly away from hotels and beaches but easily accessible to the well-informed excursionist exploring the remoter areas of the islands.

The members of this flora form the major vegetation zones of the islands, the dry *tabaibales* (spurge-bush scrubland) and semi-deserts of the scrub coastal zones; the forests of the moist northern slopes, the pine woodlands of drier mountain regions and the spectacular mountain vegetation of the highest volcanic peaks, perhaps the most distinctive landscape of the Canaries.

Even though these vegetation types are found throughout the Canaries there is a sharp botanical contrast between the western and eastern provinces of the archipelago, with the central island of Gran Canaria more or less intermediate between the two extremes.

Lanzarote and Fuerteventura, which lie closest to the African coast, have a semi-desert flora very similar to that of the western fringes of the Sahara desert and the impression of a desert landscape is greatly enhanced on Fuerteventura by the sand-dune systems at Matas Blancas on the Jandia isthmus and at the Dunas de Corralejo natural park on the northeast corner of the island.

In the "moon-scape" volcanic scenery of the National Park at Timanfaya on Lanzarote plants are generally conspicuous by their absence and found only in small havens of

sparse vegetation known as *islotes* amongst the barren lava, thus enhancing the sensation of desert. Timanfaya is largely off-limits for the visitor, however, who has to stick to proscribed roads and paths.

Fuerteventura: The island has not always been such a dry, barren place. Thanks to the best efforts of man, his omnivorous and rapacious domestic goats and his need for fuel-wood the former thickets of *Pistacia* trees and wild olives have been destroyed and the vegetation altered to its present semi-

desert scrub form.

The landscape of the island is dominated by low, heavily eroded, rolling hills sparsely covered with succulent-leaved salt bush and the barbed wire-like aulaga with Canary palms and tamarix shrubs in the beds of dry, ephemeral streams. The cliffs and peaks of the southern Jandía region, however, are high enough to intercept the trade-wind clouds and the moist north-faces are home for several very localised rare species of viper's bubloss (*Echium handiense*) and Paris daisy (*Argyranthemum winteri*).

On the south slopes of Jandía one of the rarest Canarian plants, the Cardón de Jandía, a cactus-like spurge (*Euphorbia handiensis*) is found. This plant has its closest relatives on the western edge of the Sahara between the Anti-Atlas and the Moroccan coast along with several other Fuerteventura plants such as botonera (*Asteriscus schultzii*) and rare, tree-like sow-thistle (*Sonchus pinnatifidus*), which also occurs on Lanzarote as well as on the North African coast.

Lanzarote: With its extensive areas of recent lava and cinder fields, many of them only in the initial processes of colonisation by plants, Lanzarote is superficially uninteresting from a botanical point of view. There are, however, a few areas, particularly towards the north of the island, where the the Hermita of Las Nieves and the high cliffs near Mirador del Rio, the restaurant and viewpoint designed by César Manrique.

Gran Canaria: Unlike Lanzarote and Fuerteventura, Gran Canaria is an island of considerable contrasts, ranging from sand-dunes in the extreme south through xerophytic vegetation often resembling that of the eastern islands to pine forest and mountain vegetation in the centre of the island. In addition it has a few relict patches of humid laurel forests which still survive precariously on the northern slopes.

The coastal plant communities are similar to those of the eastern islands with a number of rare local endemics in isolated areas such

vegetation is more luxuriant. The palm-groves of the valley of Haría and the *tabaibales* (spurge-covered scrubland) covering the old lava of the *malpais* La Corona are quite rich in local species but the floristic centre of Lanzarote is located on the slopes and cliffs of the Famara Massif.

In this area virtually all the endemic species of the island are found including two species of siempreviva or statice (*Limonium arborescens*) a very decorative yellow flowered daisy bush (*Argyranthemum ochroleucum*) and a host of cliff plants occurring nowhere else on the planet. Many of these can be seen on the rocks surrounding as Arinaga or Melenara.

The succulent spurge vegetation, especially the candelabra spurge *Euphorbia canariensis* with four-sided stems, is dominant over extensive areas of the south. Usually it is interspersed with palm-groves in side-valleys such as at Fataga, Artenara and Los Palmitos.

Higher up the mountain slopes the palms and candelabra spurges merge into a pine forest zone in which a single, endemic pine species (*Pinus canariensis*) is dominant. The Canary pine is an ancient species, fossils of which have been found in the Mediterranean region from Pliocene deposits over two million years old. Its nearest living relative occurs in the Himalaya region and this suggests that both are the last survivors of a massive warm temperate pine belt which once extended right across the Mediterranean region and the Near and Middle East, before the world's climate changed.

Fine examples of Canary pine can be seen at Pilancones and at the Mirador de Los Pinos de Galdar. The pine is very fire-resistant because it evolved in a volcanic environment and the heart wood (Tea) provides an excellent timber for construction work.

Several other species including a shrubby pink rock-rose (*Cistus symphytifolius*) and various forms of bird's-foot trefoil (*Lotus*

(*Sideritis* species), strongly scented thyme-like *Micromeria* species, and the alehli or wild Canarian wall flower, one of the most common species of all, along with the dwarf yellow broom (*Teline microphylla*) which is the dominant plant over large areas of the mountain slopes.

Below the pine forests on the northern slopes of the island is an area of intensive agriculture which occupies the rich soils of the former laurel forest zone. Very little (probably less than five percent) of the original forest still survives and even this is in a rather degraded form. A few very rare local species such as the orange-flowered foxglove (*Isoplexis chalcantha*) and *Sideritis*

species) are important elements of the pine forest community. Bird's-foot trefoil species occur in almost all habitats on Gran Canaria from the coast to the highest mountains and are absent only from the more humid laurel forests. Many of them are highly appreciated as forage plants.

Above the pine forests, the high mountain zone with its deeply eroded landscape has been described as a petrified storm and in spring and early summer the area is covered by a host of wild flowers such as wild sage

Hardy plants. Left, a cochineal cactus in bloom, and above, the Canary pine.

discolor, a member of the sage family, still survive in the small pocket of forest at Los Tilos de Moya in an area now protected as a nature reserve.

Birds, bees and bats: As on most oceanic islands, birds, reptiles and insects are the main faunistic elements to have successfully colonised the Canarian archipelago. All the modern mammals other than bats appear to have been introduced by man, though recent finds of fossilised bones of a large rat-like creature suggest that perhaps some mammals may have reached the islands before humans. Quite how they arrived is a subject for speculation.

Currently, brown and black rats, mice and rabbits are widespread and the North African hedgehog has reached all the islands except La Palma. Amongst the most interesting mammals, however, are the recently discovered nocturnal shrew which is probably more common than previously thought, and the North African ground squirrel which was introduced to the island of Fuerteventura as a single pair in 1965 and is now one of the most common animals on the island living amongst rocks, stones and in stone walls. In fact the squirrel is rapidly becoming a problem for the farmers who already have the sufficiently difficult task of cultivating the poor land on the island.

The birds of the Canary Islands can be divided into two groups: the resident, breeding ones of which there are about 70 species, and the regular or occasional non-breeding visitors which number about 200. Some of the residents have become very well adapted to living in the urban environment of the main tourist centres and can frequently be seen amongst the hibiscus hedges and palms of hotel and public gardens. These include the ubiquitous chiff-chaff, blackcaps, blue tits and warblers as well as the Spanish sparrow and recently arrived green-finch.

In contrast, however, other birds are much more rare and only occasionally seen. The most interesting of these are the houbara bustard of the flat, rolling plains of Fuerteventura, a species now recovering after many years of persecution by hunters, and the blue chaffinch and spotted woodpecker of the pine forests of Gran Canaria. The blue chaffinch, which occurs only in the Canary Islands, is a shy bird feeding mainly on pine-seeds and hiding away in the remotest parts of the centre of the island. Only the most dedicated of watchers will ever see it.

Equally shy and difficult to observe is the Fuerteventura chat found only in palm and tamarisk thickets in dry stream beds particularly on the eastern side of the island (Puerto de la Peña, Barranco de Esquinzo). This native species is related to the European winchat and stone chat which are also very occasional visitors to the island.

Two species of frogs are native to the Canaries and are found on all three islands in the eastern province, Lanzarote, Fuerteventura and Gran Canaria. The small green tree frog (*Hyla meridionalis*) is sometimes encountered in humid corners of hotel gardens whereas the common brown frog (*Rana perezil*) lives close to pools, water tanks or permanent streams.

Small geckos of the genus *Tarentola* occur on all the islands and are usually seen at night hunting mosquitos. On Gran Canaria skinks (*Chalcides* species) are common and frequently found basking on walls on sunny days. The skink from the south of the island is remarkable for its bright metallic blue-green tail. Wall lizards of up to 24 ins (60 cm) (*Gallotia* species) are ubiquitous on Gran Canaria but rather rare on Lanzarote and Fuerteventura, where the much smaller *Gallotia atlantica* occurs.

The invertebrate fauna of all three islands is very rich with a myriad of small beetles, grasshoppers, Mantis species as well as butterflies and moths. Most notable amongst the latter group are the large monarch butterflies which are commonly seen even in city gardens; the day-flying, hummingbird hawkmoth often seen hovering amongst nectar-bearing flowers and the nocturnal death's head hawkmoth whose lava frequently occurs on garden plants such as bignonia and datura.

Left, pigeons in Las Palmas. Right, Serinus canarius, or the Canary, by Marianne North.

THE VERDINO

About 2,000 years ago a galley loaded with explorers from Roman Mauritania reached Gran Canaria. The explorers found a fertile land with soaring mountains and exotic flowers and trees.... and dogs such as they had never seen before.

Dogs everywhere—slender, sinuous, tiger-striped. Dogs that were wild but not savage, intelligent, beautiful to look at, easy to train and quick to obey.

The explorers chose a pair of pups and took them back to King Juba II of Mauritania. The boy-king Juba had been educated in Rome and had returned home with a thirst for discovery which brought him fame, and it was he and his people who put the Canary Islands onto the map of the world with a name that has never changed—the island of *canes*, of dogs.

This theory of the naming of the islands is the most widely accepted by historians and scholars through the ages, starting with the Roman naturalist Pliny. There are other, less attractive theories. Thomas Nichols, the first Englishman to describe the islands, suggests that the islanders actually lived on dog flesh. Historian Francisco Gomara says there were no dogs at all when the conquistadores came from Spain, and that the island was named after a red grape *uva canina*.

The 19th-century Spanish writer and naturalist Viera y Clavijo had two theories; first, that the vassals of the Italian kings, Cranus and Crana, settled in one of the islands and named it Cranaria. His second was that Canarias derived its name from the Latin verbs *canere* or *cantare*, to sing, and that canary birds are thus responsible for the islands' naming. In addition many archaeologists now believe the name of the island group comes from a North African tribe, the Canarii, from whom the islanders are descended.

An awesome creature: The Canary mastiff, known as the Verdino (also called the Bardino, the letters V and B being almost interchangeable in Spanish) because of its green shading (*Verde* = green), has probably

Left and right, man and his dog, ancient and modern.

been on the islands for 2,000 years. It is presently an unregistered breed, although the Spanish Kennel Club has recognised it and is setting standards by which to judge a true specimen.

The Verdino is a rustic, smooth-haired, heavy guard-type dog with a broad jaw, usually brindle coloured in stripes, or sometimes golden with white flashes on the chest. It weighs in at between 90 and 110 lbs (40 and 50 kilos). At its best it is an awesome creature of obvious strength and it has all the

characteristics of a dog which has for centuries been assisting man in all manner of agricultural work; it is affectionate to known friends, highly faithful, but also highly territorial.

Whether or not the dogs so admired by King Juba were true Verdinos is open to discussion. Certainly there were other dogs on the islands, and that of Fuerteventura has its own tradition, being commonly longer and leaner in the body and faster across the ground. Every major incoming influence since has brought with it more dogs; the conquistadores imported their own favourites, and the preponderance of small lap-dogs and variations on a Pekinese theme in the streets of Puerto de la Cruz on Tenerife are descendents of the sofa dogs brought out to Puerto by holidaying ladies of gentility earlier this century.

Despite all these influences and cross-breeds the Verdino is championed as the true Canarian dog unique to the islands, possibly because it is yet another symbol of the independence of the islands from the mainland.

Dr Luis Felipe Jurado, professor of the La Laguna (Tenerife) veterinary faculty of the university, has studied the Verdino for many years. He accepts the Juba theory of the naming of the islands, and is convinced that

been glaringly ignored by the islanders, judging by the number of times it was made public and the fines that were imposed. Offenders faced being scourged, but they continued to keep and protect their precious dogs. However, with many of the original islanders dead as a result of conquest, some of the Verdinos turned savage and attacked herds of goats. A price was put on their heads and they were termed "worse than wolves".

At one stage a gold coin was paid to anyone producing the head of a Verdino, but eight years later the Spanish ruler Castellano, who was in love with a Guanche princess, annulled the order, saying that the Verdino was "an honourable dog and that he

the dogs preceeded men on the Canaries. How did they get here? On rafts from Africa, he theorises; not man-made ones but great storm-knarled platforms of fallen trees and bushes that drifted here after floods in the rivers of the mainland.

Dogs of prey: However they came, whenever they came, history accepts the Verdino as an integral part of the islands' past and a sad one at times. The conquistadores so feared these animals that in Tenerife they condemned most of them to death, allowing each shepherd only one to guard his flock.

This law, issued in May 1499, must have

(Castellano) didn't wish to judge it".

But life was difficult and death almost inevitable for the dogs during those bad years. In Fuerteventura where for centuries they had guarded goats and sheep, a general "licence to kill" was issued against dogs of prey, as they were termed. One was allowed for each flock, with the proviso that a young boy should stand guard over it.

Somehow the Verdino managed to survive, only to face a new threat in the last century when British and German dog-fighting enthusiasts settled in the islands, bringing with them the bull terrier. Cross-breeding to produce stronger, fiercer animals in this cruel sport threatened the purity of the breed.

The dog-fighting is officially outlawed now, and staged fights are rare. Lovers of the Verdino are also fighting, to preserve the purity of the breed. Most are strongly opposed to selective breeding, but choose— with care and difficulty—mates that are not closely related, because of the dangers of interbreeding. Verdino owners and organizations such as Solidaridad Canario are generally stimulating public awareness and interest in the Canarian breed.

Lack of money is a continual problem, and Verdino enthusiasts, professional or otherwise, often disagree on all but the most

basic issues. Efforts to breed the dog, to "follow through" on pups and to arouse government interest have all been hampered by so many difficulties that today it seems the Verdino banner is flown by individuals, not groups.

However public awareness and interest in the dogs is flourishing and the price of a pure-bred Verdino pup (about £250) has increased accordingly—even if the owner would part with it. Shepherds and goatherds

Left, faithful, strong, and unique to the islands. Above, an early representation of the Fuerteventuran dog.

in Fuerteventura, where the Verdino is still a working dog, have replaced the basic *gofio* and water diet with a higher-protein one, and are careful to remove ticks and other parasites which have always sapped the dogs' strength.

Rescued breed: A brighter day is dawning for the Verdinos. These days they are guarded as zealously and lovingly as they once guarded their masters.

In Tenerife the Club Español del Presa Canario ("presa" literally means bulldog) arranges regular meetings and competitions of Verdinos, which take place in the main square of La Laguna, in Geneto, Tegueste and other venues.

It isn't easy to find a Verdino, at least not in Gran Canaria, where they are now pets-cum-guard dogs. Veterinary surgeon Enrique Rodriguez Grau Bassas has acquired one from Fuerteventura (where he carried out in-depth genetic research on the dog for the University of Cordoba some years ago); Ico—named after a legendary Lanzarote princess, daughter of a Guanche queen and a Spanish nobleman—is six years old and hopefully will be a mother of many Verdino pups. She is quite small—the average height of a bitch is 22 ins (57 cms) from neck to ground, but over the past ten years Verdinos have grown and with a good diet will further increase in size.

Like all her breed, Ico likes to sleep by day and is active at night. She growls but doesn't bite. She has lovely gold-flecked eyes and is friendly but not fawning, demonstrative only with her owner. But beware that friendliness– she would attack anyone approaching her owner's house or car. She is as agile as the mountain goats her ancestors guarded, and resistant to disease. She has, says Dr Rodriguez, a certain daintiness—on her first visit to a restaurant she sat quietly behind him and delicately accepted the food he passed to her.

The writer and historian Viera y Clavijo describes this dog better than any other: "...apart from its svelte figure, vivacity, courage and speed, it possesses that delicate and exquisite sentiment that allows it to enter society with man. The Verdino understands man's desires, fights for his security, obeys and helps him, defends and loves him, and .... knows exactly how to gain the love of his owner."

Of the eastern Canary Islands, Lanzarote has the most impressive volcanic scenery—equal to that of Hawaii or Iceland. This landscape was formed as recently as the early 18th century when eruptions buried a large area of the island beneath a layer of lava and ash.

At the end of the 16th century, a European visitor described the part of Lanzarote soon to disappear as "a pretty and cheerful plain with a population of farmers cultivating the land." But in a few apocalyptic years, between 1730 and 1736, a third of the island and most of the local community was devastated. Hundreds of people fled their homes and their animals and fields were smothered by boiling lava.

Flight from Lanzarote: After a year of suffering and trauma the local parish priest finally led his terrified flock to a new life on nearby Gran Canaria. He left a vivid account.

"On 1 September, between nine and ten at night, the land suddenly opened up near Timanfaya, some two leagues from Yaiza. During the first night an enormous mountain rose out of the bosom of the Earth. From its top flames belched out and continued burning for 19 days."

He went on to describe the lava flowing first like water, later running sluggishly like honey. The inhabitants were terrified by the darkness of the days due to the ash being thrown into the skies, and by the horrendous noises from explosions and the advancing lava. Huge quantities of dead fish, including strange, previously unknown varieties were washed up on the shore.

Ten days after the eruption began, lava and ash reached the sea, having engulfed villages, roads and fields. A period of calm followed and the people believed the worst was over. But the middle of October brought further emissions. Much of the islanders' livestock was suffocated by the sulphurous gases. In December new islands emerged from the sea. More dead fish were washed up

Preceding pages: layered lava formation. Left, the most recent eruption, on La Palma in 1971. Right, Cueva de los Verdes, a cavern on Lanzarote created by the eruptions.

and even more farmland was smothered.

"On 17 January 1731," the priest continues, "new eruptions came and over-ran all the earlier ones. Incandescent streams of lava together with the densest smoke came from openings which had formed on the mountain. The clouds of smoke were frequently rent by brilliant flashes of red and blue light, followed by violent thunder, just like a great storm."

Clearly Lanzarote suffered one of the most violent types of volcanic eruption possible, a

mere 250 years ago—geologically speaking, only yesterday.

A period of calm after 1736 ended with small earthquakes during 1812. These rumbled on until 1824, when, between 31 July and 25 October, Lanzarote's most recent volcanic eruptions took place. Three craters opened up—the Volcán de Tao, Tinguatón and Montaña del Fuego. This last crater now forms the focus of the National Park of Timanfaya. Since 1824, the island has slipped into a geological slumber—but by no means a deep one.

The National Park of Timanfaya: One of only nine such areas of preservation in Spain,

Timanfaya covers nearly 20 sq miles (5,000 hectares), about one quarter of the recent lava fields. A well-surfaced road leads off from the Tinayo-Yaiza road to the Islote de Hilario where parking, a shop and a restaurant are provided for visitors. On the way the route passes several spatter conelets poking out of the lava—one has been christened the "little cup of chocolate".

From the restaurant there are sweeping views across the *malpais,* the "badland", a storm-tossed sea of coal-black lava, pock-marked with cones and craters. Useless for farming and almost too rough to walk on, it is a fragile and unique landscape, and visitors are not allowed to wander freely over the

Beneath the Islote de Hilario is a "hot spot", an area just below the surface where temperatures are still extremely high; only a few inches down water boils, and at a depth of a 30 feet or so lead would melt.

Watchers never fail to be impressed, and a little unnerved, as a park ranger tips a bucket-full of water down a hole in the ground and steps back quickly, out of the path of a jet of steam shooting back out again a few seconds later. The superheated spume of water is spat high into the air.

Dry twigs pushed into a nearby trench burst into flames of their own accord—barely a couple of feet below the ground it's hot enough to burn fingers and hands.

park. In view of the number of visitors it is a necessary rule; however there are a number of marked paths near the visitor centre that you are free to walk without a guide.

Otherwise, the curious can see the main sights from the comfort of a tour bus or hire-car or, perhaps most memorably, from the bonebreaking back of a camel, although this is usually only available for those who are part of a pre-booked tour.

Before starting to explore, go to the restaurant where you can dine on meat grilled over heat rising straight out of the ground. As you leave you are treated to more demonstrations of Timanfaya's barely-suppressed energy.

The *ruta de los volcanes* is a circular tour, some nine miles (14 km) long, through some of the most apocalyptic scenery of the park. A park ranger on a motorbike leads a convoy of cars through the volcanoes, stopping every so often so you can take photos. The whole trip takes about an hour, and is the easiest way into the heart of this spine-chillingly beautiful waste-land.

Within the stark, eerie landscape of Timanfaya National Park, the lava takes on weird shapes and textures. Its different surfaces are likened to elephant hide, shark skin and rope patterns formed on the thin crust of cooling lava by the molten rock flowing beneath. Thicker, slow-moving lava formed Cyclopean blocks—and, as it ground its way across country it screeched, roared, bellowed and spat.

Most of the lava within the Park is sombre black or grey, but some is dark red or even yellowish; some looks green due to the lichen spreading over the surface of the rock—even after 250 years life has only a tenuous hold here.

The classic volcano, with a circular crater topping a cone of different lava flows and ash, is hard to find on Lanzarote. But instead there are innumerable little cones formed of ash, cinder and volcanic bombs. The lava did not have the power to rise up to the lip of the

crater, but sought another way out through the sides leaving lava streams between slag-heap islands.

Most of the *lapilli*—the material spewed out of the cones—is fine and cindery and has been banked up and rippled by the wind into dark and desolate sand-dunes.

The lava bombs—not to be removed from the National Park area—look like large spindles with "twisted tails". They are formed as solid chunks of rock, are hurled through liquid lava in the throat of the vol-

**Left, a ranger demonstrates underground heat.
Above, a collapsed volcanic tube.**

cano. Their crusts are usually crazed, revealing an inner skin of frothy lava—like petrified crusty bread buns. They can be any size from a fist to a football.

Tubes and Caves: Collapsed volcanic tubes snake their way through the lava flows of Timanfaya, though the tunnels and trenches of the Park are not accessible to the visitor. But one of the longest and most complex volcanic tubes in the world is found elsewhere on Lanzarote—Cueva de los Verdes, up in the northeast of the island, in lava flows much older than Timanfaya's. Cueva de los Verdes is open to the public, who can experience the eerie beauty by joining a guided tour. Subtle lighting and haunting music either add to the atmosphere or destroy it, according to your point of view.

Where the roof of one of these tubes has collapsed, the void created is known as a *jameo*. An excellent example is Jameos del Agua, not far from Cueva de los Verdes. Really these are two *jameos* separated by a surviving stretch of volcanic tunnel. The whole area has been landscaped and contains a restaurant, concert area and swimming pool. Within the volcanic tube is a large rock-pool which is home for unique, tiny white crabs.

Although they look like the limestone caverns found in northern Europe and the States, these tubes and trenches were not carved out by underground streams. They were formed by still-liquid lava running out from beneath a cooling and solidifying crust of superheated rock.

The cave lining would have remained liquified for some time because of the hot gases which filled the cave after the original contents had drained out. This liquid rock oozed and dripped, and eventually froze into "lava tears" hanging from the roof, or blunt stakes growing up from the floor. Hot waters, rich in mineral salts, have painted them unworldly colours—a chilling place where the island women and children once hid from the Barbary pirates.

Crater Land: The islands of Gran Canaria and Fuerteventura have not witnessed volcanic eruptions for at least the last 500 years, but you don't need a doctorate in geology to notice fresh volcanic remains lying around on both islands.

Fuerteventura's dry climate has preserved some of its volcanoes in almost pristine condition, even though they erupted some two million years ago. Las Casillas del Angel, for example, is a low shield volcano of non-violent origin—unusual in the Canaries. The island also has extensive zones of *malpais* including the Malpaiz de la Corona and parts of Isla de Lobos—both important conservation areas, though you wouldn't think so from the number of apartments and holiday homes going up.

One of Gran Canaria's most famous volcanic landmarks is the Pico de Bandama, a huge ash cone, now topped by café and souvenir shop and provided with a terrace, from where coffee-sipping customers can look down on the whole northwest corner of the

bottom of the crater, makes this a likely suggestion.

Or perhaps rather than the *caldera* creating the peak, the peak created the *caldera*. The original volcano may have sprouted a parasitic cone on one side, and as this cone grew out of all proportion it drained the original volcano, leaving a hollow "heart" into which the old volcano eventually collapsed.

Whatever its origin, Bandama is an awe-inspiring reminder of the power of nature—and the hot spot just below the surface suggests that its active life is not yet over. The prospect does not seem to worry the lone farmer in the tiny house at the bottom.

Gran Canaria is a land of *calderas*. Pinos

island. The road spirals upwards round the cone—and then, just beyond the turn off towards the golf course, is the *caldera*. An enormous crater, nearly a mile across and over 650 ft (200 metres) deep. All around the lip of this steep-sided pit are layers of ash and *lapilli*, the same material that makes up the cone itself.

How the *caldera* was formed remains a subject for debate. Perhaps a massive explosion blew the heart out of a former volcano. Trapped ground-water could have been superheated, building up enough pressure to rip the rock "lid" apart. Certainly the existence of a "hot spot", just a few feet below the

de Gáldár, high up on the road between Cruz de Tejeda and Artenara, is a classic crater sitting atop a volcanic cone, whereas the *caldera* of Los Marteles, almost in the very centre of the island, was formed by the collapse of the volcano back into the magma chamber beneath it.

These craters are relatively small basins, and are found at or near the tops of volcanic cones. Bandama is the largest of this type.

On a grander scale are the *calderas* created by erosion, like that of Tirajana which encloses the town of San Bartolome. These are the product of occasional torrential downpours on badly faulted lava-flows—over the course of several million years huge slabs of rock and earth have slumped down into the *barranco,* leaving a series of high cliffs all round the Tirajana basin.

But the grandest crater of them all is the Caldera de Tejeda. This huge structure embraces almost all of northeast Gran Canaria, and was formed when much of ancient Tamaràn—the prototype of the present island—collapsed back into the magma chamber beneath. As the centre of Tamaràn gradually sank in on itself, some time between four and five million years ago, fresh lava was squeezed out through the faulted rock to leave a series of concentric basalt dykes. From Cruz de Tejeda or Artenara you

can see the vertical walls of this vast basin curving round beyond the distinctive peaks of Roque Nublo and Bentaiga. The stubby finger of Roque Nublo is the resistant core of an ancient volcano.

Anyone based in Las Palmas does not need to leave his or her sun-bed to appreciate the natural forces that made Gran Canaria. Las Canteras beach would not exist but for the protective reef of lava clearly visible just off-shore; to the left is the isolated volcanic cone of Arucas; and to the right, at the far end of

Left, the crater at Bandama, Gran Canaria. Above, Roque Nublo with Mount Teide behind.

the beach, are the barren cones of the Isleta. But the cones are forbidden territory—the army still uses the area as a training ground, even though it has been declared a Natural Park by virtue of its geological and botanical importance.

Volcanic Origins: How did the islands come into being in the first place? Certainly not through the drowning of Atlantis. Quite the reverse, although geologists would argue over the details.

The general view relies on the theory of plate tectonics. Essentially the world's surface is made up of a number of thick slabs or plates of rock which are constantly moving—slowly—relative to one another. These movements are caused by the inter-action of currents of heat generated within the molten core of the Earth itself.

Over hundreds of millions of years the plates on which Africa and South America sit drifted apart, forming the Atlantic Ocean. As Africa rubbed along the southern edge of Europe the enormous pressures built up here folded up the Atlas Mountains in North Africa, and as the Atlas chain was folded, huge blocks of rock in the Atlantic were shoved upwards. Local releases of pressure around these blocks let white hot liquid rock flow upwards through cracks in these blocks. Volcanoes formed where the cracks reached the surface.

Beneath the two easternmost islands—Lanzarote and Fuerteventura—parts of these blocks have been located. These are the oldest rocks in the Canary Islands, dating back 37 million years. Both these islands were probably once part of the African land mass—there is only a short, shallow channel between the two islands and Africa, and fossil ostrich eggs have been found on Fuerteventura.

On the other hand Gran Canaria and the four western islands are purely volcanic. They are separated from each other by deep-water trenches and almost certainly were never linked to the continent of Africa.

And the chances of seeing an eruption? Fairly remote—the last was on the island of La Palma in 1971—but still possible. Teide on Tenerife still oozes sulphurous trails of smoke and Timanfaya burns away just beneath your feet. It is just a matter of time—next week, next month, next year, next century, or maybe not for another million years.

CANARY WRESTLING AND STICK-FIGHTING

Judging by match attendance Canary wrestling or *lucha canaria* is the third most popular sport of the islands. But among the native-born islanders it is a clear favourite. Wrestling clubs and rings are on all the islands—there are, for example, 15 clubs on Fuerteventura alone, one club for every 1,200 *majoreros*.

The sport's governing body has tried to get the wrestling recognised for the 1992 Olympics to be held in Barcelona, arguing that *lucha canaria* is international because Canarian emigrants introduced it throughout South and Central America as well as mainland Spain. The rejection of the proposal by the Olympic Committee is seen as yet another slight by Madrid on *lo nuestro*, "our own", though cutting the televised final bouts of the 1986 inter-island championship match caused more obvious indignation at the time.

How Canarian *lucha canaria* is may be an open question, but it certainly has pre-Spanish origins. Nevertheless similar styles of wrestling can be seen in northern Spain, the Swiss Alps, western Britain and even in parts of Africa.

Ancient and modern: The 17th-century poet, Viana, described a wrestling match held in Tenerife just before the conquest in such detail that it is possible to identify all three throws that the winner used. The prose chroniclers recorded notable bouts too, like that held in Tenoya, Gran Canaria, between Adargoma of Gáldar and Gariragua representing Telde. The two champions fought over the two kingdoms' grazing rights. In the best traditions of *lucha*, both wrestlers claimed the other had won. This must be one of the most gentlemanly and chivalrous contact sports.

These pre-conquest matches generally took the form of personal duels or trials of combat, like the Tenoya fight. Wrestling was also a form of training for war and an entertainment at festivities—the bouts described by Viana formed part of the official merry-making at a royal wedding.

According to the early European writers, special places were set aside for native wrestling bouts. "They had public places outside the villages where they had their duels, which was a circle enclosed by a stone wall and a place made high where they might be seen," wrote one visitor.

In its modern form, *lucha canaria* is no longer an individual contest but a team sport. There are 12 wrestlers in each team, only one man from each team fighting at any one time.

The individual bouts or *bregas* are fought within a sand-covered ring between 30 and 33 ft (nine to 10 metres) in diameter.

The rings—often built and owned by the local town council—are known as *terreros*, a word of Portuguese origin and probably acquired during the various temporary alliances of native islanders and Portuguese against the Spanish.

At the start of a *brega* the wrestler takes his opponent's right hand in his and grasps the rolled hem of his opponent's shorts with his left. As the two wrestlers come together their right hands brush the sand-covered floor of the *terrero* and the *brega* is under way.

Left, stick-fighting, vicious and skilful. Right, *lucha canaria* is part of the islands' heritage.

Using a combination of trips, lifts and sheer weight each man tries to unbalance his opponent, gripping onto shorts or shirt. The *brega* is lost if any part of the wrestler's body—except, of course, his feet—touches the ground. If both wrestlers are toppled the man who hits the ground first is the loser. Each team member must grapple to win the best of three *bregas* or bouts to gain a point for his side.

Until the Spanish Civil War *lucha canaria* retained much of its original character. A style of wrestling similar to Cumbrian wrestling from the north-west of England was to be found in Tenerife and other stylistic differences occurred on other islands. The presence of foreign residents—two German brothers, brought up in the islands, are members of the Hierro team.

Sport or art?: Less common as a tradition on the islands is *juego del palo* or stick-fighting (known as *banot* in Tenerife), though it is currently undergoing a revival. A controlling body for the sport—or perhaps art form—has been set up, and classes are now being given in branches of the *Universidad Laboral* throughout the islands.

In pre-conquest days stick-fighting formed part of a more dangerous game. When two Canarios challenged each other to a duel, they went to the place agreed upon, which was a raised arena with a flat stone, big

ence of a *comisionado*, or wrestler's second, harked back to the duels of pre-conquest days. In Gran Canaria the two opposing teams used to be known as North and South—preserving the former ancient division of the island into two separate Guanche kingdoms.

In the 1920's *lucha* was the sport of the country people practised on the grain-threshing circles. These days threshing floors are few and far between, but even the modern city-dwelling Canario will occasionally wrestle with a friend or cousin during a Sunday barbecue in the country. And *lucha* has even been taken up by some for-

enough for a man to stand upright on at each end. Both competitors stood on their stones, with three stones each for throwing and with three more which served for wounding, and with the stave called a *magodo* or *amodeghe*.

First they threw the stones, which they dodged with skill, weaving their bodies without moving their feet. After that they stepped down to the ground and faced each other with the *magodos*, trying to smash each others' forearms and using the thin stones between their fingers as a kind of vicious knuckle-duster.

The stone throwing preliminaries and the stone knuckle-dusters went out of fashion years ago, but the stick-fight has survived—just—in areas like Fuerteventura, where goat-herding still plays an important role in the economy.

The staff is about six ft (1.8 meters) long and about an inch (2.5 cm) thick. Almost any wood can be used as long as it will provide a straight staff and will not shatter easily. The Canary Island bush, *membrillo*, or the introduced cherry are preferred.

A pole of appropriate length is cut green, stripped of its bark and left to season. The seasoned pole is then cured with pig fat to make it more resilient—linseed oil is sometimes used, though few practitioners of the sport would readily admit to using a manu-

factured product.

As with wrestling there are differences between the islands. The Fuerteventuran "school" prefers a defensive style, sacrificing speed for power, whilst adherents of the Tenerife style go for speed. Even the name of the staff varies from island to island—in Gran Canaria it is called a *garrote*, on Tenerife a *banot* and in Fuerteventura it is known as a *lata*. Throughout the islands herdsmen still carry these staves.

Juego del palo (stick-fighting) was a rural

Left, he who hits the ground first, loses. Above, a form of combat with a long history.

sport, like wrestling, though the practitioners were mainly goat-herders. In living memory herdsmen in Fuerteventura met occasionally in a "Corral Council" to resolve disputes between individual herders. If agreement could not be reached by negotiation the matter was eventually determined by a stick-fight between the two men or their representatives.'

Banned and forgotten: A variant on the theme was developed in the last century when camels were first introduced to Fuerteventura as beasts of burden or for ploughing. In this type of stick-fight a camel-driver's crop, a stick of about three feet long (one metre) is used.

In 1860 Pedro Pestano introduced the *palo camellero* to Tenerife and by the 1920s there was a thriving group of stick-fighters on the island who used the short stick. This style, however, has all but died out.

And the same almost occurred with *garrote* on Gran Canaria. This was banned after the conquest by a Spanish law which forbade native islanders from carrying weapons, although goat-herders were exempt on the grounds that they needed a suitable stick to protect their flocks.

Lucha was more difficult to control. Indeed in 1527 wrestling bouts were held in Tenerife as part of the festivities to mark the birth of Felipe II of Spain.

By the 19th century, however, the *cultos* (cultured) of society were of the opinion that "spectacles of this kind should figure only in the memory". With the Franco era *lucha* generally met with malign neglect but, since the democracy was re-established in 1976 much more public interest—and money—has been invested in the sport. Nowadays most of the main *luchaderos* (rings) are modern buildings.

Demonstrations of both *lucha* and *juego del palo* are given during most festivals, and Fuerteventura offers the best chance of coming across a wrestling match in a local *luchadero*. Otherwise look for posters in bars off the tourist run—or on the wall of the Lopez Socas stadium in Las Palmas, Gran Canaria, near which is a bronze statue of two wrestlers set in a bleak park off the Avenida Escaleritas.

Matches are televised surprisingly regularly on the local TV channel; check the local papers for details.

No serious visitor to the Canaries will remain ignorant of the existence of a major street event comparable in splendour and extravagance to *carnaval* in Rio de Janeiro, an event that has made its entry into the *Guinness Book of Records* as the largest open air ball in the world. Perhaps because they were deprived of it for so long—festival celebrations were banned under Franco's rule—the people of Gran Canaria are *carnaval*-crazy, and some spend the entire year working on their costumes or rehearsing song-and-dance routines for just one event.

And yet, even during the Franco years carnival was discreetly celebrated under the guise of a "Spring festival" or a saint's day in most villages, while the people of La Isleta in the north of Gran Canaria, a law unto themselves, held their own little *carnaval* ban or no ban.

Soon after Franco's death *carnaval* was reborn, and in Gran Canaria these days it has spread from La Isleta right down to Maspalomas. The grand procession, usually towards the end of *carnaval*, parades through the streets of Las Palmas for several hours and is a magnificent sight, though more people participate than watch.

The magic of *carnaval* is that it brings out the child in everyone; donning masks is a signal to shed inhibitions, to laugh and dance with total strangers. For two weeks there are contests and *verbenas* (dances) and many tourists bring their own costumes. Dates vary; officially Gran Canaria celebrates during the last two weeks of February though in fact *carnaval* here tends to begin when Tenerife's has finished. In Lanzarote the **Carnival Fiesta** (the second Tuesday) is early March, and Fuerteventura's is two weeks later.

A feast of Fiestas: *Carnaval* is the greatest of them all, but in these Catholic islands there are hundreds more fiestas. A few are deeply religious, most are a mixture of religion and sheer fun, and a few have strong Guanche origins. To list them all isn't possible, but here are the main ones.

The first and most joyous is the feast of the **Three Kings** on 5 January, the eve of the Canarian Christmas. In major towns the Three Kings parade on camels, followed by a huge excited crowd that later return to their homes and exchange customary gifts over family dinners.

On 20 January, Aguimes, Guia and Gáldar (Gran Canaria) celebrate **St Sebastian's Day** with a solemn High Mass followed by folklore performances, dancing, drinking and general merrymaking. Depending on the weather, a lovely **Almond Festival** is held in the main almond growing areas of Tejeda and Valsequillo in late February. Visitors come from all over the island to see the sporting competitions, hear the music, join in the dancing and so on. Almond-based products like marzipan are sold—along with as much food and drink as you like from the many stalls.

Easter usually falls in March which is a quiet month for fiestas except for **St Joseph's Day**, 19 March, which is **Father's Day**. Check whether this is a national holiday, because it is sometimes "swopped" for *carnaval* Tuesday.

May Day is a holiday, and there's a charming fiesta on the first Sunday of the month (which incidentally is Mother's Day in Spain) known as **The Neighbours** in Fontanela, near Moya (Gran Canaria). The fiesta is to thank St Bartholomew for ending a terrible drought several centuries ago, celebrated with religious plus general festivity with a street market as well. There's a similar fiesta in San Mateo on 13 May, in honour of Our Lady of Fatima; look out for lovely floral displays.

On 15 May **St Isidor's Day** is celebrated in several Gran Canarian villages—Teror, Galdar, Sta Lucia and St Nicolas de Tolentino. It's a very colourful, happy day, a kind of rustic May Day. The month ends with another holiday, the **Day of the Canaries** on 30 May, and most people make for the beach. This is also the feast of **San Fernando**, the dormitory suburb of the development at Playa del Inglés, so head south.

Preceding pages: festive blooms; the faces of *Carnaval*. Left, already a fiesta veteran.

Ascension Day is a moveable feast, and not a public holiday; but there's a lovely ceremony, the throwing of rose petals outside the Cathedral in Las Palmas, which is unique in Spain. Three weeks later *Corpus Christi* is a public holiday, and the very best place to be is Las Palmas because the streets of Vegueta around the Cathedral are exquisitely decorated into patterns using pebbles, sand, grass and flowers.

The feast of **St Antony of Padua** is celebrated with great gusto in Tias and St Bartholomew (Lanzarote) and Mogán, Moya and Sta Brigida (Gran Canaria) on 13 June, followed by the day of **St John the Baptist** on 24 June in Artenara, Arucas,

July, when the people gather at the simple little shrine of **San Marcial of Rubicon**, built on the mountainside. Fuertaventura honours its patron saint St Buenaventura on 14 July, and the 16th is a great day for the whole of the Canaries. This is the fiesta of **Our Lady of Carmen**, patron saint of seamen. No village is far from a port, so head for the nearest one to see a statue of the Virgin being put in a beautifully-decorated boat; a priest goes out to sea with the statue, to bless the waters that provide the islanders' living, half in thanksgiving for the previous year and half as a prayer that the coming year will be as fruitful—and safe.

There is a public holiday on 25 July in

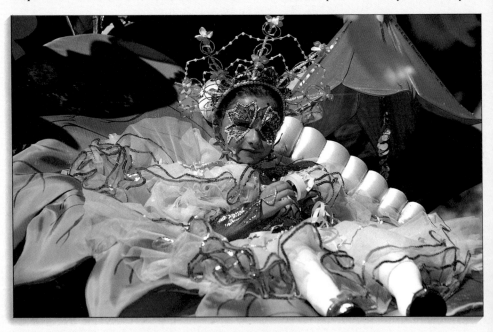

Telde and Firgas (Gran Canaria); wherever you go there'll be sporting contests, processions and country produce for sale as well as music and dancing.

Busy month: July is positively bursting with fiestas; the main ones are **St Isidor's** in Teror (Gran Canaria) where small children wear toy crowns and charming costumes. On the same island the **apricot harvest** is held in Fataga later this month but the exact date depends on the weather. The fiesta includes contests for the best stalls and cookery, and all the usual shows and rides in a delightful mountain setting.

There's a fiesta in Femes (Lanzarote) on 7

honour of **Santiago**, patron saint of Spain (Santiago was the battle cry of olden days) and the 26th is dedicated to **Sta Ana**, Las Palmas' own patron saint.

There's a most colourful spectacle in Agaete (Gran Canaria) on 4 August, the festival of **Rama**, "bringing down the branches" from Tamadaba Forest as an offering to Our Lady of the Snows (Virgen de las Nieves). Half the island goes to this fiesta, which is officially recommended as an event of tourist interest and lasts two days.

On the same island there are related ceremonies in Marzagan and Lomo Magullo, Telde, where a large cattle fair is held. On 12 August Telde celebrates again with **"the bringing of the water"**, inspired by the Guanche prayers to their god Alcorar, to send rain. Young people in ancient costumes carrying pottery vessels sprinkle the precious liquid in imitation of the Guanche ceremonies.

Other August fiestas are **San Roque** on the 16th in Tinojo (Lanzarote), Guia, Firgas and Telde (Gran Canaria) where the cattle join in. **St Bartholomew's Day** is joyfully celebrated on the 24th in the village of that name in Gran Canaria and in Betancuria, Fuerteventura.

Lanzarote spends most of August fêting **St Gines** (principal day 26th) and there's an

Locals celebrate in a big way over in San Nicolas de Tolentino for two weeks in September (main day 11th) especially the **Festival of the Pool**. In 1788 the church banned fishing in the nude and ever since the townspeople have gone fishing—wearing shoes! There's a lovely picnic area.

The **Dance of the Branches** in Guia (Gran Canaria) on 12 September dates back two centuries to when a swarm of locusts threatened the crops but miraculously (after everyone had grabbed a branch to beat them off) torrential rain killed the invaders. Great fun, this one, with a *verbena*, or local dance.

The big day in October is the second Saturday (the 12th is Spanish National Day)

extensive programme of events all over the island. In Artenara (Gran Canaria) on the last Sunday of the month there's a torchlit procession to a cave shrine, the **Virgin of the Little Cave**.

In September the main fiestas are the **Waters of Teror** (Gran Canaria) on the second day of the month. But the most important of the year is on 8 September: **The Virgin of the Pines** fiesta is officially recommended to tourists; thousands gather in pilgrimage on this wholly religious day.

Left, in *Carnaval*, the more elaborate the better. Above, persuading the livestock to join in.

when Fuerteventura and Gran Canaria celebrate (and sometimes re-enact) beating off the British "pirate" Sir Francis Drake— there's usually a maritime procession. The religious feast of **All Souls** is on 1 November and 8 December is a national holiday, the **Immaculate Conception**. **Constitution Day** falls on 27 December, also a holiday.

Of special interest to tourists is **Sta Lucia's feast** on 13 December; a young girl comes from Sweden to reign over the festivities in which all Scandinavians participate and so, of course, does the southern mountain village of Sta Lucia on Gran Canaria.

TRAVEL TIPS

GETTING THERE

The Canarian archipelago, variously called "The Land of Eternal Spring", "The Garden of the Hesperides", or "The Fortunate Isles", stretches out in a chain of seven main islands and three smaller ones, some 300 miles (480 km) long. The nearest point to the African coast—only 60 miles (96 km) away—is the island of Fuerteventura, sometimes described as a piece of the Sahara that drifted away.

BY AIR

All but one of the seven largest islands has an airport; Gomera, the exception, can be reached by ferry only at the moment. All others are linked by frequent inter-island flights, and by far the busiest airports are Reina Sofia (South Tenerife) and Gando in Gran Canaria, into which principal scheduled international air traffic comes. Spain's national airline Iberia has regular services to Tenerife and Gran Canaria from most major European cities, with daily flights to and from Amsterdam, Brussels, Düsseldorf, Frankfurt, Geneva, London, Paris, Rome, Vienna and Zurich. Iberia's HQ in the UK is at 130, Regent Street, London W1 (tel. (1)-437 9822). From the UK the principal charter—and limited scheduled—flights are operated by Air Europe, Britannia Airways, Monarch and Dan-Air.

BY SEA

The ferry company Trasmediterranea runs between Cadiz and Santa Cruz (Tenerife) or Las Palmas (Gran Canaria) three times a week, with a journey time of 36 hours. Sailings go on to Lanzarote once a week. Ferries link all seven islands with frequent sailings between Tenerife and Las Palmas, Gran Canaria.

A regular jet-foil service runs (except when the sea is too rough) between Santa Cruz and Las Palmas, and, three times weekly, to Morro Jable in the south of Fuerteventura. This is also operated by Trasmediterranea and is much quicker than travelling by conventional ferry, the hydrofoil "flight" between Santa Cruz and Las Palmas taking just 80 minutes.

The island of La Gomera is linked to Tenerife by Ferry Gomera (a subsidiary of the Fred Olsen Scandinavian ferry company) which piles between Los Cristianos (Tenerife) and San Sebastian de la Gomera.

RMS ST Helena sails from Avonmouth to Cape Town every 60 days, with stops in Tenerife, Ascension Island and St Helena. The trip from England to Tenerife takes five days.

Cruise ships such as *QE2*, *Canberra* and those of the Fred Olsen line also call occasionally at the two main ports. Compania Trasmediterranea: Marina 59, Santa Cruz de Tenerife – tel. 277300; Muelle Ribera Este, Las Palmas de Gran Canaria – tel. 267766; St Helena Shipping Co. Ltd., Helston, Cornwall, UK. – tel. (326) 563434.

BY RAIL

Being rugged and mountainous, the Canaries have no rail network, but the Spanish national rail system (RENFE) will deliver passengers to the station at Cádiz. From there to the islands, see the above section "By Sea".

BY ROAD

Road users travel through mainland Spain to Cádiz and thence by ferry to Tenerife or Gran Canaria, and the other islands.

Any size of vehicle can be brought across and most standards of accommodation are available on board. Pets are charged extra. Imported vehicles used on the islands for more than six months will need Spanish licence plates. The importation of foreign vehicles involves much red tape, such as an International Driving Licence, car registration papers, a Green Card and a Spanish bail bond.

The principal French **tour operators** are: FRAM, Nouvel Horizon and Jet Tours, each with offices in the provincial capitals and holiday resorts. For detailed information regarding scheduled flights to Tenerife and Gran Canaria, contact Air France agents: there are daily flights between various French airports and the Canaries.

German tour operators such as Turistik Union International, Neckermann Reisen and Tjaereborg are also well represented in the archipelago, while the German airline Lufthansa runs a regular scheduled service to and from the major airports.

Apart from the Cadiz ferry, there are no fixed sailings between mainland Europe and the islands, other than cruise ships which, as already mentioned, call at irregular intervals at the ports of Las Palmas and Santa Cruz.

TRAVEL ESSENTIALS

VISAS AND PASSPORTS

Spain joined the European Economic Community on 1 January 1986 and will become a full member state on 31 December 1992, so citizens of EEC countries, the USA and Canada need only valid passports, while visitors from Australia, New Zealand and South Africa must have a **visa**. Make sure your passport is stamped on entry, especially if you intend to stay for more than three months. If this is the case you must obtain a visa from a Spanish Consulate at home, and later, a *permanencia* from the offices of the Civil Governor of the province and the police station of your local town.

The Canary Islands have different **customs regulations** to mainland Spain, and passengers' personal baggage from Europe is not normally subjected to Customs inspection. Prohibited goods, however, include narcotics and pornographic material—both incidentally readily available in the cities and tourist areas.

PORTER SERVICE

Do not expect **porter service**, except at the best hotels. One can usually ferret out a luggage trolley at the main airports, although there is an inexplicable lack of them at Tenerife's Reina Sofia airport.

HEALTH

Tips for a **healthy stay** are: drink bottled water and beware the origin of ice-cubes, don't overdo the sun-worshipping, it's only too easy to become badly burned in the Canaries' unusually clear atmosphere; take care over eating and drinking (measures of spirits are much larger than in other countries and generally far cheaper, too).

Visitors with severe respiratory complaints should avoid the major cities of Las Palmas and Santa Cruz because of the high level of petrol and diesel fumes and dust, some of it from the Sahara, and anyone with heart trouble on Tenerife would be well advised to give the trip to Teide (Spain's highest mountain) a miss.

Citizens of EEC countries enjoy reciprocal **medical benefits** (in your home country, the local social security office will provide you with a form E111 for temporary visitors, or E121 for pensioners). State facilities generally mean adequate treatment and medical skills, but lengthy waits for out-patients, with few nurses and doctors speaking anything other than Spanish. However, names of doctors with some knowledge of a foreign language are available at local tourist bureaux and in English and German newspapers and magazines.

Private medical care is preferred by foreign visitors and usually implies prompt attention, good standards, staff who speak foreign languages, but relatively high costs. Foreign visitors should arrange sickness and accident insurance before departure and cover of £10,000 is not excessive.

Recently a few foreign doctors (mostly British or German) have begun to practice in the Canaries, though this is by no means the norm. Bear in mind, that in both state and private hospitals, a patient's family is expected to help out with basic nursing duties, which could prove problematical if on one's own.

ANIMAL QUARANTINE

There are no quarantine regulations as such for those bringing their **pets**, but you will need the usual vaccination certificates issued by your veterinary surgeon back home, and preferably translated by a Spanish consular official in the country of origin.

Dogs need a current certificate to prove that they have been inoculated against rabies—though no case of the disease has been reported in the Islands since 1927. Dogs are not allowed on beaches, in taxis, buses or restaurants. Pets arriving at airports in the Canaries are treated as baggage (meaning they are simply collected from the luggage carousels) assuming they have travelled on the same flight as their owner. If they have flown out unaccompanied, they are treated as freight and cannot be released from the airport until passed as fit by the airport veterinary officer.

GETTING ACQUAINTED

GOVERNMENT AND ECONOMY

The Canaries form two of Spain's 50 provinces. The province of Santa Cruz de Tenerife, consists of the islands of Tenerife, La Palma, Gomera and Hierro; and the province of Las Palmas de Gran Canaria, comprises the islands of Gran Canaria, Lanzarote and Fuerteventura.

Although an integral part of the Spanish state which reverted to being a monarchy after the death of General Franco in 1975, the Canaries became an autonomous region on 16 August 1982. Governed by the Gobierno de Canarias, which is responsible for strictly Canarian decisions, it has various councils in the role of local ministries called *consejerías* and the members of the parliament are of several different political colours and persuasions.

A *cabildo*, or local council, deals with matters related to each island. Each municipality has a mayor (*alcalde*) whose well-paid job it is to take an active and positive interest in his town's life and development. The town hall deals with purely urban matters, such as the town's police force (mainly concerned with traffic control nowadays), rates, fines, permits (foreign residents can now obtain a 30 percent discount when travelling by Trasmediterranea or Iberia, between the Canaries and mainland Spain, or 10 percent in the case of inter-island travel) and various taxes and charges levied on businesses. Further, each province has both a civil governor and a military governor, appointed from Madrid.

The **economy** relies on tourism, commerce and agriculture—bananas, tomatoes and avocado pears being the principal products exported to mainland Spain and Europe besides being grown for home consumption. Tourism is by far the biggest growth industry with an annual increase approaching 20 percent, each province receiving around 1-1/2 million visitors every year. Both Las Palmas (Gran Canaria) and Santa Cruz (Tenerife) have large ports, each handling more than 50 million tonnes of shipping annually.

GEOGRAPHY AND POPULATION

Totalling 870,000 inhabitants, the province of Las Palmas (Gran Canaris, Lanzarote and Fuerteventura) is the more populous, while that of Santa Cruz (Tenerife and the other islands) has some 700,000 residents. The islands of Tenerife and Gran Canaria are the most densely populated of the seven.

The total area of the archipelago is just under 3,000 square miles (7,770 sq. km) and the geography, while based on volcanic activity, is infinitely varied; the lunar **landscape** of the crater of Teide in Tenerife, which was the location for the film *One Million BC*, starring Raquel Welch in 1966; Lanzarote, which the first American Apollo astronauts visited as the place in the world most closely resembling the moon; the fertile valleys of La Palma and Hierro; the sandy desert of Fuerteventura; the grass-covered mountains of Gran Canaria; the pine forests of Gomera and Tenerife—the list is endless.

Some 700 miles (1,100 km) southwest of the Peninsula, as the Canarios refer to mainland Spain, the islands lie between 27 and 29 degrees north latitude and 13 and 18 degrees west longitude.

CLIMATE

The **climate** has made the islands very popular in recent years. At the turn of the century, the Grand Hotel Orotava and the Hotel Taoro Park in Puerto de la Cruz (Tenerife) and the Santa Catalina in Las Palmas (Gran Canaria) received the wealthy and the invalids from northern Europe. Nowadays the islands boast hundreds of hotels and apartment blocks of every level. Once a winter sunshine destination, the Canaries have become popular the year round.

There is little variation in temperatures between the four seasons (which do not have noticeable changes as happens in more northerly climes), ranging from 17 degrees centigrade in February, to 24.8 degrees centigrade in August.

However, between November and March, the temperature can fall quite sharply. Generally, the southern part of each island tends to be a few degrees warmer than the northern part, while at high altitudes the days and nights can be very cold in winter. Temporary visitors need not bring heavy clothing, and winter wear such as overcoats, gloves and boots is unnecessary, certainly in the tourist resorts.

TIME ZONES

The archipelago follows GMT. At noon in London and the Canaries, it is 1.00 p.m. in Madrid, 4.00 a.m. in Los Angeles and 7.00 a.m. in New York.

WEIGHTS AND MEASURES

Weights and measures are decimal (grams, kilos, centimetres, metres, kilometres, litres). Electrical current is 220 volts in modern buildings, and 110 volts in older properties, and it is unreliable, an *apagón* (power-cut) being quite frequent, especially in windy or rainy conditions. The better hotels and apartments, however, normally have their own generators.

HOLIDAYS

Fiestas, usually religious and sometimes merely historical, are celebrated in every hamlet, village, town and city in Spain, the Canaries being no exception, with each island having public holidays peculiar to itself. The bank holidays, when everything stops, are religious with just two exceptions and all apply to mainland Spain as well. January has two, the 1st (New Year's day) and the 6th (Epiphany or 12th Night or *Reyes*) when children receive their Christmas presents.

19 March is St Joseph's (Father's Day), while 7 May is Labour Day; 25 July celebrates St James' Day (he is the patron saint of Spain), and Santa Cruz fêtes its victory over Lord Nelson's attack on that day; 15 August, besides being the Feast of Our Lady of Candelaria (Candelaria is the patron saint of the Canaries), is the religious fiesta of the Holy Assumption.

Two months later, on 12 October, the *Día de la Hispanidad* celebrates Columbus' discovery of America on the same day in 1492: this date is commemorated in Latin America, too. 1 November is All Saints' Day (or "Day of the Defunct", when graves and tombs are garlanded with flowers). 6 December, day of the Constitution, is followed closely by the Immaculate Conception on 8 December. Christmas Day (25 December) ends the annual calendar of national holidays.

More parochially, the islands have a full timetable of **fiestas**, probably the most outstanding being carnival: the *Carnaval* (literally "goodbye to meat") processions and festivities of February in Puerto de la Cruz, Santa Cruz (both Tenerife) and Las Palmas (Gran Canaria)—the latter the most spectacular—are renowned and rival those of Río de Janeiro.

Noteworthy also is Corpus Christi in May or June, with the intricate sand- and flower-carpets of La Orotava and La Laguna in Tenerife.

In mid-September, *Las Fiestas del Santísimo Cristo* (the festival of the Most Holy Christ in La Laguna and Tacoronte in Tenerife), include firework displays, cattle shows, Canarian folklore and South American musical groups, *lucha canaria* (Canarian wrestling), a veteran car rally round the island and photographic exhibitions.

In June every fifth year in Santa Cruz de La Palma (La Palma), and every fourth year in Valverde, capital of Hierro, the "Descent of the Virgin" honours a 14th-century terracotta statue, when a religious procession accompanies this oldest of Canarian relics from the Sanctuary of the Holy Virgin of the Snows down to the capital, Santa Cruz de La Palma.

The calendar of fiestas and festivals is too full to be detailed, but local tourist offices (*Oficinas de Turismo*) can provide a breakdown. In brief, Tenerife can boast some 30; La Palma, eight; Gomera, five; Hierro, three; while in the province of Las Palmas, Gran Canaria can reckon on 24, Fuerteventura, six and Lanzarote, nine.

This count does not include every village feast day (it has been said there's one every day of the year somewhere), while some of those listed above last a week or more. The principal tourist offices are at: Santa Cruz, Plaza de España, tel. 242227; Puerto de la Cruz, Plaza de la Iglesia, tel. 384328; Las Palmas, Parque Santa Catalina, tel. 264623; Lanzarote, Parque Municipal, Arrecife, tel. 811860.

RELIGIOUS SERVICES

Spain, including the Canary Islands, is predominantly a Roman Catholic country and every town has its Catholic church. There are cathedrals in Las Palmas and La Laguna (previously the capital city of Tenerife and whose grid system of streets was used as the model for many Latin American cities on their foundation).

Today, the Roman Catholic authorities are much more tolerant and ecumenical vis-á-vis other religious denominations and sects. Long gone are the bad old days when Protestants who died on the islands were buried in the beaches, head down.

For 80 years there have been Anglican churches in Puerto de la Cruz (All Saints' Church, Taoro Park. Tel. 384038); Santa Cruz (St George's, Plaza 25 de Julio, behind the Civil Governor's residence); and in Las Palmas (Holy Trinity Church, *Ciudad Jardín* or Garden City); each having a resident chaplain. An Anglican Service is held every Sunday at 5.00 p.m. at the San Eugenio Church, Pueblo Canario, Playa de las Américas, Tenerife, tel. 387039, and Evangelical Services are held at 10.00 a.m. on Sundays in the TV Room of the Hotel Princesa Dacil in Los Cristianos and at the Tenerife Christian Centre, Apartamentos Teide, Calle Iriarte 6, Puerto de la Cruz, tel. 383179.

Tenerife and Gran Canaria both have Protestant cemeteries. The long-established and prosperous Indian community was allowed to build its own crematorium in Santa Cruz in 1988 to enable its dead to be burnt according to custom, although the practice had already existed for many years, during which time funeral pyres had been used for cremation purposes. The practice of burning the dead was of course long frowned upon by the Roman Catholic church. Other sects (for example the Jehovah's Witnesses) have increased in numbers in recent years.

LANGUAGE

While the language of the islands is Spanish, there are some variations on classical Castilian Spanish. The purest Castilian is reckoned to be still used in tiny Hierro, a heritage of westwardbound *conquistadores*.

Visitors familiar with the Spanish of the mainland, especially Castile, Leon and La Mancha, may notice the shorthand Spanish of the islanders: the endings of words are frequently dropped and the "th" quality of "proper" Spanish becomes an "s" sound. But that's how it's pronounced in South and Central America and even southern Spain itself.

Vocabulary peculiar to the Canaries includes *guagua* (bus), *malpaís* (lava-covered badlands), *papas* (potatoes), *bubango* (marrow), *luz* (for electricity generally) and *chicharerro* (an inhabitant of Santa Cruz).

COMMUNICATIONS

MEDIA

The islands, Tenerife in particular, are well served by English language and German language **newspapers** and **magazines**. For German-speaking readers the two magazines, the weekly *Teneriffa Woche* and the monthly *Teneriffa Monat*, are complemented by *Wochenspiegel*, a fortnightly newspaper printed, as is its English language counterpart *Here and Now*, by one of Tenerife's daily papers *Diario de Avisos*.

Magazines for English-speaking readers are the monthly *Tenerife Today* and *Island Gazette*, both of general interest with useful tips, telephone numbers, addresses and what-to-see sections, while *Tenerife Property Scene*, as its name suggests, is the island's only comprehensive property guide: all three are published and printed in Tenerife and widely distributed there and abroad. Other Tenerife-based Spanish-language newspapers are *El Día*, a daily, while *Jornada* appears on Mondays and concentrates on the weekend's sports results.

Gran Canaria has three newspapers— *Canarias 7*, *La Provincia* and *Diario de Las Palmas*. All major European daily newspapers are on the news-stands the day following publication.

Radio reception of European and American short-wave programmes is generally good, while *Radio Cadena* broadcasts in English, German and Swedish on weekdays from Las Palmas at 8.50 a.m. (Saturdays at 8.20 a.m.), giving local events, regional information, tourist tips, world news, weather, sports and exchange rates: tune in to 747 KHz, medium wave.

Spanish television offers two commercial channels, most of the programmes being relayed by satellite from mainland Spain and picked up by relay stations on Tenerife, La Palma and Gran Canaria. Some news bulletins and programmes of local interest originate from studios in Santa Cruz or Las Palmas. All are in Spanish, even the vast majority of non-Spanish programmes being dubbed.

POSTAL SERVICES

The **postal service** (*correos*) is normally quite efficient, although long delays can occur within the same island and between the islands. The price of a standard letter is seven pesetas (to a destination in the same town), 19 pesetas (within Spanish territory) and 45 pesetas inside Europe. A week is an average time for mail to and from other parts of Europe.

TELEPHONE AND TELEX

The **telephone service** Telefónica or Compañia Telefónica de España, has not been able to keep up with the demand for installation of new telephone lines. It is not unusual for private subscribers to wait more than two years for a telephone to be connected, and it is often easier (and clearer) to make a call to Europe than to ring another part of the same island.

Telefónica receive 2,000 complaints a week from dissatisfied customers in the Canaries. However, a welcome innovation has been the mushrooming of manned multi-cabin telephone centres, open from 9.00 a.m. to 9.00 p.m., though some stay open later. They are cheaper than kiosks, do away with the need to have precise change, are usually comfortable and the assistant does normally assist.

Telefónica also run a fax service in the major cities in case you do not have access to a private system. In Las Palmas (Gran Canaria) this is at Avenida 1º de Mayo 62, tel. (928) 371551, and in Santa Cruz (Tenerife), in the Plaza de España, tel. (922) 231202.

Also starting to appear on the islands, notably on Tenerife, Lanzarote and Gran Canaria, are satellite dishes able to pick up European and, soon, American television stations.

Dialling codes are 922- for Tenerife province numbers and 928- for Gran Canaria province when dialled from elsewhere within' Spain. International callers should ignore the 9.

EMERGENCIES

SECURITY AND CRIME

There was a time when it was usual to be able to leave houses and cars unlocked without risk, there being little or no robbery on the islands. Not so now. Crime is on the increase, especially petty theft, as the writer discovered to his cost when four wheels of a mini-car were removed one night. To finance drug-addiction, burglaries and *tirón* (handbag snatching from pedestrians in the street) are rife.

Police and consular advice is emphatic. Never carry large sums of money, passports or important documents—use the hotel's safe or security box—and never leave anything in a car, especially a rented one, as even the boot can easily be broken into.

Las Palmas (Gran Canaria) has the worst record for crime at the time of writing, to the extent that some British, German and Scandinavian tour operators have threatened to find alternative holiday destinations if something is not done.

Popular resorts in Tenerife, such as Playa de las Américas, Los Cristianos and Puerto de la Cruz, are not far behind, it must be added. This, interestingly, is in spite of newspaper reports that Canarian police are almost top of the league in Spain for solving crimes.

If a visitor or resident is the victim of a theft or other criminal activity, there are several options available. If you are on a package holiday, contact your representative or guide who should take control of the situation. Others who are residing or travelling under their own steam should contact the nearest consulate (between 9.00 a.m. and 1.00 p.m.) by telephone: in Tenerife province the British Consulate is at Plaza Weyler

8, First Floor, Santa Cruz—tel. 286863, while Gran Canaria province is covered from Luis Morote 6, Third Floor, Puerto de la Luz, Las Palmas—tel. 262508, 262512 and 262516.

Outside of these hours, find an interpreter with a good working knowledge of Spanish and your own language (your hotel reception should be able to help) and report your loss to the nearest Policía Nacional or Guardia Civil police station. These can be found in the telephone directory or in daily newspapers. Full insurance cover for property lost or stolen is indispensable, especially as only a tiny percentage is ever recovered.

If you are involved in an accident, the police must be informed immediately—the nearest telephone kiosk will list local telephone numbers to contact the fire brigade, ambulance services and police (both Guardia Civil and Policía Nacional). Try to ensure that injured people are not moved until either an ambulance or police-van arrives on the scene. If there are no personal injuries, still make sure that insurance details are exchanged. Do not have your car repaired until given the go-ahead after a mechanic's assessment of damage.

MEDICAL SERVICES

Where there are no facilities for dealing with serious illnesses or accidents, such as in Lanzarote and the smaller islands, helicopters are used to airlift patients to the larger and medically better-equipped islands. Private clinics in Tenerife include the Tamaragua, whose 24-hour emergency service can be contacted by telephoning 383551 or 380512 in Puerto de la Cruz; the Bellevue (permanent medical service, telephone 383551—5 lines) also in Puerto de la Cruz; the San Miguel (330550, 333712 or 333798 for 24-hour service) in La Orotava; and the International Health Centre in Playa de las Américas (791600).

In Gran Canaria the British American Clinic is in Las Palmas (telephone 264538, 262059 and 270751); the Queen Victoria Hospital (telephone 254243); and the International Clinic (telephone 245643) also in Las Palmas. There are no clinics in Lan-

zarote or in Fuerteventura.

The alternative to paying the very high costs of private medical treatment, unless you have a very comprehensive insurance cover, is the Social Security sector (see *Health* section above).

Another option is the *Centros Médicos* (Medical Centres) which are often open 24 hours a day and which can cope with first aid, injections, X-rays and even basic dental treatment (a very expensive consideration in the Canaries, being entirely private). If, however, you are in urgent need of more skilled dentistry than a simple extraction, you should go to an *odontólogo/estomatólogo* (dental surgeon).

GETTING AROUND

In recent years, a profusion of maps and guides of varying quality and to suit various tastes has appeared on the bookstalls and in the *librerías* (bookshops/stationers). The first, and still the most accurate, is Spain's equivalent to Britain Ordnance Survey series. Previously available only from the military headquarters of the provincial capitals, these *mapas militares* can now be bought in leading bookshops.

Editorial Everest produce annotated maps in different languages and the Firestone set of three road-maps (the whole archipelago, T32; Santa Cruz province, E50; and Las Palmas province, E49) are more than adequate for the holidaymaker.

For the botanist, Hubert Moeller's *What's Blooming Where on Tenerife?* or Editorial Everest's *Exotic Flora of the Canary Islands* and David and Zoe Bramwell's *Wild Flowers of the Canary Islands* should prove satisfying; for the more energetic, the island governments (*Cabildos*) in conjunction with ICONA (the Nature Conservation Institute) have produced maps of forest and mountain trails for walkers. The *Landscape* series covers Gran Canaria, Tenerife and La Gomera, giving car tours, walks and picnic suggestions and is produced by Sunflower Books of 12, Kendrick Mews, London SW7 3HG. The historically-minded should obtain Salvador Lopez Herrera's *The Canary Islands Through History*, published by Gráficas Tenerife, or *All the Canary Islands*, the Escudo de Oro edition.

PRIVATE TRANSPORT

Car hire: international rental companies such as Avis (with offices on all seven islands) and Hertz (on all save Gomera) are probably the best bet. Every major town will have at least one and, as is the case in tourist areas, many, car hire firms.

Beware back-street concerns, with just one or two cars and incredibly cheap terms. Take care even with reputable companies as "only 2,550 pesetas per day" can mean 3,350 pesetas not counting additional insurance cover, taxes and petrol, so read the small print very carefully. Fully comprehensive insurance is a necessity.

Taxis are not strictly "private transport" as they must all carry the "SP" plate—"Servicio Público". In provincial capitals, taxis are metered but elsewhere, for longer journeys, demand to see the *tarifa* (rates between different destinations).

You can import your own car for six months in any one calendar year. British European and Japanese car manufacturers are well represented on the islands and cars are generally cheaper than in Britain. Insurance is higher, the road fund licence still very low, petrol relatively cheap, but anybody resident for more than six months must exchange their national driving licence for a Spanish one.

SHOPPING

Since the Canaries became a duty-free area in 1852, by Royal Decree, commerce has flourished. Even if the visitor of the late 1980s finds the cost of living to be generally higher than at home, some items are still a *ganga* (bargain). Imported cigarettes, wines and spirits are much cheaper (oddly, local wine is dear) and some electrical goods, cameras and watches are also cheap, due to a lower luxury tax.

Property and land prices are highest near to large urban areas such as Puerto de la Cruz, Santa Cruz and the southern Tenerife development zones, as are those close to Las Palmas and Playa del Inglés in Gran Canaria.

Shopping areas worthy of a visit in Tenerife are the Calle Castillo district in Santa Cruz, the Paseo San Telmo, and other streets near the sea in Puerto de la Cruz. In Gran Canaria the port area of Las Palmas and the Mesa y Lopez and Triana streets are the best, (the latter having the excellent department stores El Corte Inglés and Galerías Preciados). Shops and offices in the Canaries generally open between 9.00 a.m. and 1.00 p.m. and 4.00 p.m. to 8.00 p.m., although some shops stay open later than this, especially over the Christmas/New Year/ Twelfth Night period, while in the summer months, many businesses operate from 8.00 a.m. to 2.00 p.m.

Post Offices (*Correos*) dispense stamps, parcels and other business between 9.00 a.m. and 2.00 p.m. on weekdays, but larger branches stay open for telegram and giro services until 7.00 p.m. Garages (*gasolineras*) provide petrol, oil, water and air between 8.00 a.m. and midnight—all the islands have at least one 24-hour petrol ·station, the larger ones having more. Mechanical repairs are carried out in a *taller* (workshop) and bodywork in a *chapista*.

Banking hours, for many years between 8.30 a.m. or 9.00 a.m. and 2.00 p.m. (9.00 a.m. to 1.00 p.m. on Saturday) are now undergoing a change. Some 25 percent of High Street Banks will now be opening from 8.00 a.m. to 5.00 p.m. from Monday to Thursday, but with reduced staff.

COMPLAINTS

The visitor (or resident) wishing to lodge a **complaint** now has recourse to several organisations concerned with citizens' welfare. The Consumer Advice bureaux in the islands comprise the office in Las Palmas (Gran Canaria), situated in the Santa Catalina hotel (the autonomous government's department of Economy and Commerce), telephone 231422; in Santa Cruz (Tenerife) it is on the Avenida Anaga no. 39 (or alternatively at the Spanish Tourist Board in the Calle Marina no. 57); in Adeje (South Tenerife) call 793165 at Pueblo Canario in Playa de las Américas; and in Puerto de la Cruz, the number is 387060.

By law, all establishments used by the general public (hotels, bars, restaurants, apartment blocks, etc.) must have a complaints book (*Libro de Reclamaciones*) which is checked periodically by the Ministry of Tourism and Information. To register a complaint, write (in English if necessary) in the *Libro de Reclamaciones*, detailing your objections.

SPECIAL INFORMATION

DOING BUSINESS

A special visa is not necessary to start a business in the islands. It is important to secure one's residency and get a self-employed work permit (*la residencia con permiso de trabajo cuenta propia*) which does not define the business involved.

To obtain this card—which in theory should be easier after 31 December 1992 with Spain's full membership of the EEC—one should employ a *gestor* (a semi-official commercial agent). The nearest consulate's commercial attaché will advise about who to see, as *gestores* tend to specialise in different spheres of commercial activity: ring 262508, 262512 or 262516 for the British Consulate in Las Palmas and 286863 in Santa Cruz. In Las Palmas the German consulate can be contacted on 275700, in Santa Cruz telephone 284812. The French Consulate in Las Palmas can be contacted on 242371, and in Santa Cruz the number to ring is 232710.

Further information about setting up a business is contained in consular leaflets such as *Procedure and Documentation for Establishing Business in Spain* issued by the British Consul.

The consulates will also be able to provide up-to-the-minute information regarding **import and export** laws. Basically, personal and household effects (radios and TVs, fridges, electric or gas ovens, washing machines, floor polishers, bicycles and pianos, etc.) which are imported on establishing residence can be brought into the Canaries by presenting to the Customs a duplicate inventory, in Spanish and visaed by the Spanish Consul in the country of origin.

STUDENTS

Due to the number of foreign immigrants, **schools** based on British, German and American educational systems have developed since the late Sixties. The private Spanish schools in the Canaries have longer hours, Spanish-medium tuition and curricula and teaching methods very different from British, French and German systems. Parents settling in the islands may be looking for a more familiar scene than this for their children's formative years.

The British School of Gran Canaria is at El Sabinal, Carretera de Marzapan, telephone 351167; there is also the Canterbury School at Juan XXIII, 44, in Las Palmas. Lanzarote has the British School of Lanzarote in the capital, Arrecife, at José Antonio 7.

In Tenerife the British Yeoward School is at Parque Taoro, Puerto de la Cruz, telephone 384685. It was established in 1969 and, like the British School of Gran Canaria, takes children from three or four years of age through to GCE/GCSE level at age 16. In the south of Tenerife, the Wingate School, Calle Mirador de las Cumbritas, El Llano, Cabo Blanco, telephone 791002, some seven miles (12 km) from Los Cristianos and Playa de las Américas, offers a British education for children from four to 14 years of age.

The Colegio Alemán in Tenerife is in Santa Cruz at Calle Enrique Wolfson 16, telephone 273937, or in Puerto de la Cruz at San Antonio 1, telephone 384062. Both establishments provide a curriculum based on German and Spanish, as will the newer Colegio Alemán on the outskirts of Playa de las Américas.

The American School at Los Hoyos, Tafira Alta in Gran Canaria, telephone 350400, takes pupils up to the age of 18.

Tenerife has a full **university** at La Laguna, formerly the island's capital, where students from the whole of Spain and from other countries follow higher education courses. In Gran Canaria, the Polytechnic has some university faculties, such as Law.

These two higher education institutes, instead of being complementary, have too often suffered from the ingrained inter-island rivalry which also manifests itself in other walks of life.

PILGRIMAGES

Ever a traditional people, the Canarios—with their distinctive music and dancing varying slightly from island to island; their *lucha canaria* (Canarian wrestling) and regional cuisine – naturally have a long-standing religious tradition.

The section above covered fiestas in the main: however, two pilgrimages are peculiar to the principal islands of the archipelago. The whole of Gran Canaria venerates 8 September each year with the celebration of the Fiesta de la Virgen del Pino (Festival of the Virgin of the Pine-tree) when pilgrims progress, many on their knees, to the sanctuary at Teror, some 17 miles (27 km) from Las Palmas. Tradition has it that the Virgin Mary appeared to the islanders at this spot; a basilica now marks the exact place where the patron saint of Gran Canaria materialised.

The patron saint of Tenerife is Candelaria (therefore a popular name for girls and often shortened to "Candi"). Pilgrims set off on 14 August—some camping in the desolate mountains—in order to arrive at the basilica of Candelaria on the following day. The town square of Candelaria, just off the motorway to the south, is noted for its statues of the Guanche kings (or *menceys*) as well as for its basilica to the Black Virgin, and the most devout of Canarians will cross the square on their knees, taking two steps forward and one step back.

THE DISABLED

The Spanish have a very uncomplicated attitude towards the physically and mentally incapacitated. While not making a conscious effort, people accept them readily. The poorly-sighted are particularly well cared for: men and women with poor eyesight find sociable employment selling lottery tickets and the blind are cared for by Spain's most organised and effective charity—ONCE (Organización Nacional de Cieqos Españoles, or National Organisation of Spanish Blind).

GAYS

Following the advent of "democracy" since Franco's régime, many hitherto clandestine groups have emerged. Apart from the politically extreme left, who were obliged to live abroad until 1975/1976, socially and sexually different groups have also appeared. It is common now to find gay and transvestite clubs in the larger cities and tourist resorts. Live sex shows are obviously successful, and transvestites have long been accepted in the Canaries, especially at Carnival time.

FURTHER READING

Banks, F R. *Your Guide to the Canary Islands*. Redman, London 1963.

Brown, A Samler. *Madeira and the Canary Islands*. Sampson Low, London 1889.

Brown, Alfred. *Madeira and the Canary Islands*. Robert Hale, London 1963.

Cioranescu, Alejandro. *Le Canarien* (texts by Gadifer de la Salle and Jean de Béthencourt). Tenerife, 1980.

Dicks, Brian. *Lanzarote, Fire Island*. Dryad, London 1988.

Du Cane, Florence. *The Canary Islands by Du Cane*. Charles Black, London, 1911

Fernandez-Armesto, Felipe. *The Canary Islands after the Conquest*. Clarendon, Oxford 1982.

Glas, George. *History of the Canary Islands* (translation from Spanish). 1764.

Léon. *Gran Canaria, Lanzarote, Fuerteventura*. Editorial Everest, Madrid 1974.

Hayter, Judith. *Canary Island Hopping*. Sphere, London 1982.

Mercer, John. *The Canary Islanders*. Collings, London 1980.

Mason, John and Anne. *The Canary Islands*. Batsford, London 1976.

Piazzi Smyth, Charles. *Tenerife or the advantages of a residence amongst the clouds*. 1852

Stone, Olivia. *Tenerife and its six satellites*. Marcus Ward, London 1887.

Wolfel, Dominik. *Estudios Canarios*. Burgfried-Verlag, Austria 1980.

Yeoward, Eileen. *Canary Islands*. Stockwell, Ilfracombe 1975.

GETTING AROUND

A bus service operates every 40 minutes between the airport and Las Palmas, beginning at Las Palmas 5.30 a.m. (last bus 12.50 p.m.) The journey (in town, buses leave from San Telmo Park bus station) takes about 25 minutes and costs 125 pts. Most major hotels and all tour companies send coaches to the airport, and taxis are also availabe (1,800 pts to Las Palmas, 4,500 pts, or so to the south). There is no bus service to the south from the airport.

INLAND

Las Palmas has an excellent city bus service (yellow, one-man-operated) with a flat fare of 50 pts; or you can buy a card valid for ten trips called a *bono guagua* (pronounced wa-wa), price 400 pts from kiosks at bus terminals and in Santa Catalina Park. The main routes are from the port to Triana (no. 1), from the port to Plaza Cairasco (two streets north of Triana) via the Garden City (no. 2), and to the same plaza via the hilly "Higher City" (no. 3).

All major routes pass through Santa Catalina Park and if you take, for instance, the no. 30, you will have a good long ride and see how locals live away from the tourist zone. The no. 12 is an express bus along the Avda. Maritime which runs between the Bus Station and Triana. Avoid the rush hour if you can. Some 30,000 cars a day come and go at this time (8.30-9.30 a.m., 1 p.m. and around 7.30 p.m.) and the traffic is awful. City buses run from dawn till about 9.30 p.m. and there's an hourly night service on major routes.

Inter-city buses leave from the Bus Station at San Telmo Park, and are cheap and good. The green Salcai buses cover the south of the island and the blue Utinsa buses the centre and the north. Buses leave on the hour and half-hour except for the express buses marked *directo* for Maspalomas (via Playa del Inglés) and Puerto Rico. These are more frequent and tend to leave as soon as they're full. There's a special cheap day return to Maspalomas (250 pts) on Sundays and fiestas. If you want to go to Mogán, change at Puerto Rico.

WATER TRANSPORT

This is the best way of visiting the other islands since plane schedules, though frequent, are not adequate. They are being augmented in 1989 by a new inter-island shuttle service, Binter Canarias, which should be in full operation by 1991. Meantime, Trasmediterranea operates a good ferry and jetfoil service around the Canaries. There's a daily ferry to Tenerife (four hours) and four jetfoils (07.30, 09.30, 15.00 and 17.00 except Sundays, when there is no 09.30 service) and the crossing takes 80 minutes.

You can also visit Fuerteventura by jetfoil on Mondays, Thursdays and Saturdays, but be prepared to stay overnight as the jetfoil deposits its passengers and returns at once to Las Palmas.

There are three ferries a week to Lanzarote, three to Fuerteventura, one to La Palma and one to Hierro. Gomera is reached via Santa Cruz on Tenerife and a ferry from Los Cristianos in the south of the island (daily service). Check local travel agents for details of weekend mini-cruises to Tenerife and La Palma, and you will have to reserve a place on the Lanzarote or Fuerteventura ferry.

TAXIS

These are comparatively cheap. The metre reading starts at 70 pts. Expect to pay 250 to 300 pts to cross Las Palmas from Las Canteras to Triana; maximum four to a taxi. Drivers are quite flexible about longer trips and often offer special "bargain" fares to the mountains, airport and so on. These are worth accepting. But you get no bargains if you take a taxi from the airport. The present rate is 1,800 pts and it will go up soon. Taxi ranks are clearly marked with a sign, (white T on dark blue).

HIRING A CAR

Arrange this through your hotel or apartment reception, or from almost any travel agent, as well as on arrival at the airport. Most companies offer unlimited mileage. Prices range from 2,600 pts for a Ford Escort, 4,600 pts for a six-seater jeep, and so on. Insurance is usually extra and drivers must have held a licence for at least a year. Delivery and collection are free during office hours (9 a.m. to 7 p.m.) and a deposit is always required. Before hiring a car remember that parking in Las Palmas can be a nightmare and that coach excursions are first-class. But there is no way to really enjoy the hidden delights of the island without a car. Never leave anything valuable in a rented car.

WALKING

Not recommended in this mountainous island, except for the really hardy visitor who wants a six-hour hike up a mountain and who is prepared to spend a night in the open (see Sports).

HITCHIKING

Hitching is safer in Gran Canaria than almost anywhere in the world but it can take a long time. It is easier in the south because there are more tourists than in the capital—where drivers are usually businessmen in a hurry or, at weekends, well loaded down with families.

WHERE TO STAY

HOTELS

Most visitors are pleasantly surprised at the price of hotels in Gran Canaria, particularly at the first-class level. Lower-priced hotels aren't anything special, but still comparatively cheap. Prices listed here are for a double room (for two people) without breakfast. A single is about 60 to 70 percent of the price of a double. Expect to pay about 300 pts for breakfast (more in a five star hotel).

HOTELS IN LAS PALMAS
(LOCAL DIALLING CODE 928)

Melias (Cristina), Calle Gomera 6. 5 star. Tel. 366454, Tx 95161. 316 rooms. Nov-April 14,080 pts, May-Oct 12,980. Facing Las Canteras, with large pool, cocktail bar, restaurants, discotheque El Coto, convention halls, garage.

Reina Isabel, Calle Alfredo L Jones 40. 5 star. Tel. 260100, Tx 95103 HOCAS. 234 rooms, 11,000 pts. Large rooftop pool with bar and dancing nightly, restaurant, convention halls, grillroom, garage. Right on Las Canteras. Two groundfloor bars, one on promenade.

Santa Catalina Hotel, Parque Doramas. 5 star. Tel. 243040, Tx 96014 HSEA. Situated in Garden City opposite Sporting Marina, this beautiful hotel is listed as a historic building and is where the British Prince Charles and the Spanish Royal Family stay. 208 rooms, 15,000 pts. Casino, restaurant, cocktail bar, convention halls, tennis courts

and pool in lovely garden.

Los Bardinos Sol, Calle Eduardo Benot 3, 4 star. Tel. 266100, Tx 95189 DJUAN. 215 rooms, 7,550 to 9,300 pts. This is Las Palmas's highest hotel, 23 storeys built like a mini version of London's Telecom Tower with panoramic views from the Dinos disco on 22nd floor. Rooftop pool, convention halls, restaurant, bar.

Concorde, Calle Tomas Miller 8. 4 star. Tel. 262750, Tx 95593 CONCO. 127 rooms. Very central, minute from beach, with pool, bar, restaurant. 5,720 to 6,380 pts.

Iberia Sol, Maritime Avenue (North). 4 star. Tel. 361133, Tx 95413 HILP. 298 rooms. Nov-April 10,045 pts, May-Oct 8,895 pts. Sea view, at the other end of town near commercial centre, popular with businessmen; convention halls, restaurant, bars, disco.

Imperial Playa, Calle Ferreras 1. 4 star. Tel. 264854. Tx 95340. Old-established hotel at one end of Las Canteras with panoramic view of the beach. 173 rooms, 7,900 pts. Restaurant, bingo, nightclub, bar.

Rocomar, Calle Lanzarote 10, 4 star. Tel. 265600. Opposite Las Canteras, bar, restaurant, nightclub. 87 rooms, Nov-April 6,750, May-Oct 5,000 pts.

Tigaday, Calle Ripoche 4. 4 star. Tel. 264720. Overlooks Santa Catalina Park (five minutes from Las Canteras). Bar, restaurant, bingo, entertainment. 160 rooms, 5,600 pts.

Atlanta, Calle Alfredo L Jones 37. 3 star. Tel. 265062. Smallish, friendly, very central, three minutes from beach, bar. 58 rooms, 3,000 pts.

Cantur, Calle Sagasta 28. 3 star. Tel. 262304. Friendly tourist hotel on beachfront. Bar. 124 rooms, 3,500 pts.

Fataga, Calle Nestor de la Torre 21. 3 star. Tel. 270408, Tx 096221 FAGA. Central for shopping, eight minutes from beach. Bar, restaurant. 92 rooms 5,500 pts.

Faycun, Calle Nicolas Estevanez 61. 3 star. Tel. 270650, Tx 95189 DJUAN. Just off Las Canteras promenade, bar, restaurant. 61 rooms, 3,300 pts.

Gran Canaria. Paseo de Las Canteras 38. 3 star. Tel. 275078, Tx 96453. The first hotel to be built on Las Canteras. Bar, restaurant, 90 rooms 5,800 to 4,600 pts.

Las Lanzas, Bernado de las Torre 79, 3 star. Tel. 265504. Very popular with Scandinavia who blockbook winter months. One minute from beach, bar. 31 rooms, mid-Oct to mid-April 3,500 pts. Mid-April to mid-June 2,800 pts, thereafter 3,000 pts.

Miraflor, Calle Dr Grau Bassas 21. 3 star. One minute from beach. Bar, restaurant. A favourite with regulars who return year after year. Price varies with length of stay, position of room. 78 rooms, 2,400 to 4,200 pts.

Nautilus, Paseo de Las Canteras 5. 3 star. Wonderful position at top of beach near Imperial Playa. Bar, 49 rooms, 5,200 pts.

Parque, Muelle de Las Palmas 2. 3 star. Tel. 368000. At the old city end of town, very near bus station. Bar, restaurant. 119 rooms, Nov-April 5,500 pts, May-Oct 4,750 pts.

Rosalia, Calle Dr Miguel Rosas 3. 3 star. Tel. 265850. Midway between Santa Catalina Park and beach, small and friendly. 40 rooms. 2,500 pts April to July, then rising to a peak of 3,000 pts Nov-March.

Atlantida, Calle Nicolas Estevanez 64, 2 star. Tel. 376356. Close to beach. Nov-April 3,000 pts, May-Oct 2,500 pts.

Funchal, Calle Los Martinez de Escobar 66. Tel. 265578. 2 star. 35 rooms, About 3,000 pts, less in May and June.

Pujol, Calle Salvador Cuyes 5. 2 star. Tel. 274433. Very near beach, bar, 48 rooms, 3,000 pts. (a noisy street).

Verol, Calle Sagasta 25. 2 star. Tel. 262104. One minute from beach. Very popular cafeteria bar. 25 rooms, 2,900 to 3,300 pts.

Duque, Calle Ripoche 14. Tel. 263944. Very near Santa Catalina Park but no frills. With bath, 1,500 pts, with washbasin 1,200 pts. 18 rooms.

Plaza, Calle Luis Morote 16. Tel. 265212. 45 rooms, 2,500 pts with bath, 1,500 pts washbasin only. Close to beach.

Savoy, Calle 29 de Abril. Tel. 277885. Midway between beach and Sta Catalina Park. 29 rooms, 1,400 pts.

Viera, Calle Pedro de Castille 9. Tel. 269601. Close beach. 32 rooms, 1,500 pts.

OUT OF TOWN HOTELS

• Agaete

Princess Guayarmina, Los Berrazales. Tel. 898009. Picturesque location, bar, heated swimming pool. 27 rooms, 3,500 pts. Old spa hotel.

• Arucas

Bella Arehucas, Calle Panchito Hernandez 10. Tel. 600651 10 rooms, 1,200 pts.

• Bahia Feliz

Bahia Feliz ("Happy Bay") is the first of the southern tourist complexes and is most attractive, with chalets, apartments, shopping centres and **The Orchidea Hotel**, with every amenity including pools, nightclub and gardens. 4 star. Tel. 764600, Tx 96232. 252 rooms. Nov-Dec 14,900 pts, Jan-April 10,600 pts, May-Oct 7,700 pts.

• San Agustin

Tamarindos Sol, Calle Retamas 3. 5 star. Tel. 762600, Tx 95463 AHOE. An elegant and beautifully appointed hotel which for many years housed the island's only casino (now there is one in Las Palmas's Santa Catalina Hotel). Pool and tennis in beautiful gardens sloping down to beach. Restaurant, popular discotheque, convention and banqueting halls, and La Scala, the famous dance troupe (see Nightlife). 318 rooms, Nov-April, 20,120 pts, July-Oct 22,400 pts, May-June 17,690 pts.

Folias, Calle Las Retamas 17, 4 star. Tel. 762450, Tx 95660 INAT. A few minutes from San Agustin beach, this smallish hotel is very reasonably priced and justly popular. It has gardens, nightclub, bar and restaurant. 79 rooms. Oct-April 5,000 pts, May-Sept 4,000 pts.

Don Gregory, Calle Los Tabaibas 11. 4 star. Tel. 762658, Tx 96072 DGHIE. This elegant hotel backs onto a sheltered cove, just past San Agustin and within easy reach of the commercial centre. Pool, bar, restaurant, suites available. 241 rooms, Nov-April 23,000 pts, May-Oct 16,000 pts.

Ifa Beach, Calle Los Jazmines 25. 3 star. Tel. 765100. 200 rooms, Nov-April 9,500 pts, May-Oct 8,250 pts. Nightclub, pool, bar, restaurant.

• Playa Del Inglés

Las Margeritas, Avda. Gran Canaria 38, 4 star. Tel. 761112, Tx 96516. Main attraction is the large pool in exquisite shady garden; close to busy Avda. Tirijana and with its own bar, nightclub, restaurant, gym, tennis, etc. 323 rooms; prices range from 6,400 pts to 11,900 pts.

Lucana, Plaza del Sol. 4 star. Tel. 762700, Tx 96529 ANULE. Pool, garden, bar—typical of upper medium price range hotels in the south. 107 rooms. Nov-April 7,400 pts, July-Oct 6,600 pts, May-June 5,900 pts.

Don Miguel, Avda. Tirijana 36, 3 star. Tel. 761508, Tx 96307. Convention hall, bar, restaurant, garden, pool, tennis. 251 rooms. Nov-April 8,000 pts, July-Oct 7,000 pts, May-June 6,000 pts.

Continental, Avda. de Italia, 3 star. Tel. 761605, Tx 96631. Gardens, pool (another for children) bar, restaurant. 383 rooms, 7,000 pts.

Waikiki, Avda. de Gran Canaria 20, 3 star. Tel. 762300, Tx 95216 AMOEX. Circular buildings set in beautiful gardens with pools (and lots of organised entertainment), tennis, nightclub, bar and restaurant, also garden cafe/bar. 508 rooms, prices 4,350 pts to 8,800 pts.

Rey Carlos, Avda. Tirijana 14, 3 star. Tel. 760116, Tx 96307. Streamlined elegance and chic disco bar, gardens and pool. 180 rooms, Nov-April 10,000 pts, July-Oct 9,000 pts, May-June 8,000 pts.

Escorial, Avda. de Italia 6, 2 star. Tel. 761358. Oct-April 6,000 pts, May-Sept 5,300 pts.

• Maspalomas

Maspalomas Oasis, Playa de Maspalomas, 5 star. Tel. 760170, Tx 95025. Princes, presidents, playboys come here; so do film stars, pop groups, and VIPs from all over the world, to enjoy every luxury a hotel can possibly provide. The Oasis was the first and is still the best hotel in the south, possible in all of Spain, with pools and tennis courts set in a vast and exotic garden. It's a stone's throw from the magnificent Maspalomas dunes but often guests don't leave the hotel grounds. Famed for its cuisine, dancing to live music nightly. 342 rooms, Nov-April 30,000 pts, May-Oct 15,000 pts.

Hotel Faro, Playa de Maspalomas, 4 star. Tel. 760462, Tx 95295 IFARO. Relatively new, overlooking beach and dunes, with convention hall, restaurant, bar, nightclub, pool. 188 rooms. Nov-April 23,055 pts, May-Oct 11,230 pts.

Maspalomas Palm Beach, 4 star. Tel. 762920, Tx 96365. Beside the beach, it has a swimming pool used (for many years before the hotel was built) for medicinal purposes, and medical services are provided along with the usual facilities. 358 rooms. Nov-April 24,800 pts, May-Oct 16,400 pts.

APARTMENTS

Large numbers of visitors to Gran Canaria opt for an apartment. The first and most obvious reason is that for every hotel there are at least eight apartment blocks. With new developments in the south, some of them giant 6,000 bed projects, this ration is probably already changing. Apartments are much cheaper than hotels, too.

How to find an apartment: if you come on a flight-only ticket, it is best to check into a hotel for a day or two while looking around. Some travel agents will help and the Tourist Information Offices have an extensive brochure (see Useful Addresses). But even this department can't keep pace with development. Word-of-mouth or just driving around looking for *se alquiler* ("to let") signs are, along with the brochure, the best ways of finding an apartment. There are plenty available except at Christmas, New Year and Easter week periods.

Listed below are a few apartments from each resort to give you an idea of per-night prices, which are higher in the winter; a studio sleeps two, a one-bedroomed apartment three, a two-bedroomed five people. This is only a selection: complete list of apartments would fill this book and be quickly out of date.

• Las Palmas

Aguas Verde, Paseo de Las Canteras 47, Tel. 268450.
104 apts on beach (not all with sea view), studio 2,800-5,000 pts, one-bedroom 11,200-14,000 pts, two-bedroom 12,800-16,000 pts.

Farylaga Playa, Calle Alfredo L Jones 42, Tel. 271800. Luxury block, many apts having large terraces overlooking Las Canteras. 29 apts. One-bedroom 3,575-6,383 pts, two-bedroom, 4,344 to 7,377, three-bedroom 6,744-7,860 pts.

Playa Sol, Paseo de Las Canteras 74. Tel. 261480. 22 apts. One-bedroom, 2,000-3,700 pts.

Brisamar, Paseo de Las Canteras 49. Tel. 269400. 85 apts. One-bedroom 1,500-4,500 pts.

Catalina Park, Calle Tomas Miller 67, Tel. 264124. Very central, close to beach. 76 apts, studio 1,800-3,000 pts. One-bedroom 1,800-4,800 pts.

Colon Playa, Calle Alfredo L Jones 45. Tel. 265954, overlooking beach. 41 apts, one-bedroom 3,500-4,600 pts.

Turismar, Calle Sargento Llargas 33, Tel. 275808. 48 apts, studios. 2,000-2,500 pts. One minute beach.

Marmoral, Calle Dr Grau Bassas 38, Tel. 271208. One minute beach. 44 apts, studio 3,130 pts. One-bedroom 3,400 pts.

• Playa Del Inglés

(All the developments listed have swimming pools and gardens, most have bars and restaurants.)

Marieta, Avda. De Italia 15. 128 apts, one-bedroom, 5,000-7,500 pts.

Paraiso Maspalomas, Avda. Gran Canaria. Tel. 762350. Luxurious gardens and pools. 390 apts, one-bedroom 4,500-5,500 pts.

Aguila Playa, Plaoleta Hibiscus 1, Tel. 763144. 58 apts, one-bedroom 1,800-3,000 pts.

Broncemar, Avda. Italia. Tel. 762570; stunning pools. 207 apts, one-bedroom, 5,000 pts.

Las Olas, Avda. Italia 20. Tel. 764621. 70 apts, all two-bedroom, 4,000-6,000 pts.

Los Tilos, Avda. Espania 11. Tel. 761300. 118 apts, one-bedroom, 2,600-4,500 pts.

• Bahia Feliz

Las Pitas, Playa de Tarajilillo. 108 apts, studio 6,655-7,260 pts, one-bedroom 8,350-9,075 pts.

• Puerto Rico

(Some blocks here are a fair way from the beach, though all have pools.)

Rio Piedras, Avda. de Ancla 2. Tel. 745898. Luxury block with nightclub, restaurants, close to beach. 98 apts, one-bedroom, 6,000-11,500 pts. Two-bedroom 8,000-13,700 pts.

Tindaya, Calle Tasartico 17. Tel. 745725. Marvellous view but not near beach. 82 apts, one-bedroom, 2,000-3,000 pts. (All have sun terraces.)

Barlovento, Avda. Fuerteventura 12. Tel. 745184. 64 apts, one-bedroom 5,000 pts.

• Maspalomas

Sun Club, Avda. Oasis, Tel. 762897. 64 apts, one-bedroom 13,225 or 14,350 pts.

Villa Eden, Avda. Oasis. 16 apts, one-bedroom 10,000-13,000 pts. Two-bedroom 14,000-17,000 pts.

• San Agustin

Interclub Atlantico, Calle Los Jazmines 2. Tel. 760950. 264 apts, one-bedroom 8,500 pts. Two-bedroom 10,300 pts.

Solares, Calle Los Jazmines 11. Tel. 760770. 32 apts, one-bedroom 4,500 pts.

• Arguineguin/Patalavaca

Aquamarina, Patalavaca. Tel. 735125. Absolutely luxurious with beautiful gardens and pool; nautical sports. 60 apts, one-bedroom 15,200 pts. Two-bedroom 22,300 pts.

Donana, Patalavaca. Tel. 735012. 49 apts, one-bedroom 2,500 pts.

Bungalows los Canarios 1, Arguineguin. Tel. 735189. Above main road on slight hill, plenty of shops and restaurants, and a lovely view. 132 apts, one-bedroom 3,300-3,800 pts. Two-bedroom 5,500 pts.

LIVING CHEAPLY

There are no such things as boarding houses in Gran Canaria, but by some magic, the most charming and picturesque places (possibly because they haven't been overdeveloped) are the cheapest ones in which to stay. In Arguineguin, there's **Pension Léon** (behind the supermarket of that name), a fascinating maze of corridors and interior rooms with a rather fierce lady in charge. She has a heart of gold, really! The 'phone number is 735035 but it's difficult to make reservations in *pensions*. Just go and hover at the supermarket. If they are full, try **Pension Naira** at the other end of the bay.

In Mogán Port there's a small, tasteful and absolutely delightful tourist development which is also very expensive. But you too can mingle with the millionaire yachtsmen for less than 1,000 pts a night if you are patient. There are several little *pensions* in the old port, and three or four on the main road just outside it. These you can see from the bus as it enters Mogán—**Eva**, **Bartolo** (760267) **Juan Deniz** (740205) and **Magali**. Usually reservations aren't taken, it's first come and first served. Midday is the best time to try, when others vacate their rooms. The best and most beautiful is the whitewashed **Casa de Guillermo**, with great cool patios and rather dark rooms, pleasant communal kitchen and separate dining patio. The telephone number is a state secret but it is just across the road from the bus stop and a great shadowy tree. Good luck!

CAMPING

There is a caravan site just outside—and beyond—Maspalomas, on the right going towards Puerto Rico. It is about 3,000 pts to rent a caravan, less to bring your own, and there are good facilities.

The most popular camping site of all is **Guantanamo**, by Playa de Tauro; it used to be a hippies' paradise but is quite respectable now with a post office, lounge, supermarket, restaurants and bars, showers and toilets and a children's playground. The beach is a lovely half-moon cove, and the eucalyptus trees shade the path to it. Price per day, adult 175 pts, child 110 pts, small tent 175 pts, family tent 200 pts, car 175 pts, caravan 200 pts.

There's another camping site in woodland near Agüimes, 15 miles (25 kms) from Las Palmas. The address is **Temisas**, Lomo de la Cruz, and it can take 50 campers. Prices: 50 pts adults, small tent 110 pts, family tent 135 pts, car 115 pts, caravan 130 pts. Facilities include telephone, washrooms with electricity, showers, bar and swimming pool.

Be careful about camping on the many little beaches in the south, for mostly it is forbidden. However, if you feel like some mountain air and have a sleeping bag, go up to Tejeda and pick yourself a cosy cave. If in doubt, ask…a villager will probably direct you to one. But do take warm clothing, for the nights can be very cold even in summer. For other camping possibilities, see Sports (walking).

FOOD DIGEST

Eating out is the local pastime and, because Canarios are not well off, it's a cheap and endlessly enjoyable way of spending your evenings and lunches. Of course, there are a few very expensive restaurants, for businessmen, special family occasions, and well-heeled tourists. But by and large, you can eat and drink very satisfactorily for 1,000 pts, and if you want to spend more, you get candles and damask table cloths and maybe a brandy on the house!

Most restaurants have a "menu of the day" (by law they should) which consists of three courses—the third usually fruit—and including a glass of wine or water, and bread. This cost anything from 500 pts to double that price, the average for a good restaurant being about 750 pts. There is also a complaints procedure for all bars and restaurants and if you feel it is justified, ask for the *hoja de reclamaciones* (*hoja* is pronounced oh-hah). But this is a very serious step so try to sort things out before taking it.

Beware of the occasional restaurant that gives you an unpriced menu; that is a justifiable complaint and quite illegal. Every menu and bar price list should be on display and stamped by the authorities. Service is invariably included, there is no cover charge or tax, but beware the little extras like garlic bread or a "recommended" wine for it could double your bill. On the whole Canarios are honest, hospitable and courteous, so bon appetit!

The local specialities are *tapas*, on display in most Spanish-owned bars. Do not try to translate some of them literally; *ropa vieja*, a kind of stew, means "old woman's clothes". As a brief guide, *estofado* is also a stew, *conejo* is rabbit, *higado* is liver, *albondigas* are meat-balls, *salsa mojo* is a spicy garlicky sauce used with new potatoes or (the green type) with fish *(pescado)*. Words like soup, salad, potatoes, are almost the same in Spanish. These *tapas* can be delicious and very cheap; in the country you can fill up with two or three for around 250 pts. The nearer you are to a beach or resort, the more you will pay.

The next stage after a *tapa* is a *medio racion*, or a small plate. A full *racion* is usually shared by two people. Two special dishes are quite costly; cold roast leg of pork and smoked ham (j*amon cerrado*). So is the excellent local cheese (*queso*).

There are hundreds of restaurants and *tapas* bars in Las Palmas, though fewer of the latter in the south. The prices below are based on a two-course meal (as a guideline we used an avocado and seafood cocktail followed by a fillet steak, with a bottle of house wine) for two people. Menus of the day and specialities are given where possible, and day of closing. It's seldom possible to reserve a table; the customary hour for dining is late at around 10 p.m. and some restaurants close for a full month or more in the summer.

LAS PALMAS

CANARIAN COOKING

Pais de Gales, Calle Montevideo 81. A good start to exploring Canarian cuisine, for Manuel speaks English and his Welsh wife Holly is there Fridays, too. Wide range of *tapas* in small but charming bar/restaurant, open daily except Sundays from 11 a.m. to 2 a.m. Always a choice of about 15 *tapas*. A meal for two (not necessarily Canarian) 2,000 pts.

La Cascada, Calle Tomas Miller. Very long *tapas* bar with restaurant beyond. Typical Canarian plus international cuisine. Open 8 a.m. to 1 a.m. Menu of the day 525 pts. Meal for two with wine 2,000 pts. Special breakfast menu 195 pts.

Taberna O'Palleiro, Calle Capital Lucena. Popular upmarket *tapas* bar with restaurant on first floor. Famed for sea food.

Open for lunch and dinner daily. Grilled platter of various fish, 3,000 pts for two. House wine 695 pts.

Tenderete, Calle Leon y Castillo 91. Tel. 246350. Owned by famous Canarian chef Pepe Lujan, this is a magnificent—in fact royal—restaurant to visit. The King and Queen of Spain lunched here! Open daily 1 p.m. to midnight. You can spend 300 or 3,000 pts according to your choice.

TYPICAL BRITISH

El Fogon, Calle Galileo 5. Tel. 262563. Fancy roast beef and Yorkshire pudding for Sunday lunch? Or a trencherman's helping of fish and chips? Home from home for lonely British ex-pats; Tom and Liz are there daily except Mondays, lunch and dinner. About 1,800 pts.

LUXURY VENUE

The Hotel Reina Isabel's eighth floor grillroom is enchanting in shades of blue, with a panoramic view from huge picture windows overlooking the beach. The *maitre* once worked at the Caprice in London. He recommends seafood salad and steak "Reina Isabel" which, with a bottle of good wine, would come to 8,000 pts (for two, of course). Open every day.

COSMOPOLITAN

The Balalaika, Calle Fernando Guarnateme 27. Tel. 274483. Large elegant Russian restaurant, interesting menu. If you avoid the caviar, about 4,5,00 to 5,000 pts. Open midday to midnight, closed Sundays.

Le Francais, Calle Sargento Llargas 18. Tel. 268762. Very popular authentic French cuisine, small but delicious menu, steaks with mushroom or avocado sauce particularly good. 3,500 pts. Open daily except Sundays, lunch and dinner.

Anita, Calle Torres Quevedo 16. Tel. 271009. Friendly little Danish restaurant, a different "dish of the day" every evening; immaculate, homely, delicious puddings. 1,800 pts. Closed Mondays.

Kim's Steak House, Calle Alfredo L Jones 19. Tel. 264057. Owned by a British couple, this intimate little steak house has a high reputation. Various steaks and stroganoff, first class. Closed Sundays and in May and June. 3,500 pts or less.

El Cerdo que Rie (the laughing pig), Paseo de Las Canteras 31. Large basement restaurant which is everyone's favourite. Some tourists eat here every night of their stay! Locals love it too. Small bar while you wait. Large and luscious menu, flambées and fondue specialities. 3,000 pts. Open daily till 11.30 p.m.

El Gallo Feliz (the happy cockerel), Paseo de Las Canteras 35. The sister restaurant of the "Pig". Slightly less exuberant, with elegant alcoves and panelling, similar menu and prices. Usually closes for a month in the summer.

Los Cedros, Calle Los Martinez de Escobar 68. Tel. 269667. Fabulous Lebanese cuisine, pleasant decor and bar. The traditional mixed starters are too much for most people. 2,500 pts. Open for lunch and dinner, closed Mondays.

HEALTY APPETITES

La Strada, Calle Tomas Miller 58. Tel. 273351/94. Self service with a marvellous selection of hot and cold dishes, as many helpings as you please, and live music in the evenings. Superb value at around 800 pts a head (plus wine). First floor.

The International, directly opposite La Strada, offers an excellent variety of self service dishes too. About the same price. Both open daily from midday till 11 p.m.

MEALS WITH A VIEW

El Pitango (steak house) and **El Padrino** (fish) are two excellent restaurants in Los Colerados on the hillside above La Isleta. Wonderful views with food to match. The steak house is closed Mondays and the fish restaurant Thursdays. Highly recommended for hot summer nights! Indoor and outdoor dining. Take no. 42 bus from Santa Catalina Park, or taxi. Check summer closings (Pitango Tel. 263194, Padrino Tel. 272094). 3,500 pts.

ECONOMY PLUS

Kennedy, Calle Secretario Artiles 75. **Jeremiah**, next door.

Just behind Santa Catalina Park, these restaurants are open daily from midday to 11 p.m. Menu of the day 425 pts, and à la carte or *plato combinado*. Most people opt for the menu; usually there's a choice of three starters and two main courses, pudding and a large glass of wine.

VEGETARIAN

Pasta Real, Secretaria Padillo 28. Tel. 262267.
This bistro-type restaurant, renowned for its Italian food, is also about the only one that offers macro-biotic vegetarian food as well. Check for summer closing. In winter, open daily for lunch and dinner, 2,000 pts.

Hamburgo, General Orgaz 54. Tel. 222745.
Near the Imperial Playa, but take a taxi. Lots of fun and superb cuisine, German/international. Smoked platter is delicious, so is the sole *cordon bleue*. 4,000 pts. Closed Wed, Sunday and one month late autumn, check by phone. A must for gourmets. Open for lunch and dinner.

FLOATING FOOD

The Mississippi is a very authentic looking steamboat moored in the Sporting Marina in Las Palmas; it has a bar on the middle deck, dining room on the top deck, 4,000 pts. Open from 11 a.m. till 2 a.m. Great atmosphere but even on a calm day the ship rolls a bit! Closed Wednesday.

ETHNIC FOOD

Elsewhere in Las Palmas Italian restaurants abound, the best being the **Pizza Real**, a bit off the beaten track (Calle Mas de Gaminde 11. Tel. 246138). Very popular with expats, fine pizzas and mouthwatering puddings. Two Japanese restaurants are well-known: the Fuji, Calle F Guarnateme 56 and **El Presidente**, Calle Barcelona 13, both closed Sundays and a bit pricier than the many Chinese restaurants. The pick of the latter are **Casa Playa**, at the bottom of Calle Torres Quevedo overlooking the beach, and **House Ming**, Paseo de Las Canteras 30— ask for the owner's recommendations if you want a memorable meal at the latter.

There's no Indian restaurants in Las Palmas, which is surprising considering the 3,000-strong Indian community.

DOWN SOUTH

San Agustin Beach Club, San Agustin. Tel. 760400. Well known for the quality, creativity and generosity of its magnificent dishes. Imports the best shellfish. You can eat in the large dining-room or the terrace solarium. Open daily throughout the year, menu of the day (for one) 3,000 pts, average for two people 8,000 pts.

Viuda de Franco, at the top of Avda. Tirijana on the motorway, Playa del Inglés. Tel. 760371. Offers a wide variety of international dishes. The fine service and the quality of cuisine makes it a popular spot for tourists and locals alike. Menu of the day 650 pts a head, meal for two 3,000 pts; open all day and every day.

La Toja, Edificio Barbados, Avda. Tirijana, Playa del Inglés. Tel. 761196. A small but very attractive restaurant offering typical Galician food. 5,000 pts. Closed one summer month, usually mid-June to mid-July.

Casa del Abuelo, Calle Alfereces Provisionales 11, Montery Apts. Tel. 764411. One of the few places in the south where you can enjoy typical Canarian food. It's lively and very popular. Closed Mondays. 2,500 pts.

Carlos V, Commercial centre Cita (top floor). Tel. 760221. Best known for its excellently-grilled meats; the menu is long, varied and appetising. Open daily. 3,000 pts.

Las Cumbres, Avda. Tirijana 9. Apt. Taidia. Tel. 760941. Nice menu, pleasant mixture of the exotic and the mundane. Very friendly staff and good service. Open daily except May. 4,000 pts.

SANTA BRIGIDA

Mano Hierro, El Pino 25. Tel. 640388. Delicious and very filling food from a menu which is an interesting mixture of typical Canarian and German specialities. A popular meeting place for the locals and German tourists. Closed Mondays and August, menu of the day 750 pts, meal for two 3,000 pts.

TEJEDA

El Refugio, Cruz de Tejeda. Tel. 658199. A good alternative to the excellent but expensive Parador (where the menu of the day is 1,600 pts, meal for two about 4,500 pts). You can eat in the dining room or on the terrace. Menu of the day 900 pts, average for two 3,000 pts. Open all day, every day.

ARTENARA

Meson La Silla. Set on a mountain ledge and open daily from morning till sunset, this is one of the most spectacularly sited restaurants in the Canaries. There's a terrace like a sun trap plus a narrow dining room, and kitchens in the caves! Snacks from 250 pts, a full meal for two around 2,500 pts.

ARGUINEGUIN

Restaurant del Mar. Lovely garden-room restaurant in new development overlooking harbour, superb food in a spectacular setting. Open daily. 3,000 pts.

TELDE

Pablo Silva, Calle General de El Goro 1. Tel. 697455. Pablo Silva's specialities include grilled meat imported from the mainland. Cheap and reliable Canarian and international dishes. Menu of the day 300 pts, average meal for two 2,500 pts. Always open.

La Pardilla, Calle Raimundo Lulio 54. Tel. 695102. For a good meal try any of the tasty dishes offered in this friendly restaurant—Canarian and international cuisine. Menu of the day 450 pts, meal for two with wine 3,000 pts. Always open.

TAFIRA ALTA

La Masia de Canarias, Calle Murillo 36. Tel. 350120. Delightful decor to match the food, outside bar, extremely high quality. The salad Roquefort and "steak of the house" are highly recommended. Open daily, reserve at weekends. Menu of the day 1,300 pts, meal for two with wine 5,000 pts.

Jardin Canario. The large dining room has huge windows overlooking the beautiful botanical gardens in the valley below. The food is typical Canarian, the service excellent. Menu of the day 900 pts, meal for two 4,000 pts. Open daily.

TEA ROOMS

The Germans have imported the tea room idea to the Canaries—cup after cup of delicious coffee and mouthwatering gateaux; lots of these to upset calorie-counters in the south, fewer in Las Palmas. The oldest and most popular in Las Palmas is **Casa Suecia** at the corner of Calle Luis Morote and Calle Tomas Miller, a rendezvous for many foreigners living here. Open all day but closed in high summer. Another very popular meeting place is the tearoom-crêperia **La Cafetera** in Calle Alfredo L Jones 37. The crêpes are quite delicious. Closed Monday.

NIGHTLIFE

PUBS AND BARS

In Las Palmas Santa Catalina Park is one giant bar—well, seven or eight bars; the serious business begins before midday and usually winds up at about midnight. Las Canteras itself is one of the longest bars in Europe—two miles (three km) of promenade pubs!

In the south, each commercial centre provides a bewildering choice of bars, and there'll be an English one, an Irish one, a German one—or two—or three, often with videos or sing-along entertainment, unfortunately.

Las Palmas's authentic British Pub is the **Blackpool**, Paseo de Las Canteras 63, run by Blackpool-born Marian and her tri-lingual husband Paco. (Marian is usually only there at weekends). Open 8 p.m. till late, with mini pool table and darts.

The Sorimba, Calle Portugal 24, is reached by Calle Kant, which runs off Las Canteras. Very cosmopolitan, it's run by an Englishman and a Swede and is a favourite watering hole for Brits, Americans and Swedes. Elegant but not pricey, it has a separate pool, darts and TV room, and opens every day from 7 p.m. till latish.

The Tekas, Calle Sargento Llargas 20, opened in the mid-70s when the oilmen took over the city. Most of them have gone now but they left their stetsons, photos, boots and hearts behind. Antonio is your host, along with his English wife Sandra who sits on the other side of the bar. Great fun and very international but as earthy as the oilmen who

made it their home-from-home. Open 5 p.m. till 2.30 a.m.

Further up the street is the **Isa Pub**, small, crowded and friendly, where Scandinavians head for in the winter. There are also many more pubs in this area, predominantly Spanish.

Pub 39 is a pleasing, quiet bar in the Hotel Gran Canaria on the beachfront, with panelling and chintz like an English country club; open midday till midnight.

Remember that bars stay open till early morning, and that the tots are triple the British size; it's best to take a siesta and to eat before a pubcrawl. Prices are lowest in small Spanish bars, rum and brandy being very cheap indeed. *Cuba libre* (rum and coke) or *sangria* (a heady fruit punch) are "national" drinks.

DISCOS

Many and varied, especially in Playa del Inglés and Las Palmas. The entry fee (500 pts to 1,000 pts) includes the first drink; often girls are admitted free. Most popular in the south are **Joy**, **Spider**, **Chic**, **The Beach Club**, **La Bamba** and many more, especially in hotels. In the capital the most popular are **Zorba's** (Calle Luis Morote), **Wilson's** (Calle Franchy Roca 20), **Jet** (Hotel Iberia), **El Coto** (Hotel Melia), and **Dino's** (Hotel Bardinos). Often open till dawn.

NIGHTCLUBS

In the old fashioned sense of the word—dance floors and live music—there aren't any nightclubs, though some hotels do have live music. There are various cabarets which are not recommended. The nearest approach to a nightclub is English owned. It's **El Bombin** (the Bowler Hat) Calle Grau Bassas, behind the Hotel Gran Canaria. There's a spacious bar, dance floor, little alcoves, pleasant (disco) music and sometimes owner Bill Bender entertains on the piano. Favourite late night spot for tourists of all countries as well as Spaniards; open 9.30 p.m. till 3-ish, with prices not much higher than a bar's.

CABARET

The best by far is **La Scala** at the Tamarindos Hotel, San Agustin (Tel. 766828 for reservations). This is a spectacular Las Vegas type show with 50 girl dancers, Hungarian acrobats, a Spanish ballet, ice-skaters and more. There's a daily dinner show (5,700 to 7,200 pts including champagne) and a late night show with drinks at 11.30 p.m. on Thursday, Friday and Saturday (3,100 pts).

GAMBLING

Two casinos—Hotel Santa Catalina in Las Palmas and Hotel Tamarindos in San Agustin. Roulette, blackjack, baccarat, chemin du fer and slot/fruit machines. Men should wear a tie and everyone should take passport or official identity card for admission (500 pts). Open 9 p.m. till 4 a.m.

BINGO

Is at several locations (take passport or other identification).

Hotel Utiaca
Calle Albareda 35, Las Palmas.
Every day from 5 p.m. to 3.30 a.m.

Hotel Imperial Playa
Calle Ferreras 1. (Playa de las Canteras).
Every day from 5 p.m. to 3.30 a.m.

Bingo Círculo Mercantil
Plaza de San Bernardo (Las Palmas)
Every day from 5 p.m.

Unión Deportiva
Calle Rafael Cabrera 68, Las Palmas.
Every day from 5 p.m.

Hotel Concorde
Calle Tomas Miller 85. Tel. 262750. Las Palmas.
Every day from 5 p.m. to 3 a.m.

Hotel Astoria
Calle Pelayo 17 (Guanarteme)
Every day from 5 p.m. to 3 a.m.

R. Hotel Parque
Parque San Telmo, Las Palmas.
Every day from 5 p.m. to 3 a.m.

THINGS TO DO

Get your bearings: buy an island map—it'll have a map of the city on the reverse, and stroll around. Las Palmas is confusing because it's built on an isthmus and at times you can see the sea in three different directions! Visit Santa Catalina Park, explore the fascinating shopping area around it, get a bus to the Old City and Vegueta. Go south to the beaches if you' re staying north or vice-versa, and then decide upon a couple of excursions or a car-hire. If you miss the interior of the island you are missing half the joy of your holiday.

EXCURSIONS

There are a dozen excursions by coach. The principal ones are listed below. Prices in brackets are from Las Palmas, otherwise from the south. Children half price.

—The Grand Tour into the interior, full day (2,100 pts) 2,600 pts.

—Tour to Agaete via the banana route, (2,400 pts) 2,900 pts.

—Medieval Fiesta at a mock castle, with jousting, barbecue and lots of authentic trimmings, (3,900 pts) 3,900 pts.

—Wild West Night at Sioux City, with as much as you can drink and eat while you watch a bank robbery, gun fight and all the fun of the Wild West (they make films there and it's as good as the real thing). 4,200 pts, children 3,100 pts (4,700 pts, 3,500 pts from Las Palmas).

—Jeep Safari, a breathtaking drive through the mountains (Dunas Tour recommended; you get your own personal video of the excursion next day). (3,850 pts, 2,850 pts) 3,500 pts, 2,600 pts.

—Scala Cabaret and Casino night with dinner, (6,800 pts) 6,500 pts.

—Several others, including a camel safari, donkey safari, and Las Palmas shopping if you're in the south, Maspalomas bathing if you are north-based.

Book tours through any travel agency or hotel reception. There are many pick-up points.

DAY TRIP TO MOROCCO

This is expensive, and a very long day it is too, but well organised with a long shopping period, self-service lunch and dinner in a Moorish palace. 26,000 pts, children 20,000 pts, babies 2,600 pts (not recommended for babies). Take a thick sweater.

KEY ROUTES

a) North to Agaete via Arucas, Galdar; then down to San Nicolas, returning the same way; full day, about 120 miles (200 km).

b) Centre and Cruz de Tejeda via Tafira, Santa Brigida and Tejeda, on to Artenara and Tamadaba forest, returning the same way. Call in at Jardin Canario, Tafira Alta; or return bearing left through Valleseco and the mountain town of Teror, 89 miles (143 km).

c) South on the motorway via Telde, returning to motorway to pass through Playa del Inglés, Maspalomas, Puerto Rico to Mogan—swimming at any of the last three. 120 miles (200 km).

Finally, you could combine trips (a) and (c) and have a full trip round the island. 143 miles (230 km).

There are daily full- or half-day boat trips from Puerto Rico down the coast; and from Muelle Santa Catalina for a "trip around the bay". The Scala/Casino excursion and the evening Sioux City visit is best made by coach.

SPECIAL VENUES

Los Palmitos Park. Five miles (eight km) north of Maspalomas. Take a bus to the park from Playa del Inglés—they are fast, frequent and stops are clearly marked. The park is an artificial subtropical oasis with small lakes, exotic trees and plants, and some 1,200 birds. There are seven shows daily with trained parrots, and the park is a photographer's paradise.

The Rastro. A Sunday morning flea-market in Santa Catalina Park, Las Palmas, selling everything from plastic ear-rings to leather jackets, mountain bread, plants galore, second-hand goods and books—some 250 stalls, including refreshments; starts about 9 a.m., ends 2.30 p.m. Midmorning best, then a pre-lunch drink in the Park.

Reptilandia. Between Galdar and Agaete, this is the largest outdoor reptile collection in the world, with many species which were in danger of extinction. A fascinating place and very popular; in its second year (1987) 40,000 people visited it. Spiders, lizards, crocodiles, serpents and dozens more are now breeding in captivity (but in almost natural conditions) and being studied by experts.

CULTURE PLUS

Museo Canario, Calle Dr Chil. Tel. 315600. Open weekdays, mornings only Saturday and Sunday. The museum reveals how the Guanches lived, and it holds a very interesting selection of anthropological remains as well as ceramics. Notable are the idols in gallery 20, and the mysterious *pintaduras* or terracotta seals (gallery 21) found only on this island. Their purpose is still a mystery—tattooing, branding or sealing harvest stoves? Lots more of interest about the island, yesterday and today.

Casa de Colón (Columbus's House), Calle Colón 1. Tel. 311255. This was the residence of the island's first governors and it is architecturally very beautiful. A wonderful collection of objects and documents from the time of Columbus, and you can see the statue of Santa Ana where he supposedly prayed before setting out to discover the New World. Usually exhibitions of paintings and sculpture from the Prado, Madrid. Open weekdays 9.30 a.m. to 2.30 p.m., Saturdays 9.30 a.m. to 1 p.m., closed Sundays.

Casa Museo de Pérez Galdós, Calle Cano 33. Tel. 366976. This is where the great Canarian writer Pérez Galdós was born and lived. On display are a great number of personal souvenirs as well as an interesting collection of works. Open 9 a.m. to 1 p.m. except Sundays. Library open 4 p.m. to 8 p.m.

Nestor Museum. This contains the principal works of Canarian painter Nestor de la Torre as well as some of his personal possessions. It is in the grounds of the Canarian Village (Pueblo Canaria) which he created. Open 10 a.m. to noon, 4 p.m. to 7 p.m., Saturdays from 10 a.m. to noon, Sundays and fiestas 10.30 a.m. to 1.30 p.m., closed all day Wednesday.

Canarian Village, Parque Doramas. The village is symbolic of Canarian architecture and the best time to visit it is during the bi-weekly displays of folk dances and songs, Sundays 11.45 a.m. to 1.15 p.m., Thursdays 5.30 p.m. to 7 p.m.

ART GALLERIES

Centro de Arte La Regente, Calle León y Castillo, very near Sta Catalina Park.
Sala Cairasco, Plaza de Cairasco 1.
Gabinete Literario, Plaza de Cairasco.
Circulo Mercantil, Plaza de San Bernardo.
Mutua Guanarteme, Calle León y Castillo 57.
Club Nautico, Calle León y Castillo
Castillo de la Luz, Calle Juan Rejón.
Galeria Vegueta, Calle León y Joven 17.
Galeria Balos, Calle Colón 4.
Galeria Yurfa, Calle Perdomo 26.
Salas San Antonio Abad, Calle Colón.
Galeria Madelca, (in front of the Cathedral).
Cueva Pintada, Calle Pérez Galdós 19.
Galeria Radach Novar, Avda. de Tirajana 1, and Hotel Catarina Playa (Playa del Inglés).
Bar Galeria, Calle Domingo J Navarro, 19.
Galeria Malteses, Calle Malteses, 16.
Galeria de Arte Artenara, Calle Galicia 38.
Agrupacion Fotografia Gran Canaria, Calle Obispo Codina, 3.

CONCERTS

The Autonomous Government sponsors a Festival of Music each year, including such names as The London Symphony Orchestra, the Royal Philharmonic Orchestra of London, the Orpheus Chamber Orchestra of New York, and the Philharmonic Orchestra of Leningrad. The Philharmonic Orchestra of Gran Canaria gives a number of concerts between October and June. The Philharmonic Society—the oldest in Spain—also has a concert season between January and July to which world famous musicians are invited. The Spring Festival of Music in Dance is held from April to May, again bringing world famous figures to Las Palmas. All concerts are held in the Perez Galdos Theatre. Season tickets for the Festival of Music cost from 20,000 pts to 50,000 pts.

MOVIES

Nearly all films are in Spanish but the *Cabildo* (island government) sponsors an annual film festival, mainly of English and American films. It's usually held in the autumn. One or two films on TV each week have the English sound-track on radio—check the TV guide.

SPORTS

Canarios love sports, and this is a sportsman's paradise. There aren't many spectator sports—football, basketball and rally driving; even so you will find small boys (and their fathers) practising to be future football stars on any beach where it is allowed (e.g. the southern end of Las Canteras).

FOOTBALL

Matches take place at the Estadio Insular, Las Palmas, every Wednesday (junior team) and alternate Sundays (senior team, now in Spain's Division two).

BASKETBALL

A new indoor stadium which, when finished, will hold 3,500 spectators, is due to open at time of press in Cruz de Piedra, Las Palmas. Handball and volleyball will also be played there.

WATER SPORTS

Unique in the world is the *vela latina* sailing—small yachts with a triangular sail; regattas and races are held most weekends in Las Palmas and Puerto Rico. Children as young as nine or ten years old have their own mini-yachts. Training in the art of *vela latina* is given in Puerto Rico, and you couldn't find better teachers in the world—Canario Jose Doreste won a gold in sailing at the Seoul Olympics.

WINDSURFING

Enormously popular. All along the south coast there are training schools, monitors and equipment for hire; Bahia Feliz, Playa del Inglés, Melaneras, Patalavaca and Puerto Rico. At Melaneras there's a scuba-diving centre, and all kinds of nautical sports can be learnt or practised at Nautical Sports, next to the Aquamarine, Patalavaca.

FISHING

Deep sea fishing excursions are made from Santa Catalina Wharf in Las Palmas and in Puerto Rico; enquire at any travel agency. Fresh water fishing from well-stocked reservoirs is a popular weekend hobby but you must obtain a licence from the Dept. of Agriculture and Fisheries in Calle Juan XXIII, Las Palmas. Favourite reservoirs are Soria and Mi Niña.

HUNTING

August to December is the season for bird shooting.

GOLF

There are two courses, the better one being in Bandama at the Grand Canary Golf Club, Santa Brigida. Tel. 351290. Specifications: 18 holes, course 3.5 miles (5.7 km), special turf greens, par 72. The other course is in Maspalomas near the dunes, 2 miles (3.2 km), par 72. Tel. 762581.

TENNIS COURTS

—Grand Canary Tennis Club. Doramas Park, next to Santa Catalina Hotel, 4 courts. Tel. 243413.
—Olimpo Tennis Club. Carretera Gen-

eral del Norte, 195 (La Paterna). Tel. 247388. 5 courts.

—Tarahal Tennis Club. Carretera del Norte, Km 4. (Los Tarajales).Behind Shell Service Station. Tel. 206914. 3 courts.

—Villa Cornisa Apartments. Paseo de La Cornisa, 3. (Escaleritas) Tel. 253340. 1 court.

—Restaurant Las Grutas de Artiles. Las Meleguinas. (Santa Brigida). Tel. 640575. 2 courts, swimming pool.

—Restaurant Country Club. Carretera del Centro (Santa Brigida). Tel. 640089. 1 court, swimming pool.

—Los Palmitos Tennis Club. (Los Palmitos Park). Hotels on the island with tennis courts:

—Las Palmas: Santa Catalina Hotel.

—Maspalomas: Maspalomas Oasis, Hotel Palm Beach.

—San Agustin: Hotel Tamarindos, Hotel Don Gregory, Hotel Costa Canaria. Hotel Inner Club Atlantic.

—Playa del Inglés: Hotel Buenaventura, Hotel Caterina Playa, Hotel Apolo, Hotel Lucana, Hotel Parque Tropical.

RALLY DRIVING

Popular in Gran Canaria, rally driving is a year-round activity. The most important is the "El Corte Inglés" rally, because it is recognised by the European Championship. It takes place in October. The international Rally at Maspalomas is the second in importance, together with the "Gran Canaria" rally. Many top international racing drivers compete with local ones, watched by thousands of fans.

MINI-KART

The largest track in all Spain lies just south of the private airport, before San Agustin. The circuit is 1,312 yards (1,200 metres), and professionals drive karts which reach 80 mph (130 km/h). Another track inland from Playa del Inglés is perhaps more suited to beginners.

PARACHUTING

The Maspalomas Paraclub—at the private airport Aero-Club in the south—offers three-day courses in "lateral" parachuting, normal parachuting and a new sport, similar to hang gliding. The lateral parachuting is particularly popular and after the third day of the course you automatically become a member of the club, with no other fees. Jumps are at weekends on the dunes at Maspalomas (to ensure a nice soft landing!).

CANARIAN WRESTLING

A very old traditional sport based on skill and strength of the wrestler. Matches are usually held between two teams of 12 men, who are eliminated two by two. Matches are held at the Lopez Socas Stadium in Las Palmas, and in Telde, Agüimes, Guia, Gáldar and Arguineguin. Some authorities maintain that this wrestling predates the Spanish conquest and was used as a kind of trial of strength to settle disputes. The present-day wrestling is certainly held at former Guanche strongholds.

HORSE-RIDING

Can be practised at the riding schools of Marzagan, Hoya del Sabinal, Bandama Golf Club, and at the Oasis stables in Maspalomas. All arrange classes and excursions.

WALKING

The most popular part of the island for walking is the west, between Mogán Town and San Nicolas, in the area of Veneguera. From the latter village you can walk along the valley to the sea, but most people prefer to go over the mountains to Gui Gui or other little coves that are otherwise only approachable by sea. Take water as well as food as the west coast can be very hot.

USEFUL ADDRESSES

SPANISH TOURIST OFFICES

Frankfruit. Spanisches Fremden-verkehrsamt. Bethmanstrasse, 50-54. 6000 Frankfurt Main. Tel. 285760/282782. Tx 413087 TURES E.

Dusseldorf. Spanisches Fremden-verkehrsamt. Graf Adolfstrasse, 81. Dusseldorf 1. Tel. 370467. Tx 8586351 TURE.

London. Spanish National Tourist Office, 57-58 St James Street. London, SW1. Tel. 4994593/4993257. Tx 888138 TURESP-G.

CONSULATES

Germany—Calle Franchy y Roca 5 (2nd fl) Tel. 275700, 275704.

Argentina—Calle Franchy y Roca 5. Tel. 261418.

Belgium—Calle Leopoldo Matos 24, (1st fl) Tel. 230701.

Bolivia—Calle Gran Canaria, 5. Tel. 273484, 243401.

Brazil—Calle Alfredo L Jones, 33 (4th fl). Tel. 278612.

Colombia—Calle Triana, 120 (2nd fl). Tel. 361699.

Korea—Calle Luis Doreste Silva, 60. Tel. 230499, 230699.

Cuba—Calle León y Castillo, 247. Tel. 244642.

Chile—Calle Eduardo Benot, 1. Tel. 271836.

Denmark—Calle Concepción Arenal, 20. (Ed Cantabria). Tel. 231122.

El Salvador—Calle Perdomo, 11. Tel. 361200.

United States—Calle Franchy y Roca 5 (5th fl). Tel. 271259.

Philippines—Calle Doctor Chil, 20. Tel. 318000.

Finland—Calle General Mas de Gaminde, 45 (1st fl). Tel. 244354.

France—Calle Néstor de la Torre, 12. Tel. 244371

Great Britain—Calle Alfredo L Jones, 33 (6th fl). Tel. 262508

Greece—Casa Miller, Muelle Santa Catalina. Tel. 260850.

Guatemala—Calle León y Castillo, 79. Tel. 371500.

Equatorial Guinea—Calle El Cebadal. Tel. 265904.

Holland—Calle León y Castillo, 248 (4th fl). Tel. 242382.

India—Calle Triana, 33. Tel. 367950.

Italy—Calle Mariucha, 2-A. Tel. 250697.

Japan—Calle Santiago Rusiñol, 12. Tel. 244012.

Lebanon—Calle Eusebio Navarro, 25. Tel. 364375.

Liberia—Calle Paseo de Chil, 111. Tel. 362838.

Morocco—Avda. Mesa y López, 8 (2nd fl). Tel. 262859, 268850.

Mauritania—Calle Galicia, 33 (1st fl). Tel. 263412, 263513.

Monaco—Calle León y Castillo, 253. Tel. 241205.

Nicaragua—Parque H Millares, 13. Tel. 252209.

Norway—Calle Maestro Valle, 22. Tel. 249258.

Panama—Avda. Juan XXIII, 3. Tel. 311288.

Peru—Calle Dr. Chil, 33. Tel. 311773.

Portugal—Calle Alfredo L Jones, 33 (4th fl). Tel 278612.

Dominican Republic—Calle J de León y Joven, 14. Tel. 251400.

Senegal—Calle Lope de Vega, 2. Tel. 246295.

Sierra Leone—Calle Viera y Clavijo, 34 (3rd fl). Tel. 362399.

South Africa—Calle Albareda, 50. Tel. 263962.

Sweden—Calle Luis Morote, 6 (4th fl). Tel. 261751, 260884.

Switzerland—Calle El Cid, 38. Tel. 274544.

Uruguay—Calle Triana, 60 (4th fl). Tel. 370970.

CULTURE PLUS

WHERE TO STAY

FESTIVALS CALENDAR

2 February: Fiesta de Nuestra Señora de la Candelaria at La Oliva. Main event which attracts people from other islands.

Last week in February: *Carnaval* of Nuestra Señora del Rosario in Puerto del Rosario. A lot of music, dancing and *Lucha Canaria* or Canary wrestling.

2 April: Fiesta de San Vicente. In the small town of Villaverde. Typical local food and celebrations.

14 July: Fiesta de San Buenaventura. Festival of the patron saint of Fuerteventura, and therefore the most important local event on the island. Canary wrestling a major feature.

16 July: Fiestas del Carmen. Island-wide. Carmen Virgen, the mother of all fishermen, is carried around the island in a gaily-adorned boat. Onshore celebrations, in which goat meat dishes are a speciality.

26 July: Fiesta de Santa Ana, at Las Casillas del Angel.

3rd Saturday in September: Fiesta de la Virgen de la Peña. The second most important fiesta on the island.

8 December: Fiesta de la Inmaculada. In Puerto del Rosario and Betancuria.

HOTELS

Tres Islas, (****), Corralejo. Tel. (28) 866000
A 15-year-old hotel with 356 rooms, situated directly on Corralejo beach, with its white sand and clean water. Room price from 6,000 pts. Facilities include tennis court, swimming pools, supermarket, cocktail bar etc.

Casa Atlantica, (****), Matorral, Jandia. Tel. (28) 876017
One of the biggest hotels in Fuerteventura, with rooms from 5,500 pts. Quiet and good location, and all rooms have a seaview. Tennis and swimming.

Robinson Club, (****), Matorral, Jandia. Tel. (28) 876100.
A modern hotel with seaview. A good location for water sports. Prices from 4,500 pts.

Oliva Beach, (***), Corralejo. Tel. (28) 866100
A new hotel with 396 rooms, priced from 5,000 pts for a single. Same situation as the Tres Islas above, with tennis courts and swimming pool.

Los Gorriones, (***), La Barca, Jandia. Tel. (28) 870850.
La Barca has an excellent beach, and near the hotel are pubs, restaurants, shops etc, and a market complete with local produce. Room prices from 4,500 pts.

Taro Beach, (***), Canada del Rio. Tel. (28) 870776.
Quite a small hotel, with only 140 rooms.

Prices start from 3,000 pts. Clean, with good service.

Parador Nacional, (***), Playa Blanca, Puerto del Rosario. Tel. (28) 851150.

One of the most interesting hotels on the island, situated between the capital and the airport. The parador has only 50 rooms, most with Canarian balconies, and is decorated in old colonial Spanish style, with a good restaurant and swimming pool.

Valeron, (**), Calle Candelaria del Castillo, Puerto del Rosario, 2. Tel. (28) 850618.

A small hotel (16 rooms) in the capital. Basic, but well located near the shops.

Roquemar, (**), Plaza Domingo J Manrique, Puerto del Rosario, 2. Tel. (28) 850359.

Very small (nine rooms), in the middle of the town. Convenient for the port, for Alisur's trips to the islands of Lobos and Lanzarote.

Tamasite, (**), Calle Leon y Castillo, Puerto del Rosario, 9. Tel. (28) 850280.

Clean, good, small (18 rooms) and with good views.

Macario, (**), Calle Almirante Fontan Lobe, Puerto del Rosario, 12. (28) 851197.

In the west side of the town, with 12 small rooms. Easy access to the airport and beaches.

Ruben Tinguaro, (apartments), Calle Juan XXIII, Puerto del Rosario, 52. Tel. (28) 851088.

12 apartments from around 1,500 pts a night.

THINGS TO DO

EXCURSIONS

To Lobos Island: Trips organised from Corralejo include a day stay on the island, which is particularly known for its water sports and diving, complete with lunch at the only house on Lobos. Book through any travel agent listed below.

TO LANZAROTE

A regular boat leaves early every morning from the Corralejo quay. Journey time is 40 minutes. A connecting bus covers the major sights on the island, which include the Fire Mountains of Timanfaya National Park, the underground landscapes of Jameos del Agua and Cueva de los Verdes, and the lagoon El Golfo. Book through any travel agent. Alisur, the company operating the route (three crossings a day), is contactable on Tel. (28)814275.

TAXI SAFARI

An organised trip around the island which includes lunch. Departures only from the north of Fuerteventura. Book through any travel agent.

SHARK FISHING

Pick up from the Hotel Jandia, in the south. Day trips last from 10.30 a.m. till 16.30 p.m.

USEFUL ADDRESSES

RESTAURANTS

Mariquita Hierro, Calle María Hierro, Tel: (28) 868049

La Andaluza, Centro Comercial Paradiso, Playa del Matorral, Tel: (28) 876047

Café Restaurante Jandia, Calle Ntra. Sra. del Carmen, Morro Jable

Casa Andrés, Calle Ntra. Sra. del Carmen, Morro Jable, Tel: (28) 876384

Casa Charty, Plaza Cirio López, Morro Jable, Tel: (28) 876066

Casa Emilio, Avda. del Mar, Morro Jable

Casa Juan, Centro Comercial Paradiso, Playa del Matorral, Tel: (28) 876360

Casa Luis, Centro Comercial Paradiso, Playa del Matorral, Tel: (28) 876235

Cuesta de la Pared, Cuesta de la Pared

Deutsches Café, Centro Comercial Paradiso, Playa del Matorral

Dorl, Abubilia, Morro Jable, Tel: (28) 876128

Los Guanches, Calle Ntra. Sra. del Carmen, Moro Jable, Tel: (28) 876258

Jandia, Calle Senador Velázquez Cabrera, Morro Jable, Tel: (28) 876137

El Laja, Avda. del Mar, Morro Jable, Tel: (28) 876054

Mavic, Avda. de Jandia, Morro Jable

El Mesón, Centro Comercial Paradiso, Playa del Matorral, Tel: (28) 876089

Mesón La Terraza, Barranco de los Canarlos

Nonna Mia, Calle Profesor Juan Tadeo Cabrera, 17

Rayo del Sol, Calle Ntra. Sra. del Carmen, Morro Jable, Tel: (28) 876318

Rodríguez, Calle Ntra. Sra. del Carmen, Morro Jable, Tel: (28) 876032

Las Salinas, Centro Comercial Paradiso, Playa del Matorral, Tel: (28) 876037

La Taberna, Costa Calma

Taberna del Pescador, Playa del Matorral, Tel: (28) 876411

Taberna Ramenca, Senador Velázquez Cabrera, Morro Jable, Tel: (28) 876085

Toni Pinte, Avda. del Mar, Morro Jable, Tel: (28) 876392

Los Barries, Avda. Juan de Béthencourt, 175

La Cabaña, Calle Garcia Escamez, 8, Tel: (28) 850487

Casa Macarlo, Calle Almirante Fonian Lobe, 10, Tel: (28) 851197

El Granero, Calle Alcaide Alonso Patalio, 8, Tel: (28) 851453

Tinguara V, Calle Fernández Castañeyra, 7, Tel: (28) 850160

Antonio, Avda. Maritima, 4, Gran Tarajal

Martin, Calle San Diego, 5, Gran Tarajal

Tarama, Avda. Maritima, 2, Gran Tarajal, Tel: (28) 870238

Victor, (Las Playitas), Gran Tarajal, Tel: (28) 870970

Antonio, Calle Isiatra Diaz, Tarajalejo, Tel: (28) 870148

Gregoria, Calle Cabrera Martín, Tarajalejo

Enríque, Calle Cabrera Martín, Tarajalejo

Perlas del Sur, Calle Cabrera Martín

TAXI HIRE

Call the following numbers (Puerto de Rosario):
(28) 850059 or 850216

CAR RENTAL

Outside the major hotels and the airport, car rental companies are as follows:

CORRALEJO

Autos Estupiñan, Avda. del Generalísimo, 18, Tel: (28) 866048
Autos Faycan—Hertz, (Apartamentos Hoplaco), Tel: (28) 866259
Autos Guerrero, (Apartamentos Acuario), Tel: (28) 866085
Inter Rent, (Hotel Oliva Beach), Tel: (28) 866160
Autos Lajares, Avda. del Generalísimo, 17, Tel: (28) 866067
Autos Dominguez, Hotel Tres Islas, Tel: (28) 86600

LA ANTIGUA

Autos Victor, (Apartamentos El Castillo), Urbanización El Castillo, (Caleta de Fuste), Tel: (28) 878100
Autos Dominguez, El Castillo, Tel: (28) 878100

PAJARA

Autos Mendez, Calle San Buenaventura, Morro Jable, Tel: (28) 876141
Autos Soto, (Hotel Robinson Club), Playa del Matorral, Tel: (28) 876419
Autos Dominguez, Hotel Casa Atlantica, Tel: (28) 876168

TRAVEL AGENCIES

Ultramar Express Hotel Oliva Beach, Tel. (28) 866251

Viajes Canyrama Calle Carrero Blanco, Tel. (28) 866225

Viajes Donamar, Hotel Oliva Beach

CYRASA travel agency Apartmentos Stella Canarias ,Playa del Matorral, Tel. (28) 876002

Viajes Malpei Calle Almirante Lallemand, 86,Puerto del Rosario, Tel. (28) 850116

Viajes Insular Avda. Premier de Mayo, 52, Puerto del Rosario, Tel. (28) 850594

SPORTS AND CULTURAL CLUBS

Centro Cultural Las Tahonillas, Calle Los Estancos, Puerto del Rosario

Club Naútico de Fuerteventura, Calle Dr. Mena, Puerto del Rosario

Sociedad El Porvenir, Calle La Cruz, 2, Tel: (28) 851413

Centro Cultural de Tuineje, Tuineje

Club Náutico Mar Azul, Puerto Azul - Tarajalejo, Tel: (28) 870148.

Club Deportivo Gran Tarajal, Avda. Paco Hierro, Gran Tarajal

Centro Cultural de Morro Jable, Calle Del Carmen, 18, Morro Jable

Centro Cultural "Raiz del Pueblo", La Oliva

Watersports facilities are available on the following beaches:

Playa de Corralejo
Playa del Cotillo
Caleta del Fuste
Pozo Negro
Jandia
Playa del Cofete

Discoteca Freddys, Calle La Iglesia, Corralejo

DISCOTHEQUES

Discoteca Las Carmelias, Calle Crucero Canarias, 13, Corralejo

Discoteca Farna, Calle Nuestra Sra. del Carmen, Morro Jable

Discoteca Star, Calle Virgen de la Peña, 15, Puerto del Rosario

Discoteca Taifa, Calle Profesor Juan Tadeo Cabrera, 4, Puerto del Rosario, Tel: (28) 850046

Discoteca Pub Disco Roma, Playa de Gran Tarajal, Gran Tarajal

Discoteca La Taberna, (Apartamentos Taraxa), Tarajalejo, Tel: (28) 870979

MEDICAL SERVICES

Residencia Sanitaria de Fuerteventura
Carretera del Aeropuerto
Puerto del Rosario
Tel: (28) 850499

Cruz Roja Española
Avenida de la Construción, 3
Puerto del Rosario
Tel: (28) 851376

Farmacia Gonzalez Rosado
Calle 1* de Mayo, 43
Puerto del Rosario
Tel: (28) 850111

Farmacia Sanchez Velazquez
Calle Fernandez Castañeira, 15
Puerto del Rosario
Tel: (28) 850197

Farmacia Sanchez Hernandez
Calle Secundino Alonso, 49
Puerto del Rosario
Tel: (28) 850676

In case of **emergency** call the following numbers:

Policia Nacional: (28)850750
Policia Municipal: (28)850635
Guardia Civil: 851100 - (28)850503

OFFICIAL BUILDINGS

Cabildo Insular de Fuerteventura
Calle 1* de Mayo, 39
Puerto del Rosario
Tel: (28) 851400

Ayuntamiento de Fuerteventura
Calle Fernández Castañeira, 2
Puerto del Rosario
Tel: (28) 850110

Delegacion del Gobierno
Calle 1* de Mayo, 39
Puerto del Rosario
Tel: (28) 850504

TOURIST OFFICE

Patronato Insular de Turismo de Fuerte-
ventura
Calle 1* de Mayo, 33
Puerto del Rosario
Tel: (28) 851024

GETTING ACQUAINTED

ON ARRIVAL

Guasimeta airport on Lanzarote is well supplied with car hire outlets and information services. There is no bus service to Arrecife, but taxis are readily available.

CLIMATE

Despite its forbidding and sometimes sterile appearance under the sun, Lanzarote actually has a remarkably varied climate. January is warm enough for sea-bathing, although you might need a jacket in the evening; locals feel the cold in February and March, although visitors from Northern Europe would not describe it as such. This is the best time of year for flowers and remarkable natural colours in the landscape. If it rains at all during the year, it rains in February. In April and May the sun strengthens, although the wind keeps the island cool. In June, July and August it gets really hot, and the island fills with young Europeans out to enjoy the sun. September and October are better months for visitors who don't like the really hot weather; the beaches are quiet, the sea is warm, and inland the locals are harvesting the grapes for the local wine, or Malvasia. November and December are busier months, particularly December, a period of fiestas.

BANKS

Banco de Bilbao
Calle León y Castillo, 7
Arrecife
Tel: (28) 810700

Banco de Vizcaya
Calle León y Castillo, 8
Arrecife
Tel: (28) 815050

Banco Central
Calle León y Castillo, 34
Arrecife
Tel: (28) 811751

Banco Español de Credito
Calle León y Castillo, 12
Arrecife
Tel: (28) 811166

Banco Exterior de España
Calle Calvo Sotelo, 8
Arrecife
Tel: (28) 812700

Banco Hispano Americano
Calle León y Castillo, 17
Arrecife
Tel: (28) 811150

Banco de Las Islas Canarias
Avda. Gral. Franco 16
Arrecife
Tel: (28) 814100

Banco de Santander
Calle León y Castillo, 24
Arrecife
Tel: (28) 815000

Banco de Vizcaya
Calle León y Castillo, 26
Arrecife
Tel: (28) 814012

Caja Insular de Ahorros
Calle León y Castillo, 2
Arrecife
Tel: (28) 811900

Banco de Bilbao
Calle Caletón del Barranquillo
Puerto del Carmen
Tel: (28) 825926

Banco Central
Calle Juan Carlos I, 46
Puerto del Carmen
Tel: (28) 825173

Banco Exterior de España
Calle Puerto del Carmen
Puerto del Carmen
Tel: (28) 825331

Banco de Santander
Calle Avenida de las Playas, 46
Puerto del Carmen
Tel: (28) 825127

Banco de Las Islas Canarias
Apartamentos Los Molinos
Costa Teguise

Credit cards are becoming more widely accepted, as are Eurocheques. Look for the signs displayed in the shop windows.

INFORMATION

The principal tourist information office is in the Parque Municipal in front of the Post Office, Avenida General Franco (Tel. [28] 811860). There is also a tourist office in the Parador (Tel.[28] 813792).

BUS SERVICES

The island-wide bus service is divided into southern, central and northern divisions. Buses run between Puerto del Carmen and Arrecife approximately every half-hour during the day. Buses run between Arrecife and Playa Blanca in the mornings and evenings, and to Costa Teguise every two hours.

Inland services to Tinajo, Teguise, Maguez and other destinations run at least every two hours.

WHERE TO STAY

HOTELS

Hotel Las Salinas, Costa Teguise. Tel. (28) 813040.
One of the oldest hotels on the island, designed for holidaymakers, with two swimming pools, sauna, fitness centre, equestrian centre, watersports, tennis and squash courts. Room prices from 6,500 pts.

Hotel Lanzarote Princess, Playa Blanca, Yaiza.
On the seashore on the southern tip of the island. Big and comfortable.

Hotel La Geria, Playa de Matagorda, Puerto del Carmen.
Unusually built from local stone in a style reminiscent of the hollows that Lanzarotenos make in which to grow their vines, the La Geria is a distinctive building a little apart from the resort area.

Apartamentos Flamingo Club, Puerto del Carmen. Tel. (28) 825427.
Conveniently located in range of all the resort's facilities, the Flamingo apartments are also surprisingly peaceful. Most sets of rooms are extensive, designed for families, and are priced from 14,000 pts per night.

Apartamentos Morana, Puerto del Carmen. Tel. (28) 825492.
64 apartments, built in 1985. Prices from 6,660 pts per night.

Apartamentos Kontiki, Calle Guanapay 5, Puerto del Carmen. Tel. (28) 825950. Tlx 96629 KOKI E.
Built in 1985, on a small hill in Puerto del Carmen. Very popular with the English.

Prices from 9,500 pts.

Apartamentos Las Panitas y Las Calas, Centro Comercial La Panita, Puerto del Carmen. Tel. (28) 825869. Tlx 96851.
Very centrally situated in the resort.

Apartamentos La Folresta, Calle Mercurio 2, Playa de los Pocillos. Tel. (28) 826500.
Located away from the touristic centre. Very good apartments.

Apartamentos Islamar, Arrecife. Tel. (28) 811550.
On the edge of the park in the middle of the city, with excellent views.

Apartamentos Playa Club, Avenida de las Playas 99, Puerto del Carmen. Tel. (28) 826219.
Prices from 6,450 pts.

Apartamentos Club Las Gaviotas, Urbanizacion Matagorda, Puerto del Carmen.
Built in 1986, close to the beach. Prices from 7,500 pts.

Apartamentos Fayna, Calle Palagre 6, Puerto del Carmen. Tel. (28) 510813.
Close to the beach. Prices from 7,000 pts.

Apartamentos La Santa Sport, Tinajo. Tel. (28) 840101. Tlx 96415 LSFU E.
Extensive facilities, including a garden, children's playground, 10 tennis courts, supermarket, bar, snack bar, cafeteria, restaurant, hairdresser, beauty salon, currency exchange, medical service, shops, laundry service. No dogs are allowed. Prices from 12,000 pts.

Apartamentos Marivista, Puerto del Carmen. Tel. (28) 510058. Fax. (28) 510904.
All facilities. No dogs allowed. Prices from 6,000 pts.

Apartamentos El Barranquillo, Calle Arpon, Puerto del Carmen. Tel. (28) 826295.
Pleasant garden and terrace. All facilities. No dogs allowed. Prices from 5,575 pts.

Apartamentos La Cumbre, Calle Manguia 8, Puerto del Carmen. Tel. (28) 510490.
Includes a conference room. Near all facilities. Prices from 3,500 pts.

Apartamentos Costa Mar, Playa de los Pocillos, Puerto del Carmen. Tel. (28) 510410. Fax. (28) 511485.
All facilities.

Apartamentos Vista Mar, Calle Guadilama 10, Puerto del Carmen. Tel. (28) 510159.
All facilities. Prices from 5,500 pts.

GUEST HOUSES

Pension Cardona, Calle 18 de Julio, Arrecife.
Pension Espanña, Calle Gran Canaria, Arrecife.
Hostal Residencia Miramar, Avda. Rafael Gonzalez 5, Arrecife.
Pension Alespa, Calle Leon y Castillo 70, Arrecife.
Pension Rocha, Calle Gomez Ulla 10, Arrecife.

Youth Hostels and Camping sites

Neither are available on Lanzarote.

FOOD DIGEST

RESTAURANTS

IN ARRECIFE

Restaurante Marisqueria Abdon, Calle Canalejas.
Good seafood restaurant.

Restaurante Shiao, near Reducto Bay.
Very good Chinese restaurant.

Restaurante Juan Carlos, Calle Jose Antonio, 100.
New restaurant serving international cuisine.

Restaurante El Laurel, Avda. Fred Olsen.
International cuisine. Good for quick business lunches.

Restaurante Folia, Calle Jose Antonio, 99.
Canarian food. Pleasant terrace outside, also for diners.

IN PUERTO DEL CARMEN

Restaurante La Boheme, Avda. de las Playas.
Excellent international cuisine.

Restaurante El Varadero, in the old village.
International cuisine. Very good.

Restaurante Casa Colon, Playa de Matagorda.
International cuisine. Very good.

Restaurante China, Playa de los Pocillos.
Probably the best chinese restaurant on the island.

Restaurante Romantica Grill, Centro Atlantico.
Grill and barbecue a speciality.

IN TINAJO

Restaurante El Rio, La Santa Urbanizacion.
Situation by a natural salt water lake, with good views of windsurfing. International cuisine.

IN TAO

Restaurante Don Manuel de Tao, in Tao village.
Good view of La Graciosa island. Canarian and international cuisine.

Restaurante Tiagua, in Tao village.
Decorated with figures and tools from Lanzarote. Canarian food and a Canary atmosphere.

IN MACHER

Restaurante El Molino, Macher village.
International cuisine.

IN TEGUISE

Restaurante Acatife, in front of the church.
Typical Lanzarote food.

Restaurante El Pescador, Pueblo Marinero.
International and Canarian cuisine, very good.

Restaurante Malvasia Grill, club resort Los Zocos.
International and Canarian cuisine.

IN HARIA

Restaurante Los Helechos.
Excellent vista of the village. Canarian food.

IN YAIZA

Restaurante La Bocaina, on the road to Playa Blanca from Yaiza.
International cuisine, specialising in fresh fish.

IN EL GOLFO

Restaurante El Golfo, in the village.
On the shore, with excellent sunset scenery. Fresh fish menu.

IN TIMANFAYA NATIONAL PARK

Restaurante El Diablo.
Cooking done with volcanic heat. Canarian food, although visitors can bring their own food to cook on the grilles. Lanzarotenos themselves sometimes bring their own ingredients, cook their meals, and take the food to the beaches nearby.

IN FAMARA

Restaurante El Risco.
Very good Canarian food. View of La Graciosa island.

THINGS TO DO

ATTRACTIONS

Cueva de los Verdes is open from 11.00 to 18.00, hourly tours on the hour.

Jameos del Agua is open from 11.00 to 18.45 every day, and on Tuesdays, Fridays and Saturdays it reopens from 19.00 to 03.00 in the morning. Tel. (28) 811060 for more information. The complex includes a restaurant next to the natural lake.

Casa Museo El Campesino (by the Campesino monument in the centre of the island). Museum of local culture, with restaurant specialising in Canarian food—ask for Sancocho, Cerdo en adobo, and jareas…Serves wine from Lanzarote.

Parque Nacional de Timanfaya. Tel. (28) 811060. Open every day from 09.00 till 16.45. Restaurant El Diablo (see above). Bus tours every hour. Individual tours with a guide only.

Mirador Del Rio. Tel. (28) 811060. Open from 10.30 till 18.30. Bar and cafeteria, view of La Graciosa island.

Castillo de San Jose. Tel. (28) 811060. Castle with museum, converted for use as conference and exhibition venue. Museum timetable: 11.00 to 19.00. Restaurant: 13.00 to 16.00 and 20.00 to 01.00.

Teguise Market takes place every Sunday, and includes ceramics, leatherwear, table-linen, local cheeses and vegetables, locally-made craft products and more tourism oriented materials.

SPORTS

Reducto Beach in Arrecife is the centre for physical activities, and incorporates a football ground and gymnasium. In Costa Teguise all kinds of sports facilities are available at Toca Sport. Most apartment complexes have their own swimming pools, tennis courts and sometimes other sporting facilities. Club La Santa, on the western coast of the island, is an activity holiday centre, used sometimes by professional sportsmen as well as by holidaymakers. Popular with Scandinavians.

TOURS

Explora (tel. [28] 813642) organises island tours in jeeps, with departures from principal hotels in the Costa Teguise area at 08.30, from Arrecife (Gran Hotel) at 09.10 and from various apartments in Puerto del Carmen from 09.15. The excursion is aimed at giving visitors an insight into the other Lanzarote that most normal holidaymakers do not see. Lunch is included, as is a guide/interpreter with every jeep.

CULTURE PLUS

FESTIVAL CALENDAR

1 January: New Year's Day holiday.

6 January: Fiesta de Pascua in Teguise (at night).

January Fiesta de Reyes. Spain-wide celebrations.

End February: *Carnaval*. Celebrated in all the islands, **Carnaval** runs for five days, and is particularly lavish in some islands. Lanzarote has its own peculiar ceremony when involving the burial of a mock sardine in the local cemetery.

March: Holy week coincides with the end of Carnaval, and is celebrated by processions in the street.

12 May: The fiesta of the Virgin Mary, celebrated in the churches. Beautiful floral displays.

25 May: Corpus Christi. Carpets of salt (the other islands use flowers, but Lanzarote has to make do with salt) depicting scenes from the Bible are laid on the streets for the holy procession to walk over.

30 May: Canary Islands day. Displays by the military and other secular celebrations.

13 June: Fiesta of San Antonio in Tias.

24 June: Fiesta of San Juan. Fires are lit all over the island, with a effigy of San Juan hanging over them, symbolic of his death by burning. After everything is burned, the locals have a sardine grill on the ashes. The best place to witness the celebrations is Haria.

29 June: Fiesta of San Pedro, best in Macher. Dancing.

7 July: Fiesta of San Marcial in Femes. He is the patron saint of Lanzarote.

25 July: Fiesta of Santiago Apostol in Tahiche village. Dancing.

16 August: Fiesta of Nuestra Senora del Carmen. As in Fuerteventura, the image of the virgin is carried around the island by sea.

25 August: Fiesta of San Gines. The biggest single event, celebrated all over the island. *Ventorillos* (bars and restaurants made of palms, wood and stone) are erected all over the island, and local food is served. Dancing.

15 September: Fiesta Virgen de los Dolores in Tinajo.

September: During the last week of the month there are many smaller fiestas all over the island. Amongst the most important are the fiestas of Playa Honda.

12 October: Hispanidad day. Small celebration of a mainland fiesta.

6 December: Fiesta of La Constitucion Espanola, celebrated throughout Spain.

24 December: Christmas.

USEFUL ADDRESSES

IMPORTANT CONTACTS

Delegacion Del Gobierno	(28) 810188
Police	(28) 811302
Cabildo	(28) 810104
Hospital	(28) 810500
Red Cross	(28) 812062
Fire Brigade	(28) 810111
Airport	(28) 811450
Tourist Office	(28) 811860

Guardia Civil:
Arrecife	(28) 810946
Tias	(28) 825236
Yaiza	(28) 830117
Haria	(28) 835003
San Bartolome	(28) 811711
Traffic Dept	(28) 811886

Taxis
Arrecife	(28) 810283
Arrecife	(28) 810769
Arrecife	(28) 811772
Puerto Del Carmen	(28) 825035
Puerto Del Carmen	(28) 825034

PHARMACIES

Don Rogelio Tenorio de Paiz
Calle León y Castillo, 43
Arrecife

Don Alfonso Valls Diaz
Calle Garcia Escamez, 1
Arrecife

Don Manuel Medina Voltes
Calle Perez Galdos, 87
Arrecife

Doña Consuelo Paez Sanchez
Calle Mejico, 31
Arrecife

Don Juan Armas Cancio
Calle Eugenio Rijo, 11
Arrecife
Santa Coloma

Don Jose Tenorio de Paiz
Calle Pedro Barba, 4
Arrecife

Doña Olga Ferrer Espino
Calle Coronel Capaz, 36
Arrecife
Altavista

Don Franciso Matallana
Calle León y Castillo, 13
Arrecife

Don Leopoldo Cabrera Lasso
Calle General Franco, 4
Tias

Don Rafael Correa Rijo
Calle Chafari
Puerto del Carmen

ART/PHOTO CREDITS

Ann Miller Collection	51, 96, 97, 111
Beatty, David	222/223
Eames, Andrew	25, 26, 28, 30, 34, 38, 42, 44, 45, 49, 50, 54, 57, 58, 62, 70/71, 72, 81, 82, 83, 84, 86/87, 90, 93, 94/95, 171, 175, 177, 205, 207, 220, 246, 248, 249
Eddy, Mike	27, 255, 258, 260
Expo Tenerife	18/19, 31, 36, 55, 56, 63, 64, 65, 75, 80, 92, 247, 252, 261, 269
Gadifer La Salle print	32
Gatti, Tulio	3, 9, 22, 33, 40, 53, 78/79, 85,100/101, 104/105, 114, 116, 117, 118, 120/121, 123, 124/125, 126, 127, 129, 130, 131, 132, 133, 134, 135, 138, 139, 141, 142, 143, 145, 146, 147, 148, 149, 150/151, 152, 153, 154/155, 156/157, 161, 162, 164, 165, 166, 167, 168/169, 170, 172/173, 174, 179, 180, 181, 212/213, 217, 219, 228/229, 235, 238/239, 256, 257, 262/263, 270/271, 272
Godfrey, Dave	24
Gravette, Andy,	159, 176
Kanzler, Thomas	67
Kew Gardens	73, 74, 77, 241, 245
Murray, Don	48
National Portrait Gallery	76,
Naylor, Kim	224
Reuther, Joerg	46, 52, 91, 221, 233, 236, 242, 243, 244, 259, 264/265, 268
Shaw, Ian	Cover, 14/15, 59, 60/61, 122, 136/137, 140, 144, 216, 234, 240
Spanish Connection	68, 69
Spectrum	16/17, 35, 88, 89, 98/99, 102/103, 119, 144, 163, 178, 184/185, 187, 190, 191, 192, 193, 194, 195, 196, 197, 200, 201, 202/203, 206, 208, 209, 230/231, 237, 253, 254
Tony Stone	20/21, 158, 182/183, 186, 204, 211, 214/215, 218
Topham Picture Library	198/199
Wassman, Bill	43, 47, 66, 110, 115, 128, 232, 250/251, 266
Wright, George	37

INDEX